Measurement and Evaluation in the Schools

Measurement and Evaluation in the Schools

DONALD L. BEGGS
Southern Illinois University

ERNEST L. LEWIS
Southern Illinois University

Houghton Mifflin Company • Boston

Atlanta • Dallas • Hopewell, New Jersey

Geneva, Illinois • Palo Alto • London

Cover photo courtesy of Marjorie Pickens. The Michigan State University Code of Teaching Responsibility, page 4, is reprinted by permission of the University.

Printed in the U.S.A.

Library of Congress Catalog Card Number: 74–10025
ISBN: 0–395–18609–9

To Shirley and Joyce

Contents

Preface

Measurement and Evaluation in the Schools is an introduction to the measurement process with a special emphasis on its relation to the problems of educational evaluation. We have attempted to present the position that evaluation must be an integral part of overall educational planning if an evaluation is to be used effectively. Only if proper plans have been developed with respect to the measurement process, we believe, can meaningful data be gathered.

We have a great deal of confidence in the teachers in our schools today. In writing this text, we have assumed that teachers have command of their teaching disciplines and that they are well-trained in the ways that students learn. But we developed the material for the text over several years of working with teachers who, despite these qualifications, were not prepared to deal with the procedures for gaining meaningful information for educational decision-making. One of our major concerns here is to make the reader aware of the advantages and limitations of the various types of measures that are commonly used in educational evaluation.

In organizing the text, we have established a framework of four parts, subdivided into eleven chapters. Part One establishes the relationship between the measurement process and the evaluation process in the field of education. We describe several ways in which measuring devices can be used to collect meaningful information. We also present our interpretation of the role of objectives in the evaluation process, particularly the relationship between general and specific objectives. We do not attempt to provide an elaborate method for developing objectives, but rather to present a few representative examples of the kinds of variables that affect the writing of objectives.

In Part Two we discuss external measuring devices, or measuring devices developed by groups external to the classroom setting. We introduce the concept of reference systems—norm-referenced and criterion-referenced systems—as they relate to interpreting test scores. Our intention is not to encourage the use of one system over another, but rather to show readers that both systems can result in meaningful information when used appropriately. We point out that the choice of reference system, in any situation, depends on a careful consideration of the objectives.

In Part Two we also consider the criteria a teacher should apply in reviewing a test for use. We emphasize the importance of the validity of a test, encouraging the teacher to base his or her own decisions about the validity of an external test on how the test results will be used and what is to be assessed. Achievement and aptitude tests are described and information is provided about the involved process of developing these tests.

Part Three deals with the development of internal measuring devices, or measuring devices developed by the teacher within the classroom. We discuss several common types of item formats and the advantages and disadvantages of each and finally the standards that should be used for evaluating internal tests.

Part Four discusses ways to apply the material presented in the preceding parts to develop an overall testing program for a school system. Finally, we provide guidelines for applying these comprehensive test results in making decisions about school programs. We emphasize that to evaluate the school system is to evaluate the component parts of the system using criteria that are acceptable to the school system.

We acknowledge the encouragement we have received from several of our colleagues. We especially appreciate the meaningful input of our students and individuals working in the field of education. We are indebted to the reviews and criticisms of Drs. Glenn Bracht, Oliver Cummings, Robert Ebel and John Mouw. No errors can be attributed to these individuals, but much can be said about the potential errors they kept us from making. Ellen Vasu was extremely helpful in reviewing our manuscript and assisting us with the selected references found at the end of each chapter. Our many thanks to Mrs. Stephanie Clark for overcoming illegible writing and poor sentence structure in preparing the original manuscript.

D.L.B.
E.L.L.

Measurement and Evaluation in the Schools

Part One

Educational Measurement in School Evaluation

1

The Role of Measurement in Educational Evaluations

CONCERNS

1. Why evaluate?
2. What is educational evaluation?
3. How does measurement contribute to educational evaluation?
4. Why are educational objectives important to the measurement process?
5. What are some of the problems in developing educational objectives?
6. What kinds of educational measuring devices are available to educators?
7. What questions should educators ask about the educational measuring devices being used?

Why Evaluate?

One thing people of the world seem to have in common is a concern about the education children receive in schools. Complaints often take the form of the question, "What is wrong with our educational system?" Although this type of complaint is generally well intended, many educators seem to view it as a threat to their profession and quickly become defensive of current instructional practices. In the past, people questioning an educational system and people defending it have attempted to debate the matter theoretically. All too often, however, the debate has degenerated into a battle of words.

Today, concerned people approach the problem of good education from a different point of view. In many instances the taxpayers and others responsible for the funding of an educational institution require that educators be able to account for expenditures. In other words, the people paying the bills are saying to educators, "Show us that the students in your school are deriving the desired benefits from the money you are spending." While many educators may view this attitude as a threat, we feel that the requirement for *accountability* in our schools should be helpful to educators in their attempts to provide an educational system of high quality. An example of a response to the call for accountability appears in the following extract. The statement of the responsibility of teachers at Michigan State University is typical of the concerns and actions of education at all levels of education throughout the country.

Michigan State University
Code of Teaching Responsibility

The teaching responsibilities of the instructional staff are among those many areas of university life which have for generations been a part of the unwritten code of "scholars and gentlemen." Now, however, along with other formerly unwritten contracts, it seems appropriate to set forth these responsibilities in the form of a code. The provisions of such a code are so reasonable to learned and humane men that it may appear redundant or unnecessary to state them. However, the university conceives them to be so important that the performance of the instructional staff in meeting the provisions of this code shall be taken into consideration in determining salary increases, tenure, and promotion.

1. Instructional staff members are responsible for stating clearly the instructional objectives of each course they teach at the beginning of each term. It is expected that each instructional staff member will direct his instruction toward the fulfillment of these objectives and that examinations will be consistent with these objectives. Instructional staff members are responsible to orient the content of the courses they are assigned to teach to the course descriptions approved by the University Curriculum Committee and the Academic Council.
2. Instructional staff members are responsible for informing students in their classes of the methods to be employed in determining the final course grade and of any special requirements of attendance which differ from the attendance policy of the university.
3. It is expected that graded examinations and papers will be provided to the student for inspection and discussion. Thus, final examinations will be retained for one term to provide the opportunity for review with the instructor, if the student so desires. It is expected that examinations will be graded within a sufficiently appropriate time to make the examination a part of the student's learning experience.
4. All instructional staff members are expected to meet their classes regularly and at scheduled times. In case of illness or any other emergency, the instructor will notify the department chairman so that appropriate action may be taken.
5. All instructional staff members whose responsibilities involve students are expected to schedule a reasonable number of office hours for student conferences. Office hours should be scheduled at times convenient to both students and instructors with the additional option of prearranged appointments for students when there is a schedule conflict. The number of office hours is to be determined at the appropriate administrative level, and office hours should be a matter of common knowledge.
6. Instructional staff members who are responsible for academic advising are expected to be in their offices at specified hours during the period of each enrollment. Arrangements will also be made for advising during registration.

Approved by the Academic Senate
November 19, 1969

Before the demand for accountability can be met, both educators and the public must be aware of the responsibilities of the educational system. In the past, a great deal of empty rhetoric has been employed in the concern for responsibility in education, and diverse interests in the topic have sometimes died from lack of agreement. If the process of accountability is to function well, the individuals involved must solve this problem. Undoubtedly, not everyone will be satisfied with the solution, but the process of identifying the responsibilities of the educational system can only help individuals better understand the role of education in society. Having reached agreement with the public, educators can approach the question, "What is wrong with our educational system?" Knowing the responsibilities of the educational system, they can define its end product. Such a definition generally takes the form of a statement of objectives that the educational institution is designed to achieve.

Once the objectives have been described, accountability dictates that educators develop and institute procedures for measuring the extent to which they have been met. Such procedures must be explicitly described and must provide for the collection of information that will allow educators and the public to determine whether the educational system is meeting its objectives adequately. The procedures to be used are collectively called *educational evaluation.*

What Is Educational Evaluation?

The term "evaluation" is familiar in education. Teachers evaluate students when they assign grades. Principals evaluate teachers when they rate their individual teaching capabilities. Superintendents evaluate principals, and school boards evaluate superintendents. Teachers evaluate their instructional materials, and students evaluate their teachers.

Educational evaluation involves a great deal more than a simple rating of good or bad. The most appropriate definition of educational evaluation is perhaps that stated by the Phi Delta Kappan National Study Committee on Evaluation: "the *process of delineating, obtaining,* and *providing useful information* for *judging decision alternatives.*" This definition indicates that evaluation is the process of gathering information as well as the process of making decisions. Unfortunately, information-gathering is often forgotten or ignored when the term "evaluation" is used. Within the process of gathering information, educational measurement makes a significant contribution to evaluation.

To understand the Study Committee's definition of educational evaluation, one must know what each of the italicized terms means. Perhaps they can best be understood through an example of how the evaluation process might be applied in a school setting. Suppose the administrators and teachers of a graded school are considering the possibility of reorganizing their school into an ungraded structure. Educational evaluation, as defined, could provide the framework within which they could reach a decision as to whether or not to reorganize in this way. The process of educational evaluation would require that the members of the school first define the choices that are available—their *decision alternatives*. In this example, the simplest set of decision alternatives might be to:

1. retain the present system
2. adopt the ungraded system for the entire school
3. adopt the ungraded system for some aspects of the curriculum, such as mathematics, and retain the present system for other parts of the curriculum, such as science.

Once the decision alternatives have been identified, it is necessary to define criteria that can be used in *judging* or choosing among the various alternatives. This school, as do all others, has certain goals or objectives to achieve through its programs. Some of these take the form of very general statements about the entire curriculum. Other objectives are specific statements about what certain segments of the curriculum should achieve. A third category of objectives states specifically what should be accomplished in each classroom. All three levels of objective would probably consist of things students should learn as well as statements of attitudes and personal characteristics students should display. The importance of these objectives is, of course, that they provide the criteria for *judging* the various *decision alternatives* that are available to the school. If the ungraded system can achieve the school's objectives and the present organization cannot, then the school has a basis for deciding to adopt an ungraded system. Conversely, if the ungraded system can achieve the school's objectives in mathematics but not in science, then the appropriate choice would be to adopt the ungraded system in mathematics but not in science.

Before the *judging* of *decision alternatives* can occur, it is necessary to determine whether, or to what degree the school's objectives have been achieved. In other words, certain *information* must be available. The members of the school might decide that tests that can be purchased from testing companies would provide information on certain objectives. For other objectives, it might be necessary for faculty members to develop the relevant tests. For still other objectives, it might be necessary to gather subjective data from observations, interviews, and checklists. Other methods of gathering information might also be used. In any case, the information to be obtained must first be delineated and then obtained. After the information has been obtained, it must be provided in a useful form to the individuals who are directly responsible for judging the decision alternatives. The information must be understandable, dependable, and meaningful to the people using it. Once the decision makers possess useful information, they can determine the degree to which the school's objectives have been attained. It is then possible to judge the various decision alternatives as to the degree to which each alternative provides the opportunity for the school to meet its objectives.

Measurement's Role in Educational Evaluation

Educational measurement plays a very important role in evaluation. The principles of measurement provide the framework in which tests from outside the school may be chosen, tests within the school may be developed and test scores may be meaningfully interpreted and reported. In short, they are designed so that the information resulting from the testing program is meaningful, understandable, and dependable.

It may be that you, as a teacher or potential teacher, are asking yourself at this point, "All this talk about educational evaluation is fine, but what has it got to do with me?" In the example just presented, teachers were involved in the educational evaluation process. Teachers write the objectives for their classes and help determine the objectives for the school. They are involved often in the adoption of standardized tests and especially in the interpretation of the scores resulting from standardized tests. And, certainly, teachers write, administer and score tests and make judgments about decision alternatives. Although individual teachers may not often be involved in an evaluation project of the magnitude of our example, they are constantly operating as educational evaluators.

Consider the process that a teacher goes through in assigning letter grades to students at the end of a grading period, for example. The teacher is faced with a number of alternatives. Should a particular student receive A, B, C, D, or E? The teacher has five *decision alternatives* from which to choose. In order to determine which is most appropriate for each student, the teacher needs information on which to base a *judgment* of the *decision alternatives*.

The first thing this teacher would do at the beginning of the grading period is establish criteria for determining how letter grades will be assigned. These criteria generally take the form of objectives it is hoped the students will achieve, and for a given grading period these may be very specific statements. The teacher must then decide how to determine the degree to which each student has attained the various objectives. It may be that for each student scores from three tests, a grade on a term paper, and a rating of class participation are necessary to determine the degree to which the student has achieved the objectives. In determining what information will be gathered, the teacher is *delineating* the *information* to be *obtained* for *judging decision alternatives.* Once the teacher has decided on the information to be used, it must be gathered. The teacher must write, administer, and score the three tests, assign and score the term paper, and rate the student on class participation.

Not only must the information be delineated and obtained; it must also be *provided* in a *useful* form. Since the teacher alone uses the information in this example, providing the information is not a problem, but making it *useful* may be. The test scores that are to be a major part in the final decisions about grade assignments must be meaningful in the sense that they provide an accurate indication of what each student has achieved. To be *useful*, the test scores must be dependable and *provided* in a form that can be interpreted.

Each of the two examples of evaluation just presented concentrates on the outcome of an educational process. In the first example, the decision alternatives relate to whether the educators in a school system should choose an ungraded structure. The choice between decision alternatives is made on the basis of information gathered at the end of a period of ungraded organization. The second example deals with the assignment of grades at the end of a grading period. Students are to be rated on how well they have done after the opportunity to change performance has passed. <u>While evaluation of outcomes is important, it is not the only—and it is probably not the most important—type of educational evaluation.</u> It seems that the <u>primary role of education is to help students optimize their learning potential. If this is to be accomplished, *information* must be available for *judging decision alternatives* during the process of education as well as at its end.</u>

The role of educational evaluation within the educational process can be seen clearly in the system of Individually Prescribed Instruction in mathematics (IPI) which is published by Appleton-Century-Crofts. It is a system intended to manage instruction in elementary mathematics so that each student's program can be specially designed. IPI breaks elementary school mathematics into ten basic learning areas. Within each area, materials are divided into seven difficulty levels. Within each level, there are a number of educational objectives for each student. Every teacher using the IPI system is faced with a number of *decision alternatives.* To which learning area should a student be assigned? In which difficulty level within a learning area should a student be placed? On what objectives within a difficulty level in a learning area should a student work? <u>In order to *judge* these *decision alternatives,* the teacher must be *provided* with *useful information*.</u> The *process* of educational evaluation allows the teacher to *obtain* this.

<u>Part of this information is obtained through the use of a diagnostic placement test to determine the difficulty level at which a student should work within a given learning area.</u> Once the students have been placed at their difficulty levels, the teacher must choose each student's individual objectives. The teacher obtains the information on which to judge these decision alternatives through the use of a pretest. Such placement tests and pretests occur during rather than after the educational *process.*

In addition to aiding in placement, evaluation is used in IPI to monitor each student's progress through a set of worksheets with check-tests called Curriculum Embedded Tests. These *provide* the teacher with *information* on which to *judge decision alternatives* related to student progress. This information can be used along with progress and placement profiles to help the teacher decide which activities and experiences to prescribe for an individual student. <u>Of course, if the process of educational evaluation is to be valuable in the IPI system, the information that is gathered</u>

must be *useful*. It is at this point that the principles of educational measurement play an important role in evaluation.

As we have stated, the principles of educational measurement are designed to make the information provided by tests useful in the evaluation process. These principles provide the basis for judging tests that may be adopted from external agencies and for developing tests that will provide meaningful and dependable results. They provide procedures for judging the quality of test items. Finally, measurement provides the basis for interpreting test scores and determining their dependability and usability. The purpose of this book is to examine the various principles of educational measurement so that you as a teacher can ensure that the tests and scores you use will be meaningful, useful information in your evaluations.

Importance of Educational Objectives to the Measurement Process

In order to develop specific measuring devices or measurement techniques to assist in obtaining information for education evaluations, there must be well-developed reasons for obtaining the information. Usually the reasons for collecting specific types of information are found in the objectives that have been stated as a part of the evaluation. Although the process of developing educational objectives is difficult, it must be done before beginning the measurement process.

General vs. Specific Objectives

Objectives can be stated in many different ways. In this text, objectives are classified as either *general* objectives or *specific* objectives. General objectives usually do a poor job of directing an individual to the appropriate measuring technique. One common general objective for educational systems is "to advance learning." The first reaction most people make to this objective is to say that it is good and worthwhile. But how does one determine whether this objective is being met? It does not provide us with enough information to determine what criteria are appropriate to collect. What does the term "learning" mean in this objective? What do the initiators of this objective mean by the expression "to advance"?

In an effort to overcome the problems associated with general objectives, educators have encouraged the development of specific objectives. Keeping in mind that the general objective is "to advance learning," one might develop an objective such as:

Ninety-five percent of the pupils in Grade 5 will increase at least three raw-score points on the *Hawk Intellectual Capacity Skills Test* during the nine-month school year.

This objective is specific, and it will allow the evaluator to use a specific test. But although this objective is satisfactory with regard to the data to be collected, it may not be satisfactory for other reasons. For example, it may not help determine whether there has actually been an advancement in learning. Is it fair to require that only 95 percent of the students meet the minimal criterion? Is the objective so specific that the intent of the general objective is lost?

In stating specific objectives, there is a tendency to lose sight of the intent of the general objective and concentrate only on the problem of stating objectives in such a way as to make them measurable. When this occurs, specific objectives become meaningless and measurements or data based on them also become meaningless. Specific measurable objectives must be developed if direction is to be given to the measurement devices to be used, but they must be developed as subcategories of general objectives if measurement is to provide useful information for educational evaluations. The procedures for developing appropriate educational objectives will be discussed in Chapter 2.

Norm-Referenced vs. Criterion-Referenced Measurement Devices

The nature of the reference group against which results are to be compared is critical in determining whether the available data are useful. Reference groups are usually provided by test developers in the form of test norms that indicate the distribution of scores from other groups. Ideally, users want a reference group to be similar to the group that they are evaluating. For this reason, conscientious test developers provide test users with norms from a variety of reference groups from large cities, various regions of the country, inner cities, specific states, or the entire nation.

Recently some educators have been seeking a form of reference not based on norm groups. The new references are criteria established by the teacher or evaluator before data collection. This form of referencing is called *criterion-referenced* testing. From previous experience and expectations, the educator states the requirements that would define success with respect to a particular objective. The data that is obtained can then be compared with these previously stated requirements.

Some educators believe that they must choose between two reference systems when they set up an evaluation. This is unfortunate because a well-planned evaluation can employ both forms of reference system. The appropriateness of a reference system is a function of the objective being evaluated. For example, some objectives might require comparison with a known group:

A pupil receiving individual instruction will score above the median for a representative group of inner-city children on the *Hawk Intellectual Capacity Skills Test.*

In this objective, the norm reference group is inner-city children. Another objective might be:

A pupil receiving individual instruction will be able to spell the words on the fifth-grade word list.

For this objective the criterion for success has been defined in terms of words to be spelled. Students are to be compared against a minimal level set by the evaluator on the basis of his experience and expectations.

Both reference systems are appropriate in educational evaluations, but it is the responsibility of teachers and evaluators to determine a system for each objective. How does the teacher determine which system to use? If norm-referenced groups are used, how does the evaluator correctly interpret the scores available? If criterion-referenced evaluation is used, how does an evaluator determine the appropriate criterion to use as a minimal acceptance level? In Chapter 3 we provide practical responses to these questions.

Choosing the Appropriate Measuring Device

Once the objectives to be evaluated have been developed, the evaluator can pay attention to the type of information to be collected. It is quite possible that data can be obtained from *external measuring instruments,* so called because they have been developed outside the school system. External devices are often standardized tests developed by measurement specialists. The most common types of standardized test are achievement, aptitude, and attitude tests. Each provides a specific set of information. The problem is to determine which type is appropriate to the objectives being evaluated. Before the teacher can make this decision, the test must be reviewed and specific questions must be asked:

1. Are the tests measuring what they are intended to measure?
2. Does the information obtained from the tests provide an adequate description of the student?
3. Can the teacher interpret the results in a meaningful way?

These are only some of the questions that must be asked about an external or a standardized test. A thorough review must take place before selecting an externally developed test.

In many instances, objectives are such that the data to be collected cannot be obtained from standardized tests. When this is so, the teacher or evaluator must assume the responsibility of developing his own tests. These *internal measuring devices* must be reviewed much in the manner that external measures are reviewed. The fact that a test has been developed by a classroom teacher or a school curriculum specialist does not guarantee that the test is appropriate.

How do classroom teachers or groups of teachers develop good tests when the standardized tests that are available are not appropriate? What are the general requirements of an acceptable teacher-made test? How do teachers decide what type of items (essay, matching, completion, true-false, multiple-choice) to use? After results have been obtained, how should they be interpreted? All these questions are of concern to the teacher who is trying to develop tests. In Chapter 9 we present a comprehensive discussion of the standards for judging internally developed testing instruments.

Although the procedure for determining the appropriate information to be collected is complex and time consuming, it is a crucial step in educational evaluation. If the measuring devices are not appropriate to the specific objective or if the specific objective does not clearly reflect the general objective, no statistical treatment or flowing rhetoric can provide an effective evaluation. The time spent in determining the way in which information will be collected is mandatory and defensible if the measurement process is to be an integral part of an evaluation.

Reflections

1. Schools must conduct evaluations to determine whether their educational programs are fulfilling the objectives established for the educational institution. Evaluation may also provide information with respect to the value of alternative educational programs.
2. Educational evaluation is the process of delineating and obtaining information useful for judging decision alternatives.
3. The principles of educational measurement are instrumental in obtaining information useful to educational evaluation.
4. Objectives are essential to the measurement process because they specifically define the nature of the data to be collected.
5. In stating specific educational objectives, the teacher must define clearly the outcome that is desired without losing the intent of the general objective.
6. There are two main types of test available for measurement purposes: external measuring devices developed by individuals outside the local setting and internal measuring devices developed within the local setting.
7. Educators should examine their measuring devices to determine whether the devices can provide useful information.

Exercises

1. You are responsible for evaluating the class in which you are using this text. Review the various definitions of "evaluation" and determine your favorite. Put this definition in writing so that you can use it in the chapter exercises to come.

2. List the reasons you are evaluating this class.
3. Obtain the objectives of the school, college, or department in which this class is being taught.
4. List the different types of measurement that *may* be necessary to evaluate this class. Indicate which measures must be developed within the class.
5. Several references have been cited for various systems of grading. Develop the grading system that is "ideal" for this class.
6. Any educational system concerned with accountability must establish the distribution and the hierarchy of responsibility. Establish the responsibilities of the instructor of this class.

Selected References

EVALUATION DEFINITIONS

Thorndike, R. L., and E. Hagen. *Measurement and Evaluation in Psychology and Education.* New York: Wiley, 1969. Pp. 30–31, 647.

Gronlund, N. E. *Measurement and Evaluation in Teaching.* New York: Macmillan, 1971. Pp. 7–8.

Phi Delta Kappa, National Study Committee on Evaluation. *Educational Evaluation and Decision Making.* Edited by Daniel Stufflebeam. Itasca, Ill.: F. E. Peacock, 1971. Pp. 40–47.

Remmers, H. H., N. L. Gage, and J. F. Rummel. *A Practical Introduction to Measurement and Evaluation.* New York: Harper & Row, 1965. Pp. 7–10.

Ahmann, J. S., M. D. Glock, and H. L. Wardberg. *Evaluating Elementary School Pupils.* Boston: Allyn & Bacon, 1960. P. 9.

SYSTEMS OF GRADING

Ahmann, J. S. and M. D. Glock. *Evaluating Pupil Growth.* Boston: Allyn & Bacon, 1967. Different methods of reporting pupil growth and achievement are analyzed, including examples of report cards, letters to parents, and parent-teacher conferences. Emphasis is placed on cooperative participation between parents, teachers, and pupils. See especially Chapter 16.

Noll, V. H., and D. P. Scannell. *Introduction to Educational Measurement.* Boston: Houghton Mifflin, 1972. Pp. 531–39. An overview of marking is given, including the use of standardized tests for arriving at a final course grade. Five principles of marking and the use of measurement in marking are commented on and there is an

example illustrating the assignment of marks to a college class.
Remmers, H. H., N. L. Gage, and J. F. Rummel. *A Practical Introduction to Measurement and Evaluation.* New York: Harper & Row, 1965. Chapter 9 is concerned with reasons for marks, kinds of marks, kinds of marking systems and bases, criticisms, grading on the curve, assignment of course grades, and types of reporting procedure.
Thorndike, R. L., ed. *Educational Measurement.* Washnigton, D. C.: American Council on Education, 1971. Alternatives to the A–F scale are presented (p. 309). There is also a discussion of the use of the traditional grading system with reference to college admissions (pp. 684–88) and course placement (pp. 706 and 716).
Thorndike, R. L., and E. Hagen. *Measurement and Evaluation in Psychology and Education.* New York: Wiley, 1969. In Chapter 17 the authors discuss the need for and function of marks, criteria for marking, weighting of component data using a formula, categories used in grading systems, normal curve distribution, three reference systems, and an example of anchoring a specific group to the reference frame to form the "class reference group."

MEASUREMENT DEFINITIONS

Ahmann, J. S., M. D. Glock, and H. L. Wardeberg. *Evaluating Elementary School Pupils.* Boston: Allyn & Bacon, 1960. Pp. 7–9.
Greene, H. A., A. N. Jorgensen, and J. R. Gerberich. *Measurement and Evaluation in the Secondary School.* New York: Longmans, Green, 1957. Pp. 1–3.
Gronlund, N. E. *Measurement and Evaluation in Teaching.* New York: Macmillan, 1971. Pp. 7–8.
Noll, V. H., and D. P. Scannell. *Introduction to Educational Measurement.* Boston: Houghton Mifflin, 1972. Pp. 11–14.
Thorndike, R. L., ed. *Educational Measurement.* Washington, D. C.: American Council on Education, 1971. Pp. 335–55. A general analysis of the phenomena of measurement from a variety of perspectives.

DEFINING RESPONSIBILITIES WITHIN THE
EDUCATIONAL SYSTEM

Ebel, R. L. *Essentials of Educational Measurement.* Englewood Cliffs, N. J.: Prentice-Hall, 1972. Pp. 35–36. This presents the view that although school, family, and students share responsibility for education, ultimately the individual must accept responsibility for the success or failure of his education.
Stocker, J., and D. F. Wilson. "Accountability and the Classroom Teacher." *Today's Education,* 60 (March 1971), 41–56. The authors

trace the rise of accountability and assess teacher opinion on the issue.

Wilson, E. C. "Response and Responsibility in American Public Education." *Educational Horizons,* 49 (1971), 143–51. This philosophic discussion of the role of education in America emphasizes the function and responsibility of society at large.

2

Educational Objectives for Evaluating the School System

CONCERNS

1. What is the importance of objectives to educational programs?
2. What is the importance of objectives to educational evaluations?
3. What is a general objective?
4. Why are general objectives important?
5. What are the components of a good general objective?
6. What problems do general objectives pose for educational measurement?
7. What is a specific objective?
8. Why are specific objectives important?
9. What are the components of a good specific objective?
10. How are the components of a specific objective determined?
11. What are some limitations of educational objectives?

The Role of Objectives in Educational Evaluation

Educators and members of the general public are concerned that the educational system provide students with the best possible education. Generally the public remains unconcerned with how this is accomplished as long as it is accomplished. Educators, however, must deal continually with the means by which schools attempt to provide the best possible education. The one thing that can be depended on when educators consider this question is that they will disagree. Some educators argue that a school must be ungraded if it is to provide the best possible education. Some insist that team teaching is the best approach to use. Some argue for schools without walls. Each specific technique has its own proponents. But while educators disagree on approaches most agree that all instruction should be based on sound educational objectives.

An educational objective is a statement of the behavior that students should demonstrate at the end of a period of instruction. Such a statement may be very general or may specify in great detail the behavior to be expected. In either case, statements of educational objectives play an extremely important role in educational programs of all types. Objectives state the change that instruction should make in students' behavior. In other words, an objective is a statement of what instruction should actually accomplish. Once teachers and curriculum planners know the objectives, they have a basis from which to make certain important decisions. They can choose among activities to be included in the instructional process because they see that some can help achieve the objective while others cannot. Some materials will help achieve the objective better than others. Some teaching techniques will better accomplish the objective. In short, objectives provide a basis for deciding how to teach the topic in question. It is as illogical for a teacher to attempt to make such decisions without knowing what he hopes to achieve as it is for a driver to map out a route without knowing where he wants to go. Educational objectives provide teachers with the knowledge of where they want to go.

Educational objectives also play an extremely important role in educational evaluation. As we stated in Chapter 1, evaluation is supposed to provide useful information for judging decision alternatives. If the alternatives are a number of different approaches to teaching, one would like to judge their success, but to do this one must have a definition of success. Educational objectives provide this definition in that they state what instruction is to accomplish. Once objectives have been established, the evaluator need only gather data to indicate whether the objectives have been achieved and to determine whether a particular teaching technique is successful. Evaluating educational programs without knowing the objectives seems as futile as trying to determine whether a man has been successful in life without knowing what success means to him.

General Objectives

The most important function of the educational process is to bring about changes in behavior. Thus behavior must be measurable. This does not mean that we are able to measure all behavior with paper and pencil tests. It does mean that the expectation of change implies varying degrees of behavior, and this in turn suggests measurability. Not all measures are precise, however. We may at times have to employ very crude methods for measuring a particular behavior.

We might want to improve a child's artistic performance, for example. If we say that we want this improvement, then we are assuming that artistic performance can be changed through some educational program. To determine whether artistic performance has improved, we must measure it both before and after instruction. But how do we measure artistic ability? To a nonartist, artistic ability is very subjective and depends primarily on personal likes and dislikes. Since it is almost impossible for any two people to agree upon a standard definition of the concept of artistic ability, we must accept subjective judgments in our determination of artistic behavioral change.

Fortunately not all behavior is as difficult to measure as artistic ability. For example, there are very precise techniques by which we can measure whether students in a physical education class can run a mile in less than seven minutes. We have universally accepted measures of distance and time that make it easy to determine improvement in an individual's ability to run the mile.

The responsibilities set forth by an educational institution generally imply that certain behavior should improve or change, and this also implies that the behavior is measurable. "Behavior" includes knowledge, overt actions, attitudes, perceptions, and decision-making skills. Individuals who establish the goals or responsibilities of an educational institution are not usually concerned with specific behavior. They are more concerned about the general behavior that students should demonstrate on leaving the educational institution. General behavioral objectives may be universally discussed and accepted but they do not have a single, universally accepted definition.

An example of a general objective is "to advance the learning of the students." Few would disagree with the intent of this objective. It implies that the learning can be measured because it states that change (advance) should occur. But "learning" is not limited to a single, precise application and may refer to any or several of many activities. Since we do not know from the objective which behavior is to be observed, the development of appropriate measurement procedures is not possible.

Another general objective might be "the students' attitudes will improve." Here too the specific attitudes of concern are not delineated. This objective, like the one above, implies that behavior can be measured, because it indicates that improvement should be noted, but an evaluator would be unable to develop a measurement instrument to assess this objective because it lacks the definition of a precise behavior to be observed.

What is the purpose of stating general objectives for education? Probably the most important reason for stating objectives in a general way is that the people who prepare them do not have to be educational specialists. General objectives allow individuals to express their concern about the outcome of the educational enterprise in a nontechnical manner and without becoming directly involved in the process of education. The public can express its general desires and leave the specific process to trained educators. Once all the individuals responsible for the educational institution have expressed their desires as general objectives, the professional educators can map the strategies to be used in meeting them.

General objectives are not specific enough to assist in the measurement process, but they must provide elements specific enough to assist in determining whether an objective has been met. A general objective must have at least three basic components:

1. The individuals or groups who should perform the terminal behavior or outcome must be identified.

2. The direction of the change (positive or negative) must be designated.
3. A general category defining the terminal behavior or outcome must be presented.

In the two examples of general objectives, we can clearly identify the three basic components. The first objective, "to advance the learning of the students," indicates that the students are to perform the terminal behavior categorized as "learning" and the change to occur is an "advancement." The second objective, "the students' attitudes will improve," indicates that the students are the group to perform the terminal behavior generally classified as an attitude and that the change should be positive. If general objectives contain these three elements, the objective can be delineated by professional educators without losing the intent of the objective.

General objectives create several problems for an evaluator trying to develop measurement techniques for an evaluation. The third component of a general objective causes the greatest measurement problem. In the general objective "to advance the learning of the students," for example, the evaluator is not aware of the type of learning to evaluate or the specific skills to be assessed. The term "learning" may apply to academic skills, social skills, vocational skills, or some combination of these. In the second example, "the students' attitudes will improve," similar problems are evident. The type of attitude to be assessed has not been indicated and, therefore, the measurement process is delayed or stopped because the specific behavior has not been defined.

Although general objectives cause problems for the measurement process, they have a definite place in the educational evaluation process. The determination of general objectives provides an opportunity for an individual or a group to indicate its intentions for education without interfering with the educational process. A school board can develop general objectives for an entire school system without limiting the objectives to a precise application. In the same manner, a principal or a teacher committee can establish general objectives for a school without limiting the individual teacher's freedom to work toward these objectives. General objectives are relevant to a school system and they should not be discarded because they are not directly amenable to the principles of measurement.

Specific Objectives

To develop objectives that aid in the measurement process, educators must develop specific objectives. *A specific objective is a statement that is limited to a precise application.* A specific objective focuses on a specific group, a specific behavior, and a specific action that is to occur. In a specific objective, there is no possibility for subjective or variable interpretations of the precise application indicated.

Specific objectives are an outgrowth of general objectives. In other words, general objectives provide a base, or an intent, for the development of specific ones. Specific objectives allow the professional educator to delineate general objectives as meaningful educational outcomes that are both important to the educational community and measurable. But the measurability of an objective does not guarantee that it is appropriate. Not only must an objective be measurable, but the specific behavior must be determined to be an appropriate outcome of the educational program.

The general objective "to advance the learning of the students" is a statement of intent that might generate the following specific objective: "at the end of the sixth grade, all the pupils will be able to spell all the words on a seventh-grade spelling list." An immediate reaction to this objective is that it is adequate because it is measurable, but this is not enough. The behavior to be observed may be measurable, but it is not necessarily acceptable to the educator. The behavior described, "to spell all the words on a seventh-grade spelling list," is not an appropriate behavior for sixth-grade students. The terminal behavior must be measurable, and the behavior to be measured must also be educationally appropriate for the individuals involved.

Specific educational objectives are important to school systems for two reasons. First, specific objectives have precise application and are not open to broad interpretations. As a result, the educators are able to describe what is going on in the classroom. Second, specific objectives permit educational specialists to describe the specific outcome that they believe should be a product of their work. This means that the trained educator can describe the specific behavior that it is expected will occur as a result of educational experience.

Since a specific objective is a delineation of a general objective, its components can best be thought of as a product or an expansion of the components of a general objective. The first component of a general objective, to identify the individuals or groups who should perform the terminal behavior or outcome, must be made more precise. "Students" in our previous examples as a group to perform terminal behavior must be better defined. If general objectives are stated for an entire school system, then the term "students" could refer to numerous possible groupings according to grade level, age level, or social character. The specific objective must delineate the precise group to be observed.

The second component of a general objective, regarding the direction of behavioral change, should also be precisely designated. Not only must the direction of the change be stated but so must the magnitude of the change. The terms "advance" and "improve" indicated positive changes, but what is the quantity of positive change that is appropriate for these objectives? The general objective leaves this important question to the judgment of educational professionals. Because magnitude is an important issue, we must describe it in terms of the measuring devices to be employed. The term "advance" might be delineated as "to advance at least 10 raw score points" or "improve" might be specified as "to improve as judged by an outside artist." These delineations provide two very different but precise statements concerning positive change. The first, with its specific number of raw score points, implies precise objective measurement. The second, by introducing the element of artistic taste, implies a subjective measurement. In both examples, the more precise statement limits the application of a general objective.

The third component of a general objective requires that a general category defining terminal behavior be presented. "Learning" in a general objective could mean many things, depending on the precise application of the term. The term "learning" is so general that several outstanding scholars have developed differing schemes for delineating it. (See the references at the end of this chapter.) Not only must the material to be learned be described, but the level of learning must also be evident. Is learning occurring when a person can recall or recognize the terminology in a discipline, or is learning the ability to analyze a concept and meaningfully discuss its components? A specific objective must describe a specific action. The behavior or outcome must be specific enough to enable anyone who reads the objective to state the terminal behavior that is to be exhibited. Later chapters will discuss the development of measuring instruments for the different components of "learning" and "attitudes."

The relation between the components of general objectives and specific objectives may be summarized as follows:

General: Identify the group that should perform the terminal behavior or outcome.
Specific: Specify the group's age level, grade level, social class, or other characteristics.

General: Designate the direction of change.
Specific: Specify the magnitude of change.

General: Identify a general category of the desired terminal behavior.
Specific: Specify the level of the desired terminal behavior.

Throughout this discussion, it has been assumed that the educational specialist has responsibility for defining specific objectives. This is because the educational specialist has been trained to help children grow as a result of their educational experiences. The educator has had the opportunity to observe the behavior that is the desired product of education and has studied the processes that allow desired behavior to be achieved. The specialist who is aware of the intentions of the people responsible for an educational system is the individual best trained to define the specific objectives in a given area of specialization.

Limitations of Educational Objectives

It seems that every thing that is useful also has some negative aspects. Automobiles provide convenient transportation, yet engine exhaust pollutes the air. Airplanes get us where we want to go in a hurry, but environmental pollution causes considerable discomfort to people who live near the airports. Electricity provides comforts too numerous to list, but the generation of electricity also pollutes our environment. So it is with educational objectives. From the teacher's viewpoint one major limitation of educational objectives is that their development is difficult and time consuming. It seems like an overwhelming task for a teacher to sit down at the beginning of the school year to list all the objectives to be accomplished within it. Some educators have argued that objectives should therefore not be stressed because teachers have neither the time nor the inclination to undertake their statement. But it seems to us that the advantage of developing objectives, whether or not they are actually written down, is so great that they cannot be ignored. Teachers may take heart from the knowledge that once the objectives for a course have been established, probably all that will be required thereafter is periodic revision. Moreover, a number of national curriculum development centers are making the teachers' task easier by developing objectives that teachers can use either exactly as they are published or as adjustable guidelines in the preparation of individual statements of objectives.

Another limitation of educational objectives results from the necessity to state specific objectives. It is easy to lose sight of a general objective when stating specific ones. When this happens, the direction of the educational program becomes fragmented toward a large number of isolated goals for behavior with no concern for how these goals should fit together to form the over-all behavior of the students. Such education may well be worse than that achieved when educational programs are developed with no objectives at all. The teacher should remember that specific objectives are a means for achieving a more important end. If this end is forgotten and the specific objectives become ends in themselves, then the advantages of educational objectives will be lost.

A very serious problem in stating educational objectives is the decision among possible objectives. A school certainly cannot hope to achieve everything. Therefore, choice must be made. The basis from which objectives are included and excluded is sometimes nebulous. But a choice must be made if an educational program is to have sound objectives.

Once a choice of objectives has been made, educators must counteract the tendency to ignore other possible outcomes. Educational objectives designed to achieve certain behavior may also achieve others, unintended outcomes, and these are often ignored. For example, a teacher may have established a set of objectives that could reasonably be achieved through programmed instruction or through classroom discussion. An evaluation of these two teaching techniques may show that both helped accomplish the objectives that had been stated. The evaluation might also reveal that programmed instruction allowed the objective to be accomplished in less time than did classroom discussion. Given this information, the teacher would probably elect to use programmed instruction to accomplish the same objectives in the future. But the classroom discussion may well have accomplished certain unintended objectives that programmed instruction could not accomplish. For example, discussion may have helped students improve their ability to express themselves orally. If this was not one of the stated objectives, it might be overlooked in the evaluation. Consequently if programmed instruction were used with future classes to achieve the initially stated objectives, the result would probably be that the ability to help students express themselves orally would be lost.

Some programs may produce certain unintended outcomes that prove to be undesirable. If such programs are adopted because they achieve certain stated objectives, undesirable outcomes may become a part of the end result or a part of the student behavior at the end of the instructional process. Therefore educators must remain aware not only of the outcomes they expect but also of those that may also be achieved without expectation.

To determine whether desired change has occurred, educators must measure behavioral traits at the end of any given instructional process. Although objectives may state behavior in very precise terms, educational measurement has not yet developed precise measuring devices for many types of behavior. Measurement of artistic ability, for example, still relies on subjective judgments by experts. Teachers and evaluators who insist on very precise objective measurement of all objectives severely limit the number and types of objectives that can be stated. Despite the limitations, the entire school system can profit from the statement of educational objectives if all the people concerned with the educational process become involved, each to his own professional ability, in the process of developing the specific objectives.

Reflections

1. Objectives allow the members of an educational program to state precisely the impact the program is intended to have on individuals in it.
2. Objectives provide the criteria to be employed for judging decision alternatives in the educational process. In addition,

objectives describe the specific behavior to be measured in the evaluation process.

3. A general objective is a statement that is not limited to a precise set of circumstances.

4. General objectives provide an opportunity for nonspecialists to state the intent of a specific educational program or institution without describing the process by which the desired outcomes will be attained.

5. A general objective has three basic components. It must (a) identify the general group that should perform the terminal behavior or outcome, (b) designate the direction of the expected change, (c) identify a general category of the desired terminal behavior.

6. General objectives do not provide sufficient information about the behavior to be assessed. Before the principles of educational measurement can be used, the specific behavior to be assessed must be made obvious.

7. A specific objective is a statement that is limited to a precise set of circumstances and is less subject to subjective interpretation than general objectives.

8. Specific objectives provide a guideline for measurement, the criteria for educational evaluation, and the means for precisely describing the desired outcomes of teaching activities.

9. The components of a specific objective further delineate the components of a general objective as follows: (a) make the group specific by specifying the age-level, grade-level, social class, and so forth, (b) specify the magnitude of the change to occur, and (c) state the specific level of the desired terminal behavior.

10. The components of a specific objective are determined by the educational specialist most closely associated with the educational program.

11. Some limitations of educational objectives are:
    a. Developing and stating objectives is time-consuming and difficult.
    b. In the process of making an objective specific, the intent of the general objective is sometimes lost.
    c. By making the objectives of a program specific, we sometimes overlook unintended outcomes.
    d. While objectives can be stated in very specific terms, it is not always possible to measure precisely the behavior.

Exercises

1. Obtain or develop the general objectives for this course.
2. Review your general objectives. If some general objectives have been poorly stated, revise them. In what ways are the general objectives useful for your planned evaluation of the class?
3. Develop some specific objectives for the general objectives. Sharing your objectives with another member of the class, determine whether the two of you have interpreted the general objectives in the same way.
4. What are some limitations of the objectives that you have developed? Suggest ways in which the limitations could be overcome.
5. Develop a position paper on the use of behavioral objectives in your major discipline. Discuss the advantages and the limitations of behavioral objectives in your discipline.

Selected References

GRADED AND NONGRADED CLASSROOMS

Goodlad, J. I., and R. H. Anderson. *The Non-Graded Elementary School.* New York: Harcourt Brace Jovanovich, 1959. Pp. 58–59. Graded and nongraded structures are compared from a base of "internal criteria"—criteria relevant to the assumptions that underlie graded and nongraded approaches.

Brown, B. F. *The Nongraded High School.* Englewood Cliffs, N. J.: Prentice-Hall, 1963. The nongraded school and its history, variations, curriculum, advantages, and implementation are discussed.

Wang, M. C., and J. L. Yeager. "Evaluation Under Individualized Instruction" *The Elementary School Journal,* 71 (1971), 448–52. Discusses some of the problems inherent in examining rate of learning.

Lewis, J., Jr. *A Contemporary Approach to Nongraded Education.* New York: Parker, 1969. Pp. 19–32. A criticism of the graded system of education in relation to children in cultural minorities and a description of the benefits of the nongraded approach. There is an outline of a sensitivity training institute for educators.

BEHAVIORAL OBJECTIVES

Haberman, Martin. "Behavioral Objectives: Bandwagon on Breakthrough." *Journal of Teacher Education*, 19 (1968), 91–94. The values and limitations of using behavioral objectives in the classroom are discussed with examples that illustrate its benefits and its constraints.

Macdonald, J. B., and B. J. Wolfson. "A Case Against Behavioral Objectives." *The Elementary School Journal*, 71 (1970), 119–28. An argument is presented against behavioral objectives. It centers on four questions: interpreting behavior in terms of learning, the nature of human activity, the nature of knowledge, and the implications of a technological rationale for learning.

Popham, W. J., et al. "Instructional Objectives: An Analysis of Emerging Issues," *AERA Monograph Series on Curriculum Evaluation*. No. 3. Chicago: Rand McNally, 1969. Pp. 40–52. This section deals with the advantages of using precisely stated objectives. It also reviews two studies and presents and refutes ten commonly raised objections concerning behavioral objectives.

Rath, J. D. "Teaching Without Specific Objectives." *Educational Leadership*, 28 (1971), 714–20. This criticism of behavioral objectives rests on the assumption that activities can be justified in terms of criteria other than change in behavior.

Thorndike, R. L., ed. *Educational Measurement*. Washington D. C.: American Council on Education, 1971. Pp. 36–44. The author analyzes behavioral objectives under the assumption that for much of the educational process there are goals that are specifiable as behavioral outcomes.

PROCEDURES FOR DEVELOPING BEHAVIORAL OBJECTIVES

Esbensen, Thorwald. "Writing Instructional Objectives." *Phi Delta Kappan* 48 (1967), 246–47. This article details the composition of precise and well-written behavioral objectives.

Popham, W. J., et al. "Instructional Objectives." *AERA Monograph Series on Curriculum Evaluation*. No. 3, Chicago: Rand McNally, 1969. Pp. 35–38. The authors describe how to state an instructional objective and include examples of poorly and properly stated objectives.

Popham, W. J., and E. L. Baker. *Systematic Instruction*. Englewood Cliffs, N. J.: Prentice-Hall, 1970. Pp.: 20–24. The importance of stating objectives in operational terms is stressed and examples are given of vague and clear objectives.

Part Two

External Measuring Devices

3

Norm-Referenced and Criterion-Referenced Testing

CONCERNS

1. What is a reference system in educational measurement?
2. What is the purpose of a reference system?
3. What types of reference system are applicable to education?
4. What should be considered in employing a criterion-referenced system?
5. In the norm-referenced system, what is the reference group?
6. How does the teacher decide what reference group to use?
7. What types of test score are appropriate in a norm-referenced system?
8. What are the advantages and disadvantages of norm-referenced test scores?
9. What is criterion-referenced measurement?
10. How is a criterion-referenced system established?
11. How are criterion-referenced scores different from cut-off scores?
12. How are criterion-referenced scores different from content-standard scores?
13. How are scores obtained in the criterion-referenced system different from the concept of absolute interpretation of test scores?
14. What are the commonalities of norm-referenced and criterion-referenced measurement?
15. What are the differences between norm-referenced and criterion-referenced measurement?

Before educational evaluation can progress with any degree of certainty, the evaluator must decide what information he needs. Does the evaluation require information about general skills or achievement, or does it require information concerning a specific set of activities? Answers to these basic questions provide the evaluator with an indication of the types of measurement problem that must be met.

Once content of the information to be collected has been determined, the evaluator can define the area such as mathematics achievement or attitude toward adults in which data are to be collected. Given this knowledge, the specific content of examinations to be used in the gathering of information can be readily determined. The content of the information to be collected is not the only thing to be considered in preparing a test, however. A teacher may be told that Jodi received a score of 48 on a mathematics achievement test, for example. But unless this information is made meaningful, the teacher has no idea what this test score of 48 represents. Although the exam's content (mathematics achievement) is specific, the information is not useful. The teacher has been provided with nothing with which to compare the score. To give a teacher a test score without providing a reference system is like telling a moose hunter who is lost in the swamp to go north when he has no compass.

What Is a Reference System?

Reference systems in educational measurement are used to provide a basis for interpreting results obtained from a measuring device. Reference systems are the key to making useful the information that is obtained from tests. There are primarily two types of reference system available in educational measurement. The most commonly used reference system involves the use of information collected from some known group. The group is well described and its characteristics are known to the people who use it as a reference. This reference group is commonly called a norm group, and the reference system is called a norm-referenced system.

Another commonly used reference system is called a criterion-referenced system. In this there is no specifically defined group. Instead, the measuring device or test is the reference. A criterion-referenced test is constructed in such a way that either it represents the information or skills necessary to be successful at the next stage of whatever area is being assessed or it represents the terminal skills necessary to show competence. A student's score on the test is interpreted either as representing whether the student possesses the information required to move on to the next stage in the learning process or as representing whether the student possesses previously defined terminal skills.

Norm-referenced and criterion-referenced measurements are both useful in educational evaluations, and they can be used separately or simultaneously to provide useful information for an evaluation process. In general, a reference system helps the teacher interpret reported scores. In the case of Jodi, the availability of a norm group would enable the teacher to compare Jodi's score against the scores obtained by that group. If the test were to be used as the reference system, then the teacher, having full knowledge of the content of the test, and therefore of the information or skills it represents, would be able to determine whether Jodi had achieved the level of competence being sought. Until the reference systems are adequately described, however, Jodi's score is meaningless.

Norm-Referenced Groups

In evaluations in which the reference system to be used is a norm group, the usefulness of test information depends on the nature of the norm group. Its characteristics must be similar to those of the group that is being evaluated. In this regard, the most important question for the teacher or evaluator is: "What characteristics should be considered in choosing the norm group?" If achievement is the criterion being investigated, then it is important that the experiential background of the reference group be similar to that of the students being evaluated. Experiential background is extremely difficult to assess but it is very important in obtaining useful information. If all the children being evaluated are from an inner city, then the reference group for comparison should be a group of inner-city children. To say that fifth-grade children from the inner city have had educational experiences different from those of children from suburban schools is a harsh implication for today's educational system, but experience supports the hypothesis. In view of it, it is unreasonable to expect the same levels of achievement of children of the inner city and of children of the suburbs.

Other characteristics to be considered in selecting the norm group are easier to assess than is experiential background. Grade level is usually an important consideration in the assessment of achievement. The ages of the children being assessed and their overall academic ability are also characteristics to consider. In most settings, these characteristics can be measured and are usually thought of as providing information about experiential background. These classification categories provide information about the children, but they do not assure the evaluator that children in each classification have the same experiential background. Third-grade students in suburban schools undoubtedly have different experiential backgrounds from those of third-grade students in rural schools and a different norm group is needed for each.

How can an evaluator take all these norm-group characteristics into consideration? A teacher is usually dealing with a hetero-geneous group that cannot be described adequately by a single set of categories. The children in a heterogeneous classroom usually have a wide variety of experiential backgrounds. The teacher should select the most common characteristic, probably grade level, and use this characteristic to determine the appro-priate norm group.

A teacher selects a reference group from a standardized refer-ence because it is believed to be representative of the conventional classroom most like that teacher's class. Quite often this norm group is characterized as a national norm group because it is believed to represent children throughout the nation at a particular grade level. Other norm-referenced groups are provided by most publishers of standardized tests and include students from large cities, inner cities, states, specific regions, and specific ability levels. In most cases, external tests provide sufficient norm-group information to provide for the meaningful interpretation of test scores. Companies that produce standardized tests use elaborate techniques for forming a variety of norm-referenced groups, as is clearly indicated in the following description of sampling procedures.

A Description of the Norming Sample for the Standardization of the Iowa Tests of Basic Skills, Cognitive Abilities Test, and the Tests of Academic Progress

Procedures Used in the Selection of the
Standardization Sample

Seven community size categories, corresponding to the U.S. Census classification system, were employed. In each size category, a sample of approximately 0.6 per cent of pupils was to be selected. The number of sampling units to be drawn from each category and the per cent of pupils to be sampled in each unit were determined in the light of previous experience with respect to variability in school performance in communities of various sizes.

The initial specifications called for 87 public school units to be selected and sampled as follows:

Size Category	No. in Sample
1,000,000 +	5
250,000 +	8
100,000 +	11
50,000 +	12
25,000 +	15
10,000 +	18
Rural Counties	18

For each community, two facts were obtained from the 1960 census and entered on a card. These were (1) median years of education of the population 25 years old and over, and (2) median family income, in thousands of dollars. These two numbers were added together without any further weighting (they appeared to have fairly comparable variability). The resulting number which ranged from about 10 to 25, served as the basis for stratification of communities within a size category.

Within each size stratum, all communities were arranged in order on the basis of the index described above. The stack of cards was divided into as many fractions as there were communities to be drawn from that size group. Three cards were then pulled at random from the fraction, becoming, respectively, the first, second, and third choices for the sample. (The strictly random procedure was slightly modified to guarantee better regional representation. Thus, where a state was already represented, further choices from that state were rejected as first choices until every other state was also represented.)

The parochial school sample was a proportion of the total public school sample within each size and socio-economic category. The proportion of parochial school students ranged from 15% of the large city units to 3% of the public rural sample. Eighteen sampling units for parochial schools were obtained from cities and towns included in the public school sample by selecting 18 first, second, and third choice units at random from within each size and socio-economic sample.

The chief administrative school officers for both public and parochial schools designated as first choice were then contacted. The response was gratifying. Fifty-five of the 105 first-choice units agreed to participate and a total of 89 of the 105 sampling unit categories were filled.

The administrative officers who replied favorably were then asked for some form of quality rating of their schools. When these were received, a plan for sampling attendance units was worked out for each system to obtain the necessary sampling fraction of pupils. When such a quality rating was not available, units were selected at random. In some systems, all pupils were tested, and the sample was later taken from the answer sheets returned for processing.

The tests were administered, with occasional exceptions, between October 15 and November 15, 1970. The answer sheets were processed by Houghton Mifflin Scoring Service. Incomplete answer sheets (on which pupils omitted one or more tests) were processed but not included in the analyses.

Although 1960 census data were used as the basis for selecting the original public school sample, preliminary population figures for the 1970 census were obtained in November, 1970, to ascertain if any significant shifts in population occurred between 1960 and 1970. Minor changes did occur but the proportions of the population in various size categories was almost identical to the proportions observed in 1960. For example, Houston was added to the 1,000,000+ category but, because the populations in the remaining five cities increased only slightly, the percentage of the national population living in 1,000,000+ cities was slightly less in 1970 (9.2%) than in 1960 (9.8%).

In order to compensate for missing categories, and to adjust for the fact that some schools tested more or fewer than the sampling specifications called for, a weight was assigned in each grade in each building to all raw score frequencies. This weight (between 0 and 9) was assigned in such a way as to synthesize the characteristics of a missing cell or to adjust the frequency in other cells. Size of system, socio-economic status, and public-parochial balance were all simultaneously considered in assigning these weights. As a result, the weighted distributions are believed to approximate very closely those for the total population.

The appropriate norm group for an internally developed measuring device is much more difficult to find. A measuring device is usually developed at a specific time for a specific group and usually no similar reference group is available. This greatly reduces a teacher's ability to interpret exam results in a meaningful way. Where a testing instrument is used from one year to the next or in several classrooms within the same building or school system, the norm group can be the other students who have completed the test; the norm group can then be adequately defined. This procedure may be thought of as a procedure for developing local norms. While local norms are particularly useful with internally developed measures, local norms may also be developed for externally developed tests.

Interpreting Test Scores

As we indicated earlier, the crucial issue in norm-referenced testing is the similarity between the group being evaluated and the norm group. Once this similarity has been established, the nature of the interpretation of test results becomes important. Test scores can be compared to the norm-referenced group by using some scale system, or the scores can be ranked against the reference group. In a scale system, the raw scores obtained on a test are changed so that they appear in a scale of well-defined characteristics. This procedure is similar to the changing of degrees of temperature from Farenheit to Centigrade. The real difference between temperature and test scores is that raw scores, unlike temperatures, have no defined scale. The conversion to some standard scale provides a defined system in which scores can be compared. The purpose in using ranked scores is to give each score meaning by indicating how many scores in the distribution fall to each side of the score in question. Once the appropriate norm group has been established, the objectives for the evaluation indicate the score system to be used.

Percentile Rank

The most common method of interpreting norm-referenced scores is to determine the percentage of people scoring below a specific score in the norm-reference group. The percentage of scores falling below a specific score point is the percentile rank of the specific score and is a ranked score. For example, Brent may have a raw score of 17 on an arithmetic test for third-grade students. To interpret this score, the teacher might wish to compare Brent's score with the scores for a group of children who are similar to Brent. If the distribution of scores for the norm group is known, the teacher may determine that a score of 17 has a percentile rank of 93. This means that 93 percent of the students in the norm group scored below a raw score of 17.

How does a teacher interpret a percentile rank of a score? Is a percentile rank of 93 "good"? The answers to these questions depend on the nature of the reference group. If it has an experiential background similar to that of the students being observed, a percentile rank of 93 is probably acceptable in terms of how well other students did on the test. The percentile rank of a score does not tell us how well the student knows the material being assessed, however. The student with a percentile rank of 93 may or may not have adequate knowledge of the material being assessed to use the information in future learning experiences.

In the example of Brent, the score of 17 may have been obtained from a test of twenty-one items. In this case, the student correctly answered 81 percent of the questions asked. This knowledge provides for a different interpretation of Brent's score. The reference in this case is the total number of questions that were to be answered. Eighty-one percent tells us what percentage of the number of responses made were correct. This percentage case does not use the norm group in any way, but it gives the teacher a better idea of how well the student knows the material of the exam.

The concept of percentile rank is easily understood but it is occasionally misinterpreted. Sometimes people interpreting scores are discouraged when they find that the percentile rank is below fifty. This would mean that the score places the individual being tested in the lower 50 percent of the norm group. It should be realized that half of every norm group must fall below the middle of the distribution. A percentile rank below fifty does not necessarily indicate that an individual does not understand a particular area of knowledge, such as arithmetic; rather, it means that 50 percent or more of the norm group understood the knowledge being assessed better than did the individual being tested. The percentile rank of a score provides the teacher with information relative to a defined group of students, but it does not provide specific information as to whether each student understands the area of knowledge being assessed.

Grade Equivalents

In recent years, test publishers have made an effort to provide test users with scores meaningful in the environment in which the tests are used. Standardized achievement tests are developed primarily for use in the classroom. Test developers have thus created the concept of grade equivalent in order to assist evaluators in school systems that use graded classrooms. The grade equivalent is probably not useful to school systems that use nongraded classrooms.

A grade equivalent is a scale score determined from a raw score obtained on a test. The grade equivalent of a particular score is the grade level of the norm group whose median (the point below which 50 percent of the scores fall) is the same as the raw score. For example, the norm group may be a group of fifth-grade children in their fourth month of school. The raw score below which 50 percent of the scores of the norm group fall may be 14. Then the grade equivalent for the raw score of 14 would be 5.4. The grade equivalent of 5.4 represents the fifth grade and the fourth month. A grade equivalent of 6.7 would represent the sixth grade and the seventh month.

It is important to understand how a test publisher converts a raw score to a grade equivalent. The test publisher may provide, for example, for a fourth-grade reading test (the content of which has been designed for fourth-grade students) to be administered to children in grades 2 through 7. The results of this exam might be similar to those reported for the hypothetical standardized test in Table 3.1. If the Bumble Reading Test were given to the norm-referenced groups during the fourth month of the school year, then the conversion of raw score to grade equivalent would provide the grade equivalents reported in Table 3.1. A raw score of 42 would convert to a grade equivalent of 5.4, which would be interpreted to mean that an individual who scored 42 on the fourth-grade Bumble Reading Test scored the same as the median score for children in the fifth grade and the fourth month.

Table 3.1 *Median Scores and Grade Equivalents for the Bumble Reading Test*

GRADE	FOURTH-GRADE TEST MEDIAN RAW SCORE	GRADE EQUIVALENT
2	10	2.4
3	18	3.4
4	27	4.4
5	42	5.4
6	53	6.4
7	61	7.4

Figure 3.1   *Interpolation of the Scores on the Bumble Reading Test*

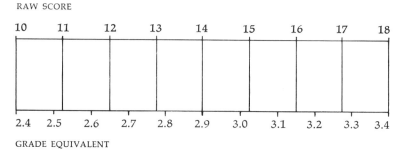

RAW SCORE

GRADE EQUIVALENT

    Historically, the school year has been ten months long. Test publishers have therefore established a ten-point scale for grade equivalents. Students could obtain fourth-grade equivalents ranging from 4.0 to 4.9, for example. A student receiving a grade equivalent of 4.0 on the Bumble Reading Test would be said to have performed as well as a student at the beginning of the fourth-grade year. A student receiving a grade equivalent of 4.9 would be said to have performed as well as a student at the end of the fourth-grade year.

    Caution must be taken in interpreting grade equivalents. In the example above, a grade equivalent of 5.4 for a fourth-grade student would *not* mean that that student can do fifth-grade work. It does mean that the student scored higher than 50 percent of the fifth-grade students in the norm group on the fourth-grade exam. Before an interpretation about the child's ability to do fifth-grade work can be made, an exam covering the content of a fifth-grade topic should be administered. Grade equivalents are determined for a norm group on a specific set of materials. The teacher should not try to extrapolate beyond the concepts covered on an exam.

    How is the grade equivalent determined for a child who earned a score of 16? Test publishers obviously, cannot administer tests monthly to obtain conversions for raw scores at each month of the school year. Therefore, they interpolate the conversions for the raw scores that do not fall at the median of a known reference group. For example, the Bumble Reading Test provides the information that a raw score of 10 converts to a grade equivalent of 2.4

and that a raw score of 18 converts to a grade equivalent of 3.4. In Figure 3.1 the distance between 10 and 18 is divided into eight equal parts and projected to the grade-equivalent scale which has been divided into ten equal parts. In this example, the raw score 16 is converted to a grade equivalent of 3.1. From Figure 3.1, the interpolation process would provide the following conversion table:

RAW SCORE	GRADE EQUIVALENT
10	2.4
11	2.5
12	2.6
13	2.7
14	2.9
15	3.0
16	3.1
17	3.2
18	3.4

Grade equivalents are useful for interpreting test scores. They provide information not contained in the percentile rank. They are useful in school systems using graded classrooms because they provide additional information as to how well a student understands the concepts being tested. But although grade equivalents can be helpful in an evaluation, they are subject to improper interpretation.

In evaluation, the teacher who seeks evidence of change must be careful in using grade equivalents. As the Bumble Reading Test example makes obvious, a change in grade-equivalent score of two points may result from a change of only one or two raw scores. In other words, the magnitude of the change in raw scores on a test cannot be obtained directly from the change in grade equivalents. The fewer the number of raw scores there is, the more obvious is the problem of determining the magnitude of change based on grade equivalents. Grade equivalents can be used to show change, but the magnitude of the change may not be meaningful. This is especially true when the grade equivalents have been obtained from two tests covering different materials. (This problem is reviewed in detail in Chapter 15 of Robert L. Thorndike's book listed in the references at the end of this chapter.)

Age Equivalents

Age equivalents are similar to grade equivalents except that years of age replace grade levels in computation and interpretation. Scale scores like these are quite useful in school systems with nongraded classrooms and in cases where school-related interpretation is not necessary. Age equivalents are extremely useful when change is expected as a result of maturation. They are meaningful when height or weight are being measured. If Scott is four feet nine inches tall and a fourth-grade student, can he be said to be tall for a fourth-grade student? Probably so, but this does not seem to be the most meaningful group to compare him with. It would be more meaningful to compare Scott with children his own age. He may be nine years and three months old. The median height for a norm group of boys nine years and three months old might be four feet five inches. Because Scott is taller than the median height for his age group, we can conclude that he is tall for his age. If age equivalents were available, we could determine the age group that Scott's height is most like.

In this example, then, the raw score is the height of the individual. To determine the age equivalent for Scott, we must find the norm-referenced group that has a median of four feet nine inches. Assume that the norm group with a median height of four feet nine inches is a group of children eleven years and five months old. The age equivalent for Scott then is 11-5. Special notice should be taken of the dash in the age equivalent. The dash is used rather than a decimal point because age equivalents are based on a twelve-month system; grade equivalents are based on a ten-month system and use the decimal point.

Age equivalent is a useful scale in situations where the variable being investigated is more closely related to age than to grade level in school. Like grade equivalents, the usefulness of age equivalents depends on the availability of appropriate norm groups, and the norm group must be similar to the group of individuals being evaluated.

Standard Scores

Another popular scale score system for representing the relative performance of a student on a test is the standard score. Standard scores provide the evaluator or teacher with information as to how a particular score relates to the average score on a test. The average performance on a test is called the "arithmetic mean" (generally abbreviated to "mean"). The *mean* is the arithmetic average of all the raw scores obtained on a test.

Since the mean is the average of all the scores in a distribution, it can be expected that most scores resulting from the test will be different from the mean. That is, there will be some variability in the test scores. The *standard deviation* of a group of scores is a measure of the variability of the scores about the mean of the group of scores. The standard deviation of a group of scores is found by using the following formula:

$$s = \sqrt{\frac{\Sigma(X_i - M)^2}{n}}$$

s = the standard deviation of the scores
X_i = an individual raw score
M = the arithmetic mean of the raw scores
n = the number of scores in the group

This equation determines the number of score points between each score in the set of scores and the mean. These distances (each number of points between scores) are then squared. The average of the squared distances is then determined. The square root of the average of the squared distances from the mean to each score is the standard deviation.

In Figure 3.2 are three graphs representing three groups that have the same mean but different standard deviations. You will notice that the only difference in the graphs is the variability of the scores. The scores are more closely grouped when the standard deviation is small, and the scores are in general farther from the mean when the standard deviation is large. Therefore, the size of the standard deviation gives the teacher an idea of the variability of the scores represented.

The purpose of a standard score is to indicate how a particular score relates to the mean of a set of scores by indicating how many standard deviations from the mean the score in question is. While there are many types of standard score in use today, the most basic standard score derived from a set of data is the *z-score*. A z-score can be determined from any distribution of raw scores. A

Figure 3.2   *Three Normal Distribution Curves with Different Stand-ard Deviations*

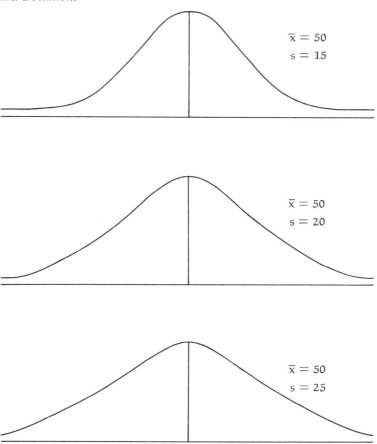

z-score is determined for each raw score in the distribution of scores. z-scores are computed with the following formula:

$$z_i = \frac{X_i - M}{s}$$

z_i = the standard score for a particular raw score
X_i = an individual raw score from any given distribution
M = the arithmetic mean of the raw scores in the distribution
s = the standard deviation of the raw scores in the distribution

We might want to know the z-score of a child for a reading exam. If the child obtained a raw score of 12, we would like to know the position of this score with respect to the remainder of the class. If we obtain the percentile rank of the score 12, we determine how many children scored less than 12, but we do not know what the score means with respect to the mean of the distribution. For this example, assume that the mean of the raw scores is 8 and the standard deviation of the raw scores is 2. Using the z-score formula, the child's z-score would be calculated as follows:

$$z_i = \frac{(X_i - M)}{s}$$

$$z_i = \frac{(12 - 8)}{2}$$

$$z_i = \frac{4}{2}$$

$$z_i = 2$$

The z-score for a raw score of 12 is 2. What does this z-score of 2 represent? It indicates that this child scored two standard deviations above the mean of the norm group. If the child had received a raw score of 6, then the z-score would have been -1, which would indicate that the child scored one standard deviation below the mean. If the child received a raw score of 5, the z-score would have been -1.5. A z-value of -1.5 would indicate that the child scored one and one-half standard deviations below the mean.

A careful inspection of the z-score formula reveals that the mean of the z-score is 0 and the standard deviation is 1. This helps the teacher to interpret the z-score results. If a student obtains a z-score of 0, that student is 0 standard deviations away from the mean of the raw scores. In another sense, a z-score of 0 indicates that the child has scored at the mean of the raw-score group.

Standard scores and percentile ranks provide different information about a set of scores. In one situation, it is possible to tie the two together to provide more information about a set of scores than either can provide independently. This very specific situation occurs when it can be assumed that the characteristic being measured by the test is distributed normally. A normal distribution is a very specific way in which the scores on a test may be distributed.

Figure 3.3   *A Normal Distribution with a Mean of 0 and a Standard Deviation of 1*

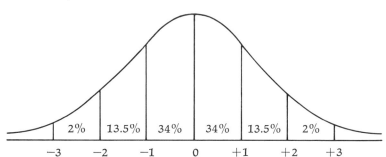

| 2% | 13.5% | 34% | 34% | 13.5% | 2% |

$$-3 \quad -2 \quad -1 \quad 0 \quad +1 \quad +2 \quad +3$$

If we know that the scores are distributed, normally, we know the percentage of individuals who fall below the various scores obtained on the test. While a normal distribution may have any value as its mean and standard deviation, the computation of a z-score for each of the scores in a normal distribution would force the normal distribution to have a mean of 0 and a standard deviation of 1. In this case, the distribution of scores would appear as in Figure 3.3

It will be noticed that 68 percent of the scores fall between $z = +1$ and $z = -1$, 95 percent of the scores fall between $z = +2$ and $z = -2$, and 99 percent of the scores fall between $z = +3$ and $z = -3$. It can also be seen that if an individual received a z-score of $+1$ on the test, he would have a percentile rank of 84. An individual receiving a z-score of -2 would have a percentile rank of 2, indicating that only 2 percent of the scores fall more than 2 standard deviations below the mean. All good statistics texts provide more specific tables for the calculation of the percentile rank of any z-value between $+3$ and -3.

Some educators do not like to use z-scores because the negative sign for all scores below the mean is viewed as damaging to the morale of the student. Educators have therefore developed other standard score scales that eliminate negative signs and decimal points. One such scale is T. The important feature of this standard score is that the mean of the T distribution is 50 and the standard deviation is 10 (whereas in the z distribution the mean is 0 and the standard deviation is 1). T can be calculated with the following equation:

$$T_i = 10(z_i) + 50$$

in which T_i is the standard T-score for an individual score and z_i is the standard z-score for an individual score.

Suppose that a child has received a raw score of 12 on a test and that the mean of the distribution of scores is 8 and the standard deviation is 2. If we wanted to determine the T-score for this child, the first step would be to determine the z-score for the score of 12. We have already determined that this score would yield a z-score of 2. The conversion to a T-score then follows:

$$T_i = 10(z_i) + 50$$

$$T_i = 10(2) + 50$$

$$T_i = 70$$

Since the mean of T-scores is 50 and the standard deviation is 10, a T-score of 70 would indicate that this child is two standard deviations above the mean. A T-score of 45 would indicate one-half a standard deviation below the mean.

Many other standard score scales are available and reported in texts. As with T, these use the z-score as the basis for the standard score system. All standard score systems are interpreted in the same manner as the z-score, and they are subject to the same limitations in the decision-making process.

Stanines

Another standard score system that is currently used by many teachers is the single-digit stanine. This has been developed from a standard nine-point scale. Stanines are very simple to use and easy to interpret. The stanine scale is not as precise as standard score scales, but many educators argue that the stanine scale is precise enough for testing situations in the schools.

Raw scores are converted to stanine scores that range from a high of 9 to a low of 1. Assuming that the raw-score distribution is normal, the conversion to the stanine scale is accomplished in such a way that the mean of the stanine scores is 5 and the standard deviation is 2. A stanine then represents a percentage of the scores. It is not a point, and for this reason it is different from the other scales discussed. The stanine conversion is as follows:

Stanine	1	2	3	4	5	6	7	8	9
Percent of scores	4	7	12	17	20	17	12	7	4

A stanine score of 1 is the stanine score for the lowest 4 percent of the raw scores. A stanine score of 4 is the appropriate score for 17 percent of the raw scores. A stanine of 9 is the appropriate score for the highest 4 percent of the scores. The stanine scale does not take into consideration the values of the raw scores in a particular stanine. This causes some problems in interpreting the data from a stanine scale. The stanine is used by individuals who believe that test scores are not as precise as the numerical scores indicate and that the stanine is a more appropriate way to report a test score.

Educators who argue for more precise information are not satisfied with the single-digit stanine. The evaluator who must determine whether change has occurred is quite restricted by the stanine scale. A student's raw score on a test could rise fifteen points from the first administration of a test to the second, but that individual could well receive the same stanine score for both administrations of the test.

Suppose on the other hand, that Pamela received a raw score of 84 on the first test administration and that this score represents the highest score in stanine 6. Suppose also, that Gregg received a raw score of 85 on the first administration of the test and that this represents the lowest score in stanine 7. If the test were administered a second time and Gregg received a score of 84 and Pamela received a score of 85, and the same conversion scale were used, Gregg would now be in stanine 6 and Pamela would be in stanine 7. It would appear to an individual looking only at the stanine scores that Pamela had demonstrated growth in the content measured by the test, because her stanine score increased from 6 to 7, and that Gregg suffered a loss in the content measured. Yet these changes in stanine occurred with changes of one raw-score point. The result of this characteristic of stanines leads to the conclusion that stanines are not appropriate for measuring the growth of individual pupils over short periods of time.

In actual practice, the determination of scaled scores from standardized tests has been made very easy. Suppose Julie had taken Level 13 in Form 5 of the Iowa Tests of Basic Skills, for example. Her raw score on each subtest could be converted to a grade-equivalent score by using the grade-equivalent conversion table in Figure 3.4. A raw score of 16 on subtest M-1 would convert to a grade equivalent of 6.4. Grade equivalents for the sum of subtests and an overall composite score for a test can be obtained by using the table in Figure 3.5. For example, if Julie scored a total of 395 points in Level 13, she would have achieved an average grade equivalent of 7.9. Once a student's raw scores have been converted to grade equivalents, the grade equivalents can be converted to percentile ranks or stanines with the use of the table in Figure 3.6. For example, Julie's grade equivalent of 6.4 in the M-1 subtest would convert to a percentile rank of 23 or a stanine of 4. Her composite grade equivalent of 7.9 would convert to a percentile rank of 57 and a stanine of 5. Notice that Figure 3.6 is designated as being appropriate for the end of year. It should be used with test results obtained from administration of the Iowa Tests of Basic Skills after March 1. Similar tables are available for administration of the test at the beginning and during the middle of the school year.

Although there are different reasons for using various scale scores, the basic issue in norm-referenced testing is the norm group. If the norm group has an experiential background similar to that of the group being evaluated, the data obtained from the norm-referenced test is useful in interpreting the results. The utility of test results is directly related to the appropriateness of the norm group.

Criterion-Referenced Testing

Need for Criterion-Referenced Measurement

Norm-referenced measurement can provide a teacher or evaluator with a great deal of valuable information about a student's abilities and achievement. All the information provided by norm-referenced measurement is relative to the norm-group, however. When norm-referenced tests are administered, the resulting raw scores are converted to a system of scaled or ranked scores before any interpretation is attempted. This conversion is made in order to determine how particular raw scores compare to the raw scores of some known group of students.

Although such comparative information can be valuable to a

Figure 3.4   *Grade-Equivalent Conversion Tables for the Iowa Tests of Basic Skills*

Grade Equivalent Conversion Tables

Level 13 – Form 5

Raw Score	V	R	L-1	L-2	L-3	L-4	W-1	W-2	W-3	M-1	M-2
0	18	20	14	15	13	19	20	22	21	25	26
1	19	21	16	17	15	21	22	24	22	27	29
2	20	23	18	19	17	23	24	27	23	29	32
3	21	24	21	22	19	26	26	31	25	31	36
4	22	25	24	25	23	30	28	35	26	33	40
5	23	26	27	28	26	33	31	40	28	35	44
6	26	27	31	31	29	37	34	44	29	38	48
7	28	28	35	34	33	41	37	49	31	40	53
8	31	29	40	37	36	45	40	55	33	43	57
9	34	30	44	41	40	50	43	60	35	46	61
10	37	32	47	44	44	55	46	65	37	49	65
11	41	34	50	48	49	59	50	69	39	52	69
12	44	35	54	51	53	64	54	73	42	54	72
13	48	37	57	54	57	68	58	75	44	57	74
14	51	38	60	56	61	72	61	78	46	59	76
15	55	40	63	58	65	76	64	81	49	61	78
16	58	42	65	61	68	79	68	83	51	64	80
17	60	44	68	63	71	82	71	86	53	66	82
18	63	46	70	66	74	85	74	89	55	68	83
19	65	48	72	69	77	87	77	91	57	70	85
20	67	50	74	72	79	90	79	94	59	71	88
21	69	52	76	74	82	93	81	97	61	73	90
22	71	54	78	76	85	95	83	101	63	75	92
23	73	55	80	79	87	97	85	105	65	76	95
24	74	57	82	82	89	99	87	108	67	78	97
25	76	59	84	84	91	101	89	110	69	80	100
26	78	60	85	87	93	103	92	113	71	81	102
27	79	62	87	89	95	106	94	115	73	82	104
28	81	63	88	92	97	108	96	117	75	84	106
29	82	65	89	94	99	111	99		76	85	109
30	84	66	91	97	101	113	101		78	87	112
31	85	67	92	99	102	116	103		79	88	114
32	86	68	94	101	103	119	105		81	89	117
33	88	69	95	103	105		107		82	91	
34	90	71	97	105	106		109		84	92	
35	91	72	98	106	108		111		86	94	
36	93	73	100	107	109		113		88	95	
37	95	74	102	109	111		115		89	97	
38	97	75	103	111	113		117		90	98	
39	99	76	104	113	114		119		92	100	
40	101	76	106	114	116		121		93	102	
41	103	77	108	116	118		123		94	104	
42	106	78	109	117	120				96	106	
43	108	79	110	119	122				97	108	
44	110	80	112						98	110	
45	112	81	113						100	112	
46	114	82	115						101	114	
47	116	83	117						103	116	
48	119	84	119						104	118	
49		85							106		
50		85							108		
51		87							110		
52		88							112		
53		89							113		
54		90							115		
55		91							117		
56		92							118		
57		93							119		
58		94							121		
59		95							122		
60		97									
61		98									
62		99									
63		100									
64		101									
65		103									
66		105									
67		107									
68		108									
69		110									
70		112									
71		115									
72		117									
73		119									
74		121									
75		123									
76		125									
77		126									
78		127									
79											
80											

Level 14 – Form 5

Raw Score	V	R	L-1	L-2	L-3	L-4	W-1	W-2	W-3	M-1	M-2
0	23	22	17	19	15	25	26	27	27	30	31
1	24	23	19	21	18	27	29	30	29	32	33
2	25	25	21	23	21	30	31	34	31	34	36
3	26	26	24	26	23	34	33	39	32	36	39
4	27	27	27	28	25	37	35	43	34	37	42
5	28	28	30	30	28	41	37	46	35	39	46
6	30	30	34	33	31	46	39	50	37	42	50
7	33	32	39	36	35	52	42	55	38	45	54
8	37	34	44	39	39	58	46	61	40	48	58
9	41	35	48	42	43	64	50	66	42	51	63
10	45	36	52	45	48	70	55	70	44	54	67
11	49	37	55	48	53	75	59	74	46	57	72
12	52	39	58	52	59	80	63	78	48	60	76
13	56	41	62	55	64	85	66	82	51	63	80
14	60	43	65	58	69	89	70	85	54	65	83
15	63	44	67	62	73	93	73	88	56	67	86
16	66	46	70	65	77	96	76	91	59	70	88
17	69	48	73	69	80	99	79	94	62	72	90
18	71	49	75	72	83	101	82	97	65	75	93
19	74	51	78	75	86	104	85	100	67	78	96
20	76	53	80	78	89	107	87	104	69	80	98
21	78	55	82	81	92	109	90	108	71	82	101
22	80	58	84	84	95	111	92	112	73	84	104
23	81	60	86	87	97	113	94	116	75	86	107
24	83	62	88	90	100	114	96	120	77	88	110
25	85	64	90	92	102	116	97	123	79	90	112
26	86	65	91	95	105	118	99	126	81	92	115
27	87	67	93	98	107	120	102	128	82	94	118
28	89	68	95	101	109	123	104	129	84	95	120
29	90	70	96	104	111	125	106		85	97	122
30	92	71	98	106	112	127	109		87	99	124
31	93	72	100	108	114	128	111		88	101	125
32	95	74	101	110	115	129	113		89	103	127
33	97	75	103	113	116		115		91	104	128
34	99	76	105	115	117		117		93	106	129
35	101	77	107	117	118		119		94	108	
36	103	79	109	119	120		121		96	109	
37	105	80	111	120	122		123		97	111	
38	107	81	113	121	123		125		99	113	
39	110	82	114	123	124		126		100	115	
40	112	84	116	125	125		127		101	117	
41	115	85	118	126	126		128		103	118	
42	118	86	119	127	127		129		104	120	
43	120	87	121	128	128				106	122	
44	122	88	122	129	129				107	123	
45	124	89	124						109	125	
46	126	90	126						110	127	
47	128	91	128						112	128	
48	129	92	129						114	129	
49		93							115		
50		94							117		
51		95							119		
52		96							121		
53		97							123		
54		98							124		
55		99							125		
56		100							126		
57		101							127		
58		102							128		
59		103							129		
60		104									
61		106									
62		107									
63		108									
64		110									
65		111									
66		112									
67		113									
68		114									
69		116									
70		119									
71		121									
72		123									
73		124									
74		125									
75		125									
76		126									
77		127									
78		128									
79		128									
80		129									

Figure 3.5 *Average Grade-Equivalent Conversion Table for the Iowa Tests of Basic Skills*

Average Grade Equivalents for Total Test Areas

Sums — Test L	Test W	Test M	Composite (C)	Average GE
515–516	386–387	258	643–645	129
510–514	383–385	255–257	638–642	128
507–509	380–382	254	633–637	127
502–506	377–379	251–253	628–632	126
499–501	374–376	250	623–627	125
494–498	371–373	247–249	618–622	124
491–493	368–370	246	613–617	123
486–490	365–367	243–245	608–612	122
483–485	362–364	242	603–607	121
478–482	359–361	239–241	598–602	120
475–477	356–358	238	593–597	119
470–474	353–355	235–237	588–592	118
467–469	350–352	234	583–587	117
462–466	347–349	231–233	578–582	116
459–461	344–346	230	573–577	115
454–458	341–343	227–229	568–572	114
451–453	338–340	226	563–567	113
446–450	335–337	223–225	558–562	112
443–445	332–334	222	553–557	111
438–442	329–331	219–221	548–552	110
435–437	326–328	218	543–547	109
430–434	323–325	215–217	538–542	108
427–429	320–322	214	533–537	107
422–426	317–319	211–213	528–532	106
419–421	314–316	210	523–527	105
414–418	311–313	207–209	518–522	104
411–413	308–310	206	513–517	103
406–410	305–307	203–205	508–512	102
403–405	302–304	202	503–507	101
398–402	299–301	199–201	498–502	100
395–397	296–298	198	493–497	99
390–394	293–295	195–197	488–492	98
387–389	290–292	194	483–487	97
382–386	287–289	191–193	478–482	96
379–381	284–286	190	473–477	95
374–378	281–283	187–189	468–472	94
371–373	278–280	186	463–467	93
366–370	275–277	183–185	458–462	92
363–365	272–274	182	453–457	91
358–362	269–271	179–181	448–452	90
355–357	266–268	178	443–447	89
350–354	263–265	175–177	438–442	88
347–349	260–262	174	433–437	87
342–346	257–259	171–173	428–432	86
339–341	254–256	170	423–427	85
334–338	251–253	167–169	418–422	84
331–333	248–250	166	413–417	83
326–330	245–247	163–165	408–412	82
323–325	242–244	162	403–407	81
318–322	239–241	159–161	398–402	80
315–317	236–238	158	393–397	79
310–314	233–235	155–157	388–392	78
307–309	230–232	154	383–387	77
302–306	227–229	151–153	378–382	76
299–301	224–226	150	373–377	75
294–298	221–223	147–149	368–372	74
291–293	218–220	146	363–367	73
286–290	215–217	143–145	358–362	72
283–285	212–214	142	353–357	71
278–282	209–211	139–141	348–352	70

Sums — Test L	Test W	Test M	Composite (C)	Average GE
275–277	206–208	138	343–347	69
270–274	203–205	135–137	338–342	68
267–269	200–202	134	333–337	67
262–266	197–199	131–133	328–332	66
259–261	194–196	130	323–327	65
254–258	191–193	127–129	318–322	64
251–253	188–190	126	313–317	63
246–250	185–187	123–125	308–312	62
243–245	182–184	122	303–307	61
238–242	179–181	119–121	298–302	60
235–237	176–178	118	293–297	59
230–234	173–175	115–117	288–292	58
227–229	170–172	114	283–287	57
222–226	167–169	111–113	278–282	56
219–221	164–166	110	273–277	55
214–218	161–163	107–109	268–272	54
211–213	158–160	106	263–267	53
206–210	155–157	103–105	258–262	52
203–205	152–154	102	253–257	51
198–202	149–151	99–101	248–252	50
195–197	146–148	98	243–247	49
190–194	143–145	95–97	238–242	48
187–189	140–142	94	233–237	47
182–186	137–139	91–93	228–232	46
179–181	134–136	90	223–227	45
174–178	131–133	87–89	218–222	44
171–173	128–130	86	213–217	43
166–170	125–127	83–85	208–212	42
163–165	122–124	82	203–207	41
158–162	119–121	79–81	198–202	40
155–157	116–118	78	193–197	39
150–154	113–115	75–77	188–192	38
147–149	110–112	74	183–187	37
142–146	107–109	71–73	178–182	36
139–141	104–106	70	173–177	35
134–138	101–103	67–69	168–172	34
131–133	98–100	66	163–167	33
126–130	95–97	63–65	158–162	32
123–125	92–94	62	153–157	31
118–122	89–91	59–61	148–152	30
115–117	86–88	58	143–147	29
110–114	83–85	55–57	138–142	28
107–109	80–82	54	133–137	27
102–106	77–79	51–53	128–132	26
99–101	74–76	50	123–127	25
94–98	71–73	47–49	118–122	24
91–93	68–70	46	113–117	23
86–90	65–67	43–45	108–112	22
83–85	62–64	42	103–107	21
78–82	59–61	39–41	98–102	20
75–77	56–58	38	93–97	19
70–74	53–55	35–37	88–92	18
67–69	50–52	34	83–87	17
62–66	47–49	31–33	78–82	16
59–61	44–46	30	73–77	15
54–58	41–43	27–29	68–72	14
51–53	38–40	26	63–67	13
46–50	35–37	23–25	59–62	12
43–45	32–34	22	53–58	11
40–42	30–31	20–21	50–52	10

From A. N. Hieronymus and E. F. Lindquist, *Teacher's Guide for Administration, Interpretation, and Use: Iowa Tests of Basic Skills.* Boston: Houghton Mifflin, 1971. Reprinted by permission of the publisher.

Figure 3.6 *Percentile Ranks and Stanine Conversion Table for Iowa Tests of Basic Skills*

7   End of Year (Mar. 1 or after) / Percentile Norms for Seventh-Grade Pupils   **7**

%-ile Rank	Test L: Language							Test W: Work-Study				Test M: Mathematics				%-ile Rank	Stanine
	L-1	L-2	L-3	L-4				W-1	W-2	W-3		M-1	M-2				
99	116	114	119	119	116	116	115	115	118	115	112	115	113	113	110	99	9
98	113	111	116	116	114	114	113	112	114	112	109	112	110	110	108	98	
97	110	108	114	115	112	112	111	110	112	110	107	109	108	107	106	97	
96	108	107	112	114	111	111	110	108	110	108	105	108	106	105	104	96	
95	106	105	111	112	110	109	108	106	108	106	104	106	104	103	103	95	8
94	105	104	110	111	109	108	107	105	107	105	103	105	103	102	102	94	
93	104	103	109	110	108	107	106	104	106	104	102	103	102	101	101	93	
92	102	102	108	109	107	107	105	103	104	103	101	102	100	100	100	92	
91	101	101	106	108	106	106	104	102	103	102	100	101	99	99	99	91	
90	100	100	105	107	105	105	103	101	102	101	99	100	98	98	98	90	
89	99	99	104	106	104	104	102	99	101	100	98	99	97	97	97	89	
88	98	98	103	–	103	103	101	98	100	–	–	98	96	96	–	88	7
87	97	97	102	105	102	–	100	–	99	99	97	–	95	–	96	87	
86	–	96	101	104	101	102	–	97	98	98	96	97	94	95	95	86	
85	96	–	100	103	–	101	99	96	97	–	95	96	–	94	–	85	
84	95	95	99	102	100	100	98	–	96	97	–	95	93	–	94	84	
83	94	94	98	101	99	–	97	95	–	96	94	95	92	93	93	83	
82	–	–	–	–	98	99	–	94	95	–	93	94	91	92	92	82	
81	93	93	97	100	–	98	96	–	94	95	–	94	–	91	91	81	
80	92	92	96	99	97	–	95	93	93	94	92	93	90	90	90	80	
79	–	–	95	98	96	97	94	–	–	–	–	–	–	–	–	79	
78	91	91	–	–	95	96	–	92	92	93	91	92	89	90	90	78	
77	–	–	94	97	–	–	93	–	91	92	–	–	–	–	89	77	
76	90	90	93	–	94	95	92	91	–	–	90	91	88	–	89	76	6
75	89	–	–	96	93	94	–	–	90	91	–	90	–	88	–	75	
74	–	89	92	–	–	–	91	90	89	90	89	–	87	–	88	74	
73	88	–	91	94	92	93	90	–	–	–	88	89	–	87	–	73	
72	–	88	–	93	91	92	–	89	88	89	–	–	86	–	87	72	
71	87	–	90	92	–	–	89	–	–	–	87	88	–	86	–	71	
70	–	87	89	91	90	91	88	88	87	88	–	–	–	86	–	70	
69	86	–	–	–	89	90	–	–	–	87	86	87	85	85	–	69	
68	–	86	88	90	–	–	87	87	86	–	–	86	–	–	85	68	
67	85	–	–	89	88	89	–	86	85	86	85	–	84	84	–	67	
66	–	85	87	88	87	88	86	–	–	85	84	85	–	–	84	66	
65	84	–	–	–	–	–	85	85	84	–	–	84	83	–	83	65	
64	–	84	86	87	86	87	–	–	–	84	83	–	–	83	–	64	
63	–	–	85	86	–	86	84	84	83	–	–	83	82	–	82	63	
62	83	83	84	85	85	–	–	83	–	83	82	–	–	81	–	62	
61	–	82	–	84	84	85	–	–	82	82	–	82	–	–	81	61	
60	82	82	83	83	83	–	82	82	–	–	81	81	80	80	–	60	
59	81	81	82	–	82	83	81	81	81	81	–	–	81	80	80	59	5
58	–	–	–	82	–	82	80	–	–	–	80	81	–	–	79	58	
57	80	80	81	81	81	–	79	80	80	80	79	80	80	79	79	57	
56	–	–	–	–	–	81	–	–	–	–	78	–	79	78	78	56	
55	79	79	80	80	80	80	78	79	79	79	77	79	–	78	77	55	
54	78	78	79	79	79	79	77	78	78	78	76	78	78	77	76	54	
53	77	–	78	78	78	78	76	77	77	77	75	77	77	–	75	53	
52	76	76	76	76	76	76	75	76	–	76	–	76	76	75	–	52	
51	75	75	75	75	75	74	74	75	75	75	74	75	75	74	74	51	
50	74	73	74	74	74	73	73	74	74	74	73	74	74	73	73	50	
49	73	72	71	71	71	71	70	72	72	72	72	73	73	72	71	49	
48	71	70	70	69	69	70	69	71	71	71	70	72	72	71	70	48	4
47	70	69	68	–	68	68	68	70	70	70	69	71	71	70	69	47	
46	69	68	67	67	67	67	67	69	69	69	68	70	70	69	68	46	
45	68	67	65	65	66	66	66	68	68	68	67	69	69	68	67	45	
44	67	66	64	64	65	64	65	67	67	67	66	68	68	67	66	44	
43	66	65	63	63	63	64	64	66	66	66	65	67	66	65	66	43	
42	65	64	62	62	62	61	62	64	64	64	64	66	65	64	65	42	
41	64	–	61	61	61	60	61	63	63	63	63	65	63	64	63	41	
40	63	62	60	60	59	58	60	62	62	62	62	64	62	62	62	40	
22	61	61	58	–	57	–	59	61	60	61	–	61	63	62	22		3
21	–	60	57	57	56	56	–	60	59	60	61	63	60	62	61	21	
20	60	–	56	56	55	55	58	59	–	58	59	62	60	61	60	20	
19	59	59	55	55	54	54	57	58	57	58	–	59	–	61	59	19	
18	58	58	54	53	53	53	–	57	56	57	59	61	58	–	59	18	
17	57	–	52	52	52	56	56	55	–	60	57	60	–	58	17		
16	56	57	53	53	51	51	55	56	55	56	58	60	56	–	58	16	
15	55	56	52	52	50	50	–	55	54	56	58	60	56	–	58	15	
14	54	55	51	51	49	49	54	54	53	55	57	–	59	57	14		
13	53	54	–	50	48	48	53	53	52	54	–	59	55	58	57	13	
12	52	–	50	49	47	47	–	52	51	–	56	–	54	–	12		
11	51	53	49	48	46	46	52	51	50	53	55	58	53	57	56	11	
10	50	52	48	47	45	45	51	50	49	52	–	57	52	56	–	10	2
9	48	51	46	46	44	44	–	49	48	51	54	56	51	–	55	9	
8	47	50	45	45	43	–	50	48	47	50	53	55	50	55	54	8	
7	46	49	43	43	41	42	49	46	46	48	52	54	49	54	–	7	
6	44	47	42	42	40	41	48	45	45	47	51	53	48	53	53	6	
5	42	46	40	40	38	40	47	43	43	45	50	51	45	52	52	5	
4	41	44	38	39	36	39	46	41	41	44	49	50	44	51	51	4	
3	39	35	35	37	34	37	44	40	40	42	48	42	50	50	3		1
2	36	41	33	35	32	36	43	38	39	40	46	47	40	48	2		
1	33	38	29	31	30	33	40	36	36	37	44	43	38	45	1		

teacher, parent, student, or guidance counselor, it does not provide all the information that may be necessary for making decisions with respect to curricula or programs of study. An extreme example may serve to illustrate this point. Suppose that Mrs. Clark administered a mathematics achievement test to her third-grade class. The results of the test show that all the students in the class scored above the 75th percentile. When the students in Mrs. Clark's class move on to the fourth grade, however, they may find mathematics extremely difficult. It is possible that if the fourth-grade teacher fails to spend a great deal of time reviewing third-grade content, Mrs. Clark's students will be totally unsuccessful in fourth-grade mathematics, despite the fact that they all scored above the 75th percentile on the third-grade mathematics achievement test.

This example is extreme and unlikely to occur, but it is not outside the realm of possibility. The reason is, of course, that the results of the achievement test indicate only how the third-graders compared to some other group of students. It may be that an inappropriate norm-group was used or the test may have suffered from any one or several of the deficiencies to be discussed in Chapter 4. What is important to notice here is that the results of the achievement test did not give an accurate indication of the students' achievement with respect to the exam content. One would generally interpret the 75th percentile as indicative of good performance, but the fact that all the students in Mrs. Clark's class scored above the 75th percentile does not necessarily indicate that they possess the skills necessary for success in fourth-grade mathematics.

The fact that norm-referenced measurement provides only information relative to norm groups must be considered a limitation. Criterion-referenced measurement has been developed in an attempt to overcome this limitation. The purpose of criterion-referenced measurement is to determine whether an individual possesses the skills and knowledge for success at the next level of whatever attribute is being measured. For example, if a criterion-referenced test rather than a norm-referenced test, had been administered to Mrs. Clark's third-grade class, the interpretation of the results would have been completely different. A criterion-referenced test would have revealed the skills and knowledge of each of Mrs. Clark's students. Assuming that the third- and fourth-grade teachers had determined what skills were necessary for a student to be successful in fourth-grade mathematics, the results of the criterion-referenced test would have shown that Mrs. Clark's students were not ready to move on to the fourth grade. In addition, the criterion-referenced test results would have indicated the areas in which Mrs. Clark would have had to concentrate for the remainder of the school year to prepare each student for the next level of instruction.

Criterion-referenced measurement helps determine whether a student possesses the skills and knowledge that he should be expected to possess at a given point in time. Mrs. Clark is concerned about her students possessing certain math skills at the end of their third school year. Another teacher might be concerned about history or spelling or any other subject taught in school. But criterion-referenced measurement is not used only in schools. It is also applied by each state in America to determine whether individuals should be issued a driver's license. It is applied by people responsible for hiring lifeguards for a swimming area. We could extend the list of users of criterion-referenced measurement almost indefinitely. But let us look more specifically at the central element in criterion-referenced tests, the test item itself.

The Test Item: The Critical Criterion

You will recall that in norm-referenced measurement, meaning is derived from test scores by comparing them to the scores of the norm-group. An individual's performance is interpreted in terms of how it compares to the performance of other individuals. Comparisons are made in criterion-referenced testing also, but the standard for comparison is the test item itself. Each item included in a criterion-referenced test is there because it represents some skill that has been determined necessary for an individual to be successful at whatever is to follow. Consider the driver's license examination administered by the states. Persons applying for a license must correctly identify each traffic sign used on the highways of that state. The reason for this is obviously that if drivers are to avoid accidents they must not fail to identify correctly even a single sign. If on the test an applicant cannot correctly identify the traffic signs, he does not possess the skill necessary to be a successful driver. He cannot be successful at the next level of achievement.

At least two assumptions are made in criterion-referenced meas-

urement that are not necessarily made in norm-referenced measurement. First, it must be assumed that it is possible to identify
the skills and knowledge that should be possessed by individuals
who are at some point in their development process. People who
write a criterion-referenced mathematics test for students who are
at the end of the third grade must be able to determine what math
skills these students must possess to be successful in fourth-grade
math. Once the skills have been identified, the second assumption
is that a test item can accurately measure whether the student
actually possesses a skill. That is, one must assume that if the
student responds correctly to the item, then he possesses the skill,
and that if he responds incorrectly he does not.

 Making the test item the reference point, as criterion-referenced
measurement does, provides the teacher or evaluator with valuable information. If the student answers an item correctly he
possesses the skill. As far as that skill is concerned, he is ready
for the next level. If an item is answered incorrectly, the student
has not yet achieved the skill measured by the item. More practice or study will be required before he can be said to possess that
skill. This interpretation presents one very important difficulty.
Suppose Mrs. Clark had felt that her third-grade students should
be able to multiply two-digit numbers before they were ready for
fourth grade. The question as to whether $\begin{array}{r} 11 \\ \times 11 \\ \hline \end{array}$ is the same as $\begin{array}{r} 69 \\ \times 99 \\ \hline \end{array}$

would have to be considered. It may be that a student could suc-
cessfully multiply $\begin{array}{r} 11 \\ \times 11 \\ \hline \end{array}$ but could not multiply $\begin{array}{r} 69 \\ \times 99 \\ \hline \end{array}$. If this is the

case, then these two items must represent different skills. Both
would have to be included in the test. If we consider the possi-
bilities that such an example presents, it can easily be seen that
the criterion-referenced test may have to include a large number
of items. The problem facing the writer of a criterion-referenced
test is to determine how many different skills are represented in
an objective such as "the student will be able to multiply correctly
two-digit numbers." Each individual skill will then have to be
represented by some item on the test. Because of the tremendous
number of skills that might have to be included, most test developers attempt to select test items that provide a representative
sample of the skills to be measured. For example, a teacher may
decide that if a student can multiply ten different sets of two-

digit numbers, he can probably multiply most pairs of two-digit numbers. As a result, the teacher may not need to include all possible skills on the test to be satisfied that a student can perform a certain category of skills.

Establishing a Criterion-Referenced Measurement System

The first step in establishing a criterion-referenced measurement system is to identify the skills to be measured. The individuals who are to write a criterion-referenced test must analyze the next level of whatever skill is under consideration to determine just what knowledge a person must possess. This knowledge must then be represented on the test as a test item. If it is answered correctly, the individual possesses that prerequisite for moving ahead successfully. If the item is answered incorrectly, the prerequisite skill is not possessed. The success of criterion-referenced measurement depends upon the test writer's ability to identify correctly the skills and knowledge and to write items that measure them.

The identification of what is to be measured by a criterion-referenced test is not simple. Consider the example of the arithmetic exam above. What skills must third-graders possess besides being able to multiply two-digit numbers? Must they be able to add, subtract, and divide? What about word problems? How about distance measurements? To further complicate the problem, one must consider how many different skills are represented within each identified requirement.

Once the skill and knowledge to be tested have been identified, the test writer faces the problem of how to write a test to measure whether a student possesses them. The fact that there can be so many skills presents the problem of writing a test that measures them all but is also of reasonable length. At the present time there are no generally accepted quantitative methods for determining whether an item written for a criterion-referenced test is good or bad. A number of attempts have been made to establish quantitative methods for determining the characteristics of good criterion-referenced test items, but none has been generally accepted by measurement specialists. (Further discussion of this is presented in Chapter 8.)

Commercial publishers have begun to recognize the difficulties of preparing criterion-referenced tests and now produce materials that allow individual school systems to identify the skills and knowledge to be assessed (see Figure 3.7), select the appropriate items for testing the stated objective (see Figure 3.8), and report the student's progress to him (see Figure 3.9). Although the use of these materials is time consuming, a school district can develop from existing files the objectives to be assessed, the items to complete the assessment, and a way of keeping a record of the progress of the student. These procedures provide an alternative to existing standardized tests.

Criterion-Referenced vs. Other Measurement Concepts

The term "criterion-referenced" is often used in conjunction with several other measurement terms. Three of these are "cut-off scores," "content-standard scores," and "absolute interpretation of test scores." The following discussion of these terms is based on rationale developed by Glaser and Nitko in Chapter 17 of Robert Thorndike's book *Educational Measurement*, listed at the end of this chapter.

Cut-off scores. One term most frequently linked with criterion-referenced measurement is *cut-off score.* The connection between them occurs because they are both used in situations in which the concern is to determine whether a student possesses certain behavior. A cut-off score is generally applied when a teacher is teaching for mastery, attempting to cause students to reach a point at which they can answer some percentage of items on a test correctly. The cut-off score is the score the student must obtain before the teacher is willing to accept that the student has mastered the topic or content under consideration. The cut-off score is further interpreted to indicate the minimal level of the skill being evaluated that the student must possess to be successful at the next level. Cut-off scores are therefore generally established at the upper end of a scale. That is, a student may be required to respond correctly to 85, 90, or 95 percent of the items. Cut-off scores and criterion-referenced measurement are frequently confused because it is popular among teachers, evaluators, and others to call the cut-off score the "criterion score."

Nothing in criterion-referenced measurement requires the use of a cut-off score. Criterion-referenced measurement is designed to determine whether an individual possesses certain skills. The

Figure 3.7   *A Section of the Behavioral Objectives Index for the Individual Pupil Monitoring System, Mathematics*

BEHAVIORAL OBJECTIVES INDEX

I. **Numeration and Number Systems**

    A. Ordering of numbers
        201. identify the cardinal number of a set with 0 through 10 members
        202. recognize the ordinal numbers first through tenth

    B. Number sentences
        207. complete number sentences, using inequality symbols
        208. complete number sentences by filling in the missing addend or symbol
        242. complete number sentences by filling in the missing addend or symbol

    C. Compact and expanded numerals
        217. read and identify numerals through 99, when expressed as compact numerals or expanded numerals.
        256. read and identify numerals to 1000, when expressed as compact numerals or expanded numerals

    D. Number theory
        261. recognize odd and even numbers

    E. Fractional numbers and fractions
        213. recognize one-half of a set
        247. recognize one-half of a region
        248. recognize one-fourth of a set
        249. recognize one-fourth of a region
        252. recognize one-third of a set
        253. recognize one-third of a region

II. **Basic Mathematical Operations**

    A. Addition
        203. solve addition problems with sums through 6, using the equation form
        205. solve addition problems with sums through 6, using the vertical form
        209. solve addition problems with sums of 7 through 10, using the equation form
        211. solve addition problems with sums of 7 through 10, using the vertical form
        216. solve addition problems with three addends, using both the equation and vertical forms: sums through 10
        218. solve addition problems with sums of 11 through 13, using the equation form
        220. solve addition problems with sums of 11 through 13, using the vertical form
        223. solve addition problems with sums of 13 and 14, using the equation form
        224. solve addition problems with sums of 13 and 14, using the vertical form
        227. solve addition problems with sums of 15 and 16, using the equation form
        228. solve addition problems with sums of 15 and 16, using the vertical form
        231. solve addition problems with sums of 17 and 18, using the equation form

---

From *Individual Pupil Monitoring System, Mathematics: Teacher's Objective Management Record.* Boston: Houghton Mifflin, 1973. Reprinted by permission of the publisher.

Figure 3.8 *Table of Contents of Level 2-A of the IPMS, Mathematics, Linking Objectives with Test Items*

<table>
<tr><th colspan="3">CONTENTS</th></tr>
<tr><th>Objective Number</th><th>Behavioral Objectives for Level 2—A</th><th>Page</th></tr>
<tr><td></td><td>Each student should be able to</td><td></td></tr>
<tr><td>201.</td><td>identify the cardinal number of a set with 0 through 10 members.</td><td>1</td></tr>
<tr><td>202.</td><td>recognize the ordinal numbers first through tenth.</td><td>2</td></tr>
<tr><td>203.</td><td>solve addition problems with sums through 6, using the equation form.</td><td>3</td></tr>
<tr><td>204.</td><td>solve subtraction problems with sums through 6, using the equation form.</td><td>4</td></tr>
<tr><td>205.</td><td>solve addition problems with sums through 6, using the vertical form.</td><td>5</td></tr>
<tr><td>206.</td><td>solve subtraction problems with sums through 6, using the vertical form.</td><td>6</td></tr>
<tr><td>207.</td><td>complete number sentences, using inequality symbols.</td><td>7</td></tr>
<tr><td>208.</td><td>complete number sentences by filling in missing addends or symbols.</td><td>8</td></tr>
<tr><td>209.</td><td>solve addition problems with sums of 7 through 10, using the equation form.</td><td>9</td></tr>
<tr><td>210.</td><td>solve subtraction problems with sums of 7 through 10, using the equation form.</td><td>10</td></tr>
<tr><td>211.</td><td>solve addition problems with sums of 7 through 10, using the vertical form.</td><td>11</td></tr>
<tr><td>212.</td><td>solve subtraction problems with sums of 7 through 10, using the vertical form.</td><td>12</td></tr>
<tr><td>213.</td><td>recognize one half of a set.</td><td>13</td></tr>
<tr><td>214.</td><td>identify time to the hour and half hour.</td><td>14</td></tr>
<tr><td>215.</td><td>recognize liquid measurement, using cups, pints, and quarts.</td><td>15</td></tr>
<tr><td>216.</td><td>solve addition problems with three addends, using both the equation and vertical forms: sums through 10.</td><td>16</td></tr>
</table>

From *Individual Pupil Monitoring System, Mathematics.* Boston: Houghton Mifflin, 1973. Reprinted by permission of the publisher.

Figure 3.9 *Pupil Progress Chart for the Individual Pupil Monitoring System, Mathematics*

TO THE PUPIL

On the front cover, ring S or T for the form you are using.

To Fill In Your Progress Chart
1. Find the right skill number.
2. Write in the number correct.
3. Fill in the same amount of boxes as the number correct.
4. Smile.

Here Is A Sample. This is how Pat filled in the chart.

201	Cardinal numbers 0-10	3
202	Number sentences—inequality symbols	5
203	Order of numbers 1-10	2

Number and Name of Skill	Number Correct	Graph				
The student is able to . . .		1	2	3	4	5
201 identify the cardinal number of a set with 0 through 10 members.						
202 recognize the ordinal numbers first through tenth.						
203 solve addition problems, sums through 6, in equation form. Ex.: $1 + 4 = \square$						
204 solve subtraction problems, sums through 6, in equation form. Ex.: $3 - 1 = \square$						
205 solve addition problems, sums through 6, in vertical form. Ex.: $\begin{array}{r}3\\+5\end{array}$						
206 solve subtraction problems, sums through 6, in vertical form. Ex.: $\begin{array}{r}6\\-2\end{array}$						
207 complete number sentences, using inequality symbols. Ex.: $4 \textcircled{<} 6$						
208 complete number sentences by filling in missing addends or symbols. Ex.: $5 \triangle 1 = 6$						
209 solve addition problems, sums 7 through 10, in equation form. Ex.: $3 + 5 = \square$						
210 solve subtraction problems, sums 7 through 10, in equation form. Ex.: $10 - 3 = \square$						
211 solve addition problems, sums 7 through 10, in vertical form. Ex.: $\begin{array}{r}6\\+3\end{array}$						
212 solve subtraction problems, sums 7 through 10, in vertical form. Ex.: $\begin{array}{r}9\\-8\end{array}$						
213 recognize one half of a set.						
214 identify time to the hour and half hour.						
215 recognize liquid measurement: cup, pint, and quart.						
216 solve addition problems with three addends, in both equation and vertical forms: sums through 10.						
217 identify compact and expanded numerals through 99. Ex.: 32　Ex.: 3 tens and 2 ones						
218 solve addition problems, sums 11 through 13, in equation form. Ex.: $6 + 7 = \square$						
219 solve subtraction problems, sums 11 through 13, in equation form. Ex.: $11 - 9 = \square$						
220 solve addition problems, sums 11 through 13, in vertical form. Ex.: $\begin{array}{r}8\\+3\end{array}$						
221 solve subtraction problems, sums 11 through 13, in vertical form. Ex.: $\begin{array}{r}13\\-5\end{array}$						
222 solve simple word problems.						

From *Individual Pupil Monitoring System, Mathematics*. Boston: Houghton Mifflin, 1973. Reprinted by permission of the publisher.

criterion in criterion-referenced measurement is the test item. A correct response indicates that the individual possesses that skill. An incorrect response indicates that the skill has not been achieved. Cut-off scores, on the other hand, indicate that the student must achieve some minimal percentage on a test. The score that the student obtains is interpreted to mean that the student has mastered that percentage of the content.

Content-standard scores. Another term linked with criterion-referenced measurement is *content-standard.* A content-standard score refers to a score derived from a test composed of items representative of the content in question. Several tests may be considered equivalent in this situation if they all contain items from the same set of content. A content-standard score means that all scores are based on the same content and that the score represents the percentage of the content that the student has mastered. The reference in this system is the content rather than the performance of other individuals as in norm-referenced measurement. A content-standard system of measurement is somewhat similar to but not the same as criterion-referenced measurement, which attempts to reveal the skills and knowledge a student possesses. Content-standard scores reveal the percentage of some content that a student has achieved. Criterion-referenced measurement attempts to locate a student in terms of skills and knowledge required at a given point in time. Content-standard measurement attempts to locate the student in terms of knowledge actually possessed at a given point in time.

Absolute interpretation of test scores. A measurement term recently introduced by L. J. Cronbach is sometimes linked with criterion-referenced measurement. This term is *absolute interpretation of test scores.* According to Cronbach, the absolute interpretation of test scores provides an indication as to what each test score means with respect to what the student can do. That is, the absolute interpretation of a test score means interpreting it as providing an indication as to what skills and knowledge an individual possesses at a given point in time. In the absolute interpretation of test scores, one is not concerned with comparison to any group of students or area of content. The test is itself the reference system. The score on the test indicates where the student stands in terms of the behavior being measured by that test.

It should be clear that such a concept is precisely what is meant by criterion-referenced measurement.

Comparison of Criterion- and Norm-Referenced Tests

Criterion-referenced tests and norm-referenced tests are similar in some respects. Either one may be a written or a performance test, taken with paper and pencil form or as an activity requiring completion of specified tasks. The driver's license examination is one example of the combination of written and performance exams. The applicant must first pass a written examination to demonstrate his knowledge of the rules of the road, and then he must actually drive a car over some predetermined course to demonstrate his ability to handle a car and perform the skills required in safe driving.

Another similarity between norm-referenced and criterion-referenced tests is that they either may be achievement tests or aptitude tests. An achievement test is intended to provide an indication of what a student has already accomplished. An aptitude test is intended to provide an indication of what the student may be expected to accomplish in the future. The scores from a criterion-referenced test certainly may be interpreted either way, and so may norm-referenced tests.

A third similarity between the two measurement systems is that they both provide information about the success of the instructional system. It is true that the information provided in each case is different, but either system can play a role in the evaluation of the educational system.

There are also many marked differences between these two measurement systems. One arises from the difference in their purpose. Norm-referenced tests are constructed to show which individuals in a group possess the most knowledge about the content being tested. Such tests are designed to force a distribution of scores, the highest score indicating the best performance and the lowest score indicating the poorest performance. A norm-referenced test is considered to be a good test only if it provides such a distribution of scores. In order to ensure a distribution of scores, items are selected for a norm-referenced test on the basis of their ability to discriminate among individuals. An item that everyone gets right is a poor item and is not used. <u>The purpose of</u> <u>constructing a norm-referenced test is to discriminate between the</u> <u>best students and the poorer students.</u> This can be done even though all students in the norm group may have essentially equal ability.

<u>A criterion-referenced test, on the other hand, attempts to</u> <u>assess the behavior possessed by the individuals being tested.</u> There is no attempt to discriminate between individuals. All may get an item right, which would mean that they all possess the behavior being measured by that item. That does not mean, as far as criterion-referenced measurement is concerned, that the item is not good. The distinction between good and bad items for a criterion-referenced test is based on whether the item does or does not assess the behavior in question.

<u>A major difference between criterion-referenced measurement</u> <u>and norm-referenced measurement is the precision required in</u> <u>determining the test items.</u> Very precise mathematical procedures have been established and accepted for determining the quality of a norm-referenced test, and the result is that we are able to place some degree of confidence in the test scores. Similar procedures have not been established for criterion-referenced measurement so that interpretation of the quality of the test depends on the judgment of the individual evaluator.

<u>Norm-referenced measurement and criterion-referenced meas-</u> <u>urement provide the teacher and evaluator with a great deal of</u> <u>information. Norm-referenced measurement indicates how a stu-</u> <u>dent's test performance compares to that of students who com-</u> <u>prise the norm group. Criterion-referenced measurement provides</u> <u>information as to what behavior the student possesses at the time</u> <u>the test is administered</u>. Each is different in purpose, but both play an important role in the evaluation of the educational system. The choice whether to use one or the other must be based on the objectives that have been established for administering the test.

Reflections

1. A reference system in educational measurement is the group, content, or other standard against which an individual's test performance is to be compared.

2. Reference systems provide a basis for interpreting the results from a measuring device in a useful and meaningful way.

3. The two types of measurement most frequently used in education are norm-referenced measurement and criterion-referenced measurement.

4. The choice of the reference system to be applied in any situation must be based on the objectives established for the measurement process.

5. The reference point in norm-referenced measurement is the norm group. The norm group is a group of individuals for whom essential characteristics are known.

6. A teacher should select a table of norms derived from a group similar in essential characteristics to the group of students being evaluated. Such characteristics are grade level, age level, experiential background, social background, geographic location, and school size and location.

7. Scores most commonly reported with norm-referenced measurement are percentile ranks, grade equivalents, age equivalets, standard scores, and stanines.

8. A major advantage of norm-referenced measurement is that it provides information as to how a student compares to other students with similar important characteristics with respect to whatever it is the test is designed to measure.

9. Norm-referenced measurement is limited to providing information relative to how individuals compare.

10. Criterion-referenced measurement is designed to determine what behaviors a student possesses at the time the test is administered.

11. In criterion-referenced measurement, the reference system is the test or test item.

12. Cut-off scores are some minimal percentage of items that a student must achieve before he can be assumed to have mastered whatever the test measures. Criterion-referenced measurement, on the other hand, attempts to determine what behaviors the student actually possesses.

13. Criterion-referenced scores attempt to show the skills and knowledge that a student possesses, and content-standard scores show the percentage of some content that a student has achieved.

14. The concept of absolute interpretation of test scores is precisely the same as criterion-referenced measurement, as long

as the content of the test is the skill or knowledge being assessed. In both cases the test is the reference system.

15. Criterion-referenced and norm-referenced measurement can be used to assess the same skills and both systems can provide information about the success of the instructional system.

16. The primary difference between norm-referenced and criterion-referenced measurement is that each reference system provides different information to the teacher and evaluator. Norm-referenced measurement provides information about students in comparison with some norm group, while criterion-referenced measurement provides information about students in comparison with the content of the measuring device.

Exercises

1. Review the list of measurements that you prepared in Chapter 1. Which type of reference system is most appropriate for each measurement listed?

2. Review the specific objectives that you prepared in Chapter 2 and determine what type of reference system is needed for each objective. If your objectives required only one type of reference system, develop some objectives that would require the second type of reference system.

3. Describe a norm group that would be an appropriate reference group for this class.

4. Present the following information to at least five individuals with children and ask them how they interpret your remarks: "Your child is in the third grade and her score on the Iowa Test of Basic Skills gives her a grade-equivalent score of sixth grade and eighth month." Write a brief summary of each interview as you complete it. Be alert for questions of clarification, inappropriate interpretations, and confidence in response.

5. Given the five scores 8, 5, 4, 4, 3,

   a. Find the mean of the scores.
   b. Find the standard deviation of the scores.
   c. Convert the scores to z-scores (and interpret the z-scores).
   d. Convert the scores to T-scores.

6. What types of scaled scores will be meaningful for evaluation in this class?

Selected References

NORMS FOR DIFFERENT GROUPS

Remmers, H. H., N. L. Gage, and J. F. Rummel. *A Practical Introduction to Measurement and Evaluation.* New York: Harper & Row, 1965. Pp. 30–31. An example illustrates how one test score can correspond to different percentiles, depending on the norm reference group.

Thorndike, R. L., and E. Hagen. *Measurement and Evaluation in Psychology and Education.* New York: Wiley, 1969. Pp. 221–22. There is a short presentation of some of the reasons for selecting different norm groups in different situations.

Womer, F. B. *Test Norms: Their Use and Interpretation.* Washington, D. C.: National Association of Secondary School Principals, 1965. The author presents a clear discussion of the characteristics of test norms, including some excellent examples as to why test norms are not absolute, not universal, and not permanent (pp. 14–23). The complete book is a clarification of the development, characteristics, and interpretation of national test norms.

TYPES OF SCALED SCORES

Nunnally, J. C. *Educational Measurement and Evaluation.* New York: McGraw-Hill, 1972. Chapter 3 begins with a clear and elementary introduction to such statistical concepts as mean, mode, and standard deviation. The concepts and utility of standard scores, T-scores, percentiles, profiles, and various types of norm are explained with cautions in interpretation.

Remmers, H. H., N. L. Gage, and J. F. Rummel. *A Practical Introduction to Measure and Evaluation.* New York: Harper & Row, 1965. Pp. 59–68. A short explanation and example is given for standard scores, T-scores, percentiles, and stanines showing how test scores can be compared. Grade norms, age norms, percentile ranks, standard scores, and quotient norms are discussed briefly along with their advantages and limitations.

Thorndike, R. L. and E. Hagen. *Measurement and Evaluation in Psychology and Education.* New York: Wiley, 1969. Pp. 212–33. This section includes definitions, explanations, and examples of age norms, grade norms, percentile norms, percentile bands, standard scores, T-scores, and IQ. There is a model of the normal curve on page 228 illustrating the equivalence of scores in different systems, and the book includes a thorough explanation of the interchangeability and interpretation of norms, including stanines.

CRITERION-REFERENCED TESTING

Cronbach, L. J. *Essentials of Psychological Testing.* New York: Harper & Row, 1970. The author presents an excellent discussion of the concepts of criterion-referenced testing and absolute scores.

Ebel, R. L. *Essentials of Educational Measurement.* Englewood Cliffs, N. J.: Prentice-Hall, 1972. Pp. 83–85. The author compares norm-referenced and criterion-referenced measures and discusses some of the limitations of the latter.

Glaser, R. "Instructional Technology and the Measurement of Learning Outcomes." *American Psychologist,* 18 (1963), 519–21. This explains the differences between norm-referenced and criterion-referenced measures with respect to purposes and test-item selection. The need for assessing existing levels of competence is briefly discussed.

Popham, W. J., and T. R. Husek. "Implications of Criterion-Referenced Measurement." *Journal of Educational Measurement,* 6 (1969), 1–9. The authors analyze thoroughly the differences between norm-referenced and criterion-referenced testing with respect to variability, item construction, reliability, validity, item analysis, and interpretation.

Thorndike, R. L., ed. *Educational Measurement.* Washington, D. C.: American Council on Education, 1971. Pp. 652–55. The authors explain various interpretations of criterion-referenced testing and discuss thoroughly the distinction between norm-referenced and criterion-referenced tests.

STATISTICAL CONCEPTS

Bartz, A. E. *Elementary Statistical Methods for Educational Measurement.* Minneapolis: Burgess, 1968. This workbook was designed to explain the statistical methods needed by the teacher for the average classroom situation. The calculations are based on a small number of scores and exercises are included in the appendix.

McFarland, S. J., and C. F. Hereford, eds. *Statistics and Measurement in the Classroom.* Dubuque: Brown, 1971. Pp. 23–42. The first six readings cover the basic statistical concepts appropriate for teachers. It includes a delightful article titled "How to Talk Back to a Statistic."

Nunnally, J. C. *Educational Measurement and Evaluation.* New York:

McGraw-Hill, 1973. Pp. 39–64. The author introduces an analysis of elementary statistical concepts imperative for teachers to grasp.

Popham, W. J. *Educational Statistics Use and Interpretation.* New York: Harper & Row, 1967. This statistics book relies on pictorial as well as verbal explanations and is designed for students not trained mathematically.

4

Standards for Judging External Measures

CONCERNS

1. What is an external measuring device?
2. What is the relationship of aptitude, achievement, and attitude measures?
3. What is the relationship between the objectives being evaluated and the content of an external test?
4. What are the requirements for choosing an external measuring device?
5. What is the validity of a test?
6. What are the different types of validity to be considered when judging the merit of an external measuring device?
7. What is the reliability of a test?
8. What are the different types of reliability to be considered when judging the merit of an external measuring device?
9. What special problems exist in determining the reliability of an attitude measure?
10. What is the usability of a test?
11. What information is provided by the standard error of measurement?
12. What is the effect of using the same students?
13. What is a true score?

Tests can be distinguished from each other by where they are prepared as well as by whether they are norm-referenced or criterion-referenced (as was discussed in Chapter 3). Most tests are prepared by the individual teacher for use in a particular classroom. Such tests, used daily in the classrooms, are called *internal measuring devices* because they are developed within a particular school for use within that school. Internal tests include tests developed by the classroom teacher, by members of a department, and by members of a school system. The majority of tests used in the educational process are internal measures, and consequently they must be developed and evaluated with extreme care. Important factors to consider in the development and evaluation of internal measures will be presented in Chapters 7–9.

In this chapter we are concerned with external measuring devices, tests developed outside the local setting. These are commonly called *standardized tests* and are generally developed by private organizations and designed to measure certain characteristics of individual students. For example, a testing company might decide to develop an arithmetic achievement test for students in grades 3 through 5. The company would gather together a group of experts to prepare a test to measure the degree to which students have attained certain concepts and skills generally considered essential in the development of mathematical ability. An externally developed test must concentrate on generally accepted goals and concepts because it is intended to be used in no specific situation. It must be equally appropriate for classrooms in California and Florida, for a school with an enrollment of 90 and a school with an enrollment of 5,000.

A standardized test is so called because the procedures for administration have been standardized so that everyone takes the test under the same conditions. The time allotted for the test is the same for everyone. The instructions, those read by the student to himself and those read to the student by the teacher, are the same everytime and everywhere the test is administered. The major reason for such standardization of administration procedures is to ensure that the scores that students attain on the test may be considered comparable because they were obtained under the same conditions. This brings us to a reason for using standardized tests. The norms that are prepared for most standardized tests provide a reference system that aids the interpretation of student scores by providing information about how some known group performed

on the test. In Chapter 3 we noticed the difficulties and misinter-
pretations that one can experience in attempting to use norms as
a standard for comparison. Norms can be used as a system for
assessing the performance of an individual student relative to the
performance of some known group, but they do not necessarily
provide an indication of the desirable or even satisfactory performance on the test.

Types of External Measuring Devices

There are three major types of externally developed tests: achievement, aptitude, and attitude. While all three categories are
actually standardized tests, each is designed to serve a different purpose or to measure a different aspect of a student's
mental characteristics.

Achievement Tests

An achievement test is designed to measure the degree to which
an individual has attained certain concepts and skills pertaining to
a particular content at a particular point in time. For example, an
arithmetic achievement test might be designed to determine the
degree to which a student can actually add, subtract, divide, multiply, solve word problems, and so on. An English achievement test
might attempt to determine a student's spelling achievement or
his ability to distinguish between nouns and verbs or his ability
to punctuate properly. An example of such a test is given in
Figure 4.1, representing a page from the primary battery of the
Iowa Tests of Basic Skills. The page is from a vocabulary subtest
for Level 8, Form 6, and is intended for students who are eight
years old.

Of course, achievement tests are developed for different levels
of achievement since one could not reasonably expect a third
grader to possess the same skills as a senior in high school.
The purpose of achievement tests is to determine the degree to
which a student possesses concepts and skills he could reasonably be expected to possess at the point in time at which he is
examined, and the skills and concepts actually tested are those
generally accepted as important by the experts who prepared the
achievement test. Interpretations of scores from a standardized

Figure 4.1   *Vocabulary Subtest from the Iowa Tests of Basic Skills*

⊘   **V: Vocabulary (continued)**

18 To keep out of sight is to . . . . ⊂⊃ leave   ⊂⊃ move   ⊂⊃ hide

19 Where you live is your . . . . ⊂⊃ address   ⊂⊃ number   ⊂⊃ space

20 Something you can see through is . . . ⊂⊃ clean   ⊂⊃ clear   ⊂⊃ seen

21 A street that is bumpy is . . . . ⊂⊃ smooth   ⊂⊃ narrow   ⊂⊃ rough

22 To take care of is to . . . . ⊂⊃ protect   ⊂⊃ defend   ⊂⊃ hide

23 A person who writes a book is an . . . ⊂⊃ editor   ⊂⊃ actor   ⊂⊃ author

24 A bend in a road is a . . . . ⊂⊃ circle   ⊂⊃ curve   ⊂⊃ bump

25 To feel pain is to . . . . . ⊂⊃ suffer   ⊂⊃ supply   ⊂⊃ touch   ⊂⊃ harm

26 A place for water to go down is a . . .
                                  ⊂⊃ sink   ⊂⊃ plug   ⊂⊃ drink   ⊂⊃ drain

27 To be quiet and not excited is to be . . .
                                  ⊂⊃ easy   ⊂⊃ noisy   ⊂⊃ nasty   ⊂⊃ calm

28 To brag is to . . . . ⊂⊃ fight   ⊂⊃ boost   ⊂⊃ boast   ⊂⊃ worry

29 To do something more than once is to . . .
                                  ⊂⊃ repeat   ⊂⊃ answer   ⊂⊃ again   ⊂⊃ reply

30 To order someone to do something is to . . . him.
                                  ⊂⊃ rule   ⊂⊃ command   ⊂⊃ control   ⊂⊃ coach

STOP

3

From A. N. Hieronymus and E. F. Lindquist, *Iowa Tests of Basic Skills*. Boston: Houghton Mifflin, 1972. Reprinted by permission of the publisher.

achievement test are generally based upon a norm-referenced system. That is, the scores resulting from standardized tests provide a basis for comparing the performance of a particular student to the performance of students who compose the norm group.

The results of achievement tests can provide a teacher with valuable information. They can aid in comparisons between the achievement of particular students and the achievement of the norm group. Such comparison can also help evaluate teaching effectiveness and it can help determine how well certain students do in comparison with others. In addition, scores from standardized achievement tests can provide information about an individual student's progress from one test administration to the next and they can be used to compare a student's achievement in one subject to his achievement in another. Standardized achievement test scores can also provide the teacher with an indication as to how a student might be expected to perform in the future.

Aptitude Tests

An aptitude test is designed to assess a student's potential for performing some task. Some aptitude tests are designed to measure very specific traits such as musical or artistic potential. Scores from these very specific aptitude tests indicate how well a student can be expected to perform in the particular task that the test is designed to measure. A student who scores high on a test of musical aptitude, for example, could reasonably be expected to perform well on tasks requiring musical ability.

The most commonly used aptitude tests are designed to measure a student's general learning capability and potential for success in learning the tasks expected in school. Aptitude tests designed to measure general learning capability are most commonly called intelligence tests, and these are the basis for a large number of decisions relative to the education of individual students.

Intelligence scores are used as one criterion for determining which students in a school system should be considered as gifted. Intelligence scores are used by school systems as the basis for grouping for instruction, for assigning students to instructional tracks, and for advising students in their choice of vocation or preparation for college study. There are many other decisions that are influenced by intelligence scores as well.

There are two different kinds of intelligence test. The first is commonly referred to as a verbal test of intelligence. Verbal intelligence tests consist of items that require the student to read and that are generally related directly to skills and concepts that a student can be expected to learn in school. A sample of the questions asked on a verbal intelligence test is presented in Figure 4.2, a page from the verbal battery of Level 4, Form A, of the Lorge-Thorndike Intelligence Tests. Level 4 is intended for use with students from grades 7 through 9.

The second type of intelligence test is nonverbal and is called a performance test. The items on it do not require the student to read and they are generally considered to be independent of school-learned skills. In many cases, the nonverbal test simply requires the student to indicate with pencil on paper the best way to match given geometric shapes. Figure 4.3 represents a page from a nonverbal intelligence test. This particular page is taken from the nonverbal battery of Level 4, Form A, of the Lorge-Thorndike Intelligence Tests and is designed for students in grades 7 through 9. Other nonverbal tests actually require the student to perform certain tasks. The proverbial task that requires an individual to match square pegs with square holes and round pegs with round holes is actually one task on a nonverbal performance test of intelligence.

Intelligence tests may be administered to a group of people or to an individual. Most verbal tests of intelligence are group tests; nonverbal tests or performance tests may be either group tests or individual tests.

Attitude Tests

Attitude tests measure an individual's attitude toward something —school, for example. Such a test would attempt to assess whether an individual likes or dislikes school or is simply indifferent to it.

Because attitudes are subjective and undoubtedly change very rapidly, the preparation of a paper and pencil instrument that measures attitude is difficult and often tedious. It is difficult to write test items that experts will agree on as measures of a particular subjective attitude. One example of a standardized attitude

Figure 4.2 *Verbal Battery from the Lorge-Thorndike Intelligence Tests*

One word has been left out of each sentence on this page. Choose the word that will make the best, the truest, and the most sensible complete sentence. Look at sample sentence 0.

0. Hot weather comes in the ————.

   A fall   B night   C summer   D winter   E snow

The best answer is **summer.** The letter before **summer** is **C,** so you should make a heavy black pencil mark in the **C** answer space for sentence 0.

Do all the sentences on this page in the same way. Try every sentence.

---

1. Fred was six years old. There were six ———— on his birthday cake.

   A candles   B boys   C girls   D parties   E children

2. The ragged ———— may prove a good horse.

   F puppy   G child   H calf   J lamb   K colt

3. No man is happy ———— he believes he is.

   L if   M unless   N dirty   P provided   Q since

4. The important thing is not so much that every child should be taught as that every child should be given the wish to ————.

   R learn   S play   T hope   U reject   V teach

5. The person who ———— another must make good the damages.

   A reforms   B improves   C instructs   D injures   E delights

6. False facts are highly ———— to the progress of science.

   F injurious   G necessary   H devoted   J useful   K instrumental

7. The shortest way to ———— a country is to give power to demagogues.

   L enjoy   M ruin   N improve   P reconstruct   Q instruct

8. ———— is a department of lying.

   R Delusion   S Exactness   T Exaggeration   U Care   V Example

9. Coal is a portable climate. It carries the ———— of the tropics to Labrador and the polar circle.

   A fuel   B heat   C energy   D humidity   E vegetation

10. The coward threatens only when he is ————.

   F afraid   G surrounded   H safe   J conquered   K happy

11. Strong affections give credit to ———— arguments.

   L precise   M weak   N strong   P perfect   Q angry

12. Grey hair is a sign of age, not of ————.

   R color   S youth   T courage   U despair   V wisdom

13. Infantry is the ———— of an army.

   A battle   B weakness   C handicap   D nerve   E luxury

14. ———— are the rightful and peaceful successors of bullets.

   F Briberies   G Revolutions   H Weapons   J Ballots   K Autocrats

15. ———— events cast their shadows before.

   L Past   M Historic   N Unreal   P Coming   Q Recent

Page 3   ***Stop!*** *Wait until you are told to go ahead to Test 3.*

Figure 4.3   *Nonverbal Battery from the Lorge-Thorndike Intelligence Tests*

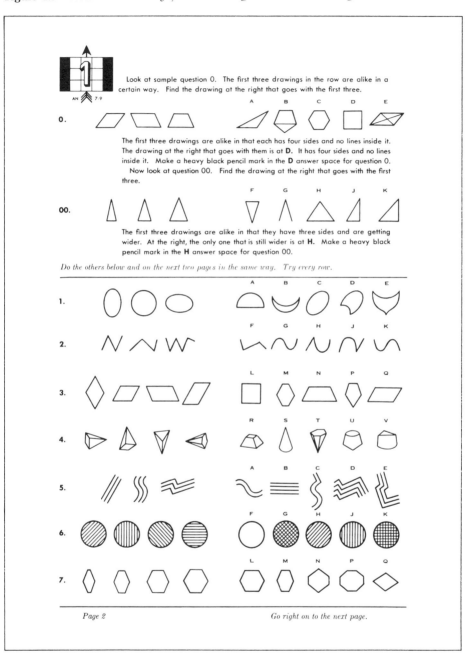

From Irving Lorge and Robert L. Thorndike, *The Lorge-Thorndike Intelligence Tests.*
Boston: Houghton Mifflin, 1954. Reprinted by permission of the publisher.

Figure 4.4 *Attitude Measure from The Jesness Inventory*

1. When you're in trouble, it's best to keep quiet about it.
2. It makes me nervous to sit still very long.
3. I get into a lot of fights.
4. I worry too much about doing the right things.
5. I always like to hang around with the same bunch of friends.
6. I am smarter than most boys I know.
7. It makes me mad that some crooks get off free.
8. My feelings get hurt easily when I am scolded or criticized.
9. Most police will try to help you.
10. Sometimes I feel like I want to beat up on somebody.

11. When somebody orders me to do something I usually feel like doing just the opposite.
12. Most people will cheat a little in order to make some money.
13. A person never knows when he will get mad, or have trouble.
14. If the police don't like you, they will try to get you for anything.
15. A person is better off if he doesn't trust people.
16. Sometimes I wish I could quit school.
17. Sometimes I feel like I don't really have a home.
18. People always seem to favor a certain boy or girl ahead of the others.
19. I never lie.
20. Most police are pretty dumb.

21. I worry about what other people think of me.
22. A person like me fights first and asks questions later.
23. I have very strange and funny thoughts in my mind.
24. It's hard to have fun unless you're with your buddies.
25. I get nervous when I ask someone to do me a favor.
26. If I could, I'd just as soon quit school right now.
27. Sometimes it's fun to steal something.
28. I notice my heart beats very fast when people keep asking me questions.
29. When I get really mad, I'll do just about anything.
30. Women seem more friendly and happy than men.

31. It is easy for me to talk to strangers.
32. Police stick their noses into a lot of things that are none of their business.
33. A lot of fathers don't seem to care if they hurt your feelings.
34. I am secretly afraid of a lot of things.
35. I hardly ever get a fair break.
36. Others seem to do things easier than I can.
37. I seem to "blow up" a lot over little things that really don't matter very much.
38. Only a baby cries when he is hurt.
39. Most adults are really very nice.
40. Winning a fight is about the best fun there is.

41. A lot of strange things happen to me.
42. I have all the friends I need.
43. I get a kick out of getting some people angry and all shook up.
44. Nowadays they make it a big crime to get into a little mischief.
45. It would be fun to work in a carnival or playland.
46. My father is too busy to worry much about me, or spend much time with me.
47. Sometimes I feel dizzy for no reason.
48. Sometimes people treat grown boys and girls like they were babies.
49. It makes me feel bad to be bawled out or criticized.
50. When things go wrong, there isn't much you can do about it.

51. If someone in your family gets into trouble it's better for you to stick together than to tell the police.
52. I can't seem to keep my mind on anything.
53. It always seems like something bad happens when I try to be good.
54. Most men are bossy and mean.
55. I don't care if people like me or not.
56. It seems like wherever I am I'd rather be somewhere else.
57. Once in a while I get angry.

measure is The Jesness Inventory, a test that was designed primarily for use with delinquents. Figure 4.4 presents the first thirty items from it. The respondent marks "true" or "false" for each item on a separate answer sheet.

Because of the difficulties in defining what an attitude is and how it can be measured, standardized tests have not been widely accepted as the best way to measure attitude. In fact, until recent years there has seemed to be doubt among educators as to whether attitudes are properly a concern of the schools. Recent movements toward concentration of education on student attitudes has made such measurement a very real concern, but agreement has not been reached on how to define and measure specific attitudes or on which attitudes the schools should be concerned with.

The difficulty inherent in developing standardized attitude tests has resulted in a rather unique development that may indicate how problems associated with attitude measurement will ultimately be resolved. The publishers of a certain standardized attitude test prepare a number of items designed to measure attitudes that the publishers feel are widely accepted among educators as important. The publishers then provide space in the test booklet and on the answer sheets in which the local school can report items that measure aspects of attitude that are considered important in that school but are not measured by the items included in the published test. Thus the concepts of external measuring devices and internal measuring devices are combined to form a single instrument designed to measure the attitudes that are considered most important by each individual school.

Choosing an External Measuring Device

When a school chooses a standardized achievement test, how can it decide between the various tests that are available? Should it choose the Iowa Test of Basic Skills or the Stanford Achievement Test? How does a school decide which intelligence tests to use? Should it purchase the Lorge-Thorndike Intelligence Tests or the Otis-Lennon Test of Mental Ability? Should the intelligence test that is administered be verbal or nonverbal or should a combination of both be administered? If an attitude test is to be given, which one should it be? These questions face the educators who are responsible for testing programs in all school districts. The remainder of this chapter will concentrate on factors that must be considered in the selection of an external measuring device.

Validity

External tests are often used to assist the school staff in placing students in classes appropriate for their ability and motivation. One ability measure used frequently is an intelligence test developed by major publishing houses. For example, members of the high school staff in Hawkville, concerned that students who have the ability or desire to go to college should be taking courses that prepare them for college, administer the Lorge-Thorndike Intelligence Tests yearly. If the staff is to use this test, they must have confidence in it. This confidence comes from being able to determine that the test is valid for use in the Hawkville School and for the purpose for which it is to be used. The manner in which a publishing house establishes confidence in an instrument is to provide evidence of its validity.

An external measure is valid if it measures what it was developed to measure. External measuring devices may be valid in one environment but not in another. In selecting an external measuring device, one must look for a test which will measure what it was developed to measure *in the setting in which it will be used.*

Validity is not a univariate concept. There are different types of validity, and a test may be valid with respect to one type of measurement but not valid with respect to another. The most frequently discussed types of validity are called content, predictive, concurrent, and construct validity. A test user must decide which type or types of validity a test must possess to meet his objectives and then determine whether the test he wishes to use possesses that validity.

Content validity. Content validity is concerned with the adequacy with which the items on a specific test measure the content area of interest. Content validity is determined by a very systematic and logical review of the items that compose a specific test. This type of validity does not require mathematical structures. Before reviewing the test for content validity, the teacher must be able to describe the content area to be covered and to state the specific objectives that the students are expected to be able to do if they have acquired the prescribed knowledge. Once the objectives are known and the content to be measured has been delineated, the determination of content validity becomes a matter of logically assessing whether the test actually measures that content. Test publishers make every attempt to inform potential users about the content covered by their tests. Technical manuals that accompany tests contain such information. In addition to what is provided by test publishers, the individuals responsible for selecting tests should review the items on each test in order to determine whether the specific behavior assessed by the test is the behavior that should be assessed. Only then can a test selector assess content validity. If an external test is to be used as a part of an evaluation plan, the test must be judged to have content validity before it can be used successfully.

The high school staff in Hawkville could very easily establish the content validity of the Iowa Test of Basic Skills. The staff knows that the general objective for administering the test is to place students with different abilities in different classes. If, upon examination of the test, the Hawkville staff decides that this test assesses the content upon which they wish to differentiate their students, then the test would be judged to have content validity for the purpose for which it is to be used at Hawkville School.

Predictive validity.   Predictive validity is concerned with the relationship between the scores attained on the day of the test and some variable assessed at a later date. For example, the staff at Hawkville should be quite concerned about the predictive validity of the Lorge-Thorndike Intelligence Tests if they wish to use the test results for assigning students to a college preparatory program of study. Evidence available from the test publisher should show that there is a strong relationship between the scores on the test and the later success in college of students who achieved those scores. That is, the evidence should indicate that students who scored high on the Lorge-Thorndike test were more successful in college than students who scored low on it. Test publishers usually provide evidence of predictive validity in the form of a correlation coefficient between test score and college success; this is an empirical indication of predictive validity. The final decision about the predictive validity of the test still rests with the school staff. Hawkville High School must decide whether the reported correlation coefficient is adequate for its purposes. To make this decision, the staff must understand what the correlation coefficient represents. (Correlation coefficient is discussed later in this chapter.) There is no coefficient uniformly agreed on that indicates that a test has predictive validity; each decision must be made by each staff.

Concurrent validity. Concurrent validity is quite similar to predictive validity and is concerned with the relationship between test scores and an accepted contemporary or current criterion of performance on the variable that the test is intended to measure. Evidence of the concurrent validity of a test is provided by a correlation coefficient between the test and the prescribed criterion. For example, Hawkville High School may have used in previous years a test battery that required four days of testing time to determine the placement of students in different classes. Since the Lorge-Thorndike requires only about two hours of testing time, the staff at Hawkville may be interested in adopting the Lorge-Thorndike to replace the present testing program, but they should do so only if the Lorge-Thorndike test does as good a job as the program presently used. The correlation between the four-day test and the two-hour test would be established if the correlation were determined to be sufficiently high, as judged by the staff. Then the Lorge-Thorndike Intelligence Tests could be said to have concurrent validity with respect to the four-day test. That is, if the Lorge-Thorndike test and the four-day test give consistent results, then the Lorge-Thorndike can be used as a replacement for the four-day test battery.

Construct validity. Construct validity is concerned with the psychological constructs measured by a particular test. This is much more difficult to understand than the other types of validity and educators often fail to consider it when they select external measuring devices. Psychological constructs are theoretically defined aspects of the human mind that may or may not exist and may or may not be practically applicable in schools. A detailed discussion of construct validity is to be found in the references at the end of this chapter.

One method commonly used for determining construct validity employs a number of judges to observe and independently rate the intelligence of a number of students. If the ratings have high correlation with the scores that the same students receive on the intelligence test, then that test probably possesses a high degree of construct validity. There is obviously a great deal of subjectivity in the determination of construct validity, and in the final analysis test users must determine whether a particular test has sufficient construct validity to make the test useful in the particular situation in which it is to be used.

Summary.   The four types of validity discussed above are independent of each other. A test may be judged as having content but not concurrent or predictive validity. A test can possess concurrent validity but not construct validity. This does not mean that such tests are inappropriate. A test does not have to be valid in all circumstances to be useful. The appropriateness of a test's validity is defined by the situation in which it is to be used. Moreover, a test is never completely valid or completely invalid. As far as validity is concerned, the choice of a test generally depends on whether it possesses or seems to possess the most validity for the purposes the school staff have in mind.

The validity of a test is crucial if it is to be used in evaluation. Evaluators and teachers must decide whether the test measures what it was intended to measure. It is the responsibility of the external test developer to provide evidence that will assist the decision maker in determining whether the test is valid for the purpose for which it is to be used. Test publishers can provide empirical and logical evidence about tests, but the teacher must eventually make a subjective decision too. If the teacher does not believe that the test is valid, then the test should not be used to evaluate students.

Reliability

Indices of reliability provide a test user with information about the consistency with which a test measures whatever it measures. An index of reliability provides not information about the material being covered but information about the consistency of the test results. There are several different ways of obtaining an index of reliability. Each index discussed in this chapter provides evidence about a different type of consistency. One provides a statistical index of the consistency of test scores from two administrations of a given test at two different times. Another provides

information about the consistency of test scores from two different testing times that used equivalent but not the same forms of
the test. The third type of reliability index indicates the degree to
which a test is internally consistent.

The correlation coefficent. To appreciate the different measures
of reliability, the potential teacher must first understand the concept of a correlation coefficient. The most commonly used index of
correlation is the Pearson Product Moment correlation coefficient.
The correlation between two variables is a statistical indication
of the relationship between them. The key to interpreting the
correlation coefficient is knowing what type of relationship is
being observed. The measure of relationship between two variables is an indication of the extent to which individuals have the
same relative position with respect to the other scores in the group
on both of the variables. If all individual test scores for the two
variables maintain the same relative position in the group, then
the correlation is generally high (approaching 1.0) and positive.
If the individuals' scores reverse their relative rank (those who
scored high on test A scored low on test B, and vice versa), the
correlation will again approach 1.0, but the sign of the index will
be negative.

The sign, positive or negative, gives the teacher an indication
of the direction of the relationship. A positive sign indicates that
individuals who are high on one variable are also high on the
other; a negative sign indicates that individuals who are high on
one variable are low on the other. The sign of the correlation
coefficient provides no indication as to the strength of the relationship. The strength of the relationship is found in the magnitude of the correlation coefficient.

If each individual's score on two tests is in the same relative
position with respect to others in the group, the correlation will
approach 1.0. If the individuals' scores on the two tests vary with
respect to relative position in a random manner, the correlation
will approach 0. Therefore, the magnitude of the correlation will
vary between 0 and 1.0. The closer the coefficient is to 1.0, the
stronger will be the relationship between the two variables.

The data presented in the first table of Figure 4.5 demonstrates
a correlation between Test A and Test B of 1.0. A careful review
of the data shows that student C scored the highest on both tests
and that the remaining students maintained the same relative

Figure 4.5   *Correlation Coefficients*

STUDENT	TEST A SCORE	TEST B SCORE
A	10	15
B	12	17
C	20	25
D	16	21
E	17	22

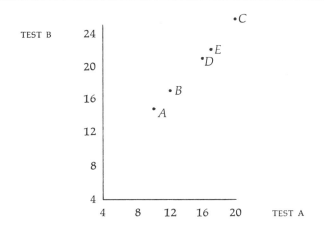

STUDENT	TEST A SCORE	TEST B SCORE
F	20	15
G	17	17
H	16	21
I	12	22
J	10	25

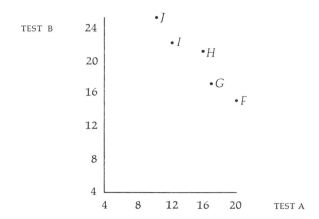

Figure 4.5 *Continued*

STUDENT	TEST A SCORE	TEST B SCORE
K	17	25
L	20	21
M	10	17
N	12	22
O	16	15

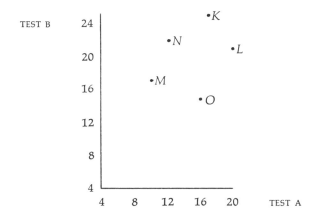

position with respect to the others in the group. (There are other numerical reasons why this correlation is exactly 1.0, and they may be found in basic statistics books.) In this example we have a perfect relationship between the two tests. Special notice should be taken that the perfect correlation means not that the student scored the same on both tests but only that the student remained in the same relative position.

The data presented in the second table demonstrates a correlation of —.95 between Test A and Test B. This correlation means that any individual scoring high on Test A will score low on Test B, and vice versa. (The reason that this correlation is not —1.0 is related to the definition of the correlation coefficient, and it can be found in a standard statistics book.) In the third table the correlation is closer to zero because there is no definite pattern in the data. When the correlation is low, it is difficult to predict whether a student who scores high on Test A will score high or low on Test B.

The reason why we discuss correlation before studying the

indices of reliability is readily apparent. The concept of consistency in test score results is supported by various types of
correlation coefficient. The term "consistent" should be interpreted in the same manner as "relationship" is defined by the
correlation coefficient. The consistency of a test score does not
mean that a test score will remain the same for an individual
from one test session to another. It does mean that the individual
will maintain the same relative position in the score distribution
from one test session to another.

Test-retest index of reliability.   The test-retest index of reliability
is determined by administering the same test to the same individual at two different times. If the trait being measured by the test
is stable, the trait should be similar from one test period to the
next. If the results of the two testing situations are consistent, the
test is reported to have test-retest reliability.

The measure of test-retest reliability is a correlation coefficient.
The closer the index of reliability approaches to 1.0, the greater
is the test-retest reliability. A high test-retest reliability index
means that the students of a group who scored higher than the
other students in that group on the first administration of the test
are likely to score higher than the other children on the second
administration as well. E. L. Lewis (see selected references) has
provided evidence that suggests that students will generally receive higher scores on the second administration of the same test
but that there is no negative effect on the reliability of the test.

Several authors have discussed the test-retest reliability index
as a stability measure of a test. In the context of interpreting
reliability coefficients the term "stability" means that students,
upon repeated measurement, maintain their same relative position
with respect to the other students in the reference group. The
concept of stability does not mean that the students will receive
the same score on each testing date. The data reported in Figure
4.6 may be helpful on this point.

The publishers of external tests are very careful to state test-
retest reliability coefficients. It is not necessary to try to describe
cut-off points between 0 and 1.0 for selecting a reliable test. If
the only criterion for using a test is its test-retest reliability, then
the potential user should compare the reliability of the various
tests that are appropriate for use in the particular situation. In
most cases, reliability is not the major reason for selecting a test.

The major reason for selecting a test is its validity; reliability adds to its credibility. The potential user must decide subjectively what value of the reliability coefficient will be sufficient. With external tests developed to measure achievement and aptitude, educators have come to expect relatively high test-retest reliability indices (above .80). In attitude assessment, it is most unusual to find a high test-retest reliability coefficient. This will be discussed in more detail later in this chapter.

Caution must be taken when evaluating the test-retest reliability index. The evaluator should carefully review and understand the time interval between the two testing periods and the conditions under which the tests were given. The circumstances ought ideally to be identical for the two administrations of the test. This is difficult to control, but the test developer must try to approximate the circumstances of the first test. R. T. Eichelberger (see selected references) has found that some students tend to lose their motivation to do well when a test is readministered. This can be controlled if the person administering the test emphasizes the relevance of the repetition. The time interval introduces the additional complexity that if it is too short the students may profit from remembering specific items or practice effects, and if it is too long they may actually change with respect to the trait being assessed. Most test publishers provide coefficients based on time intervals of two and four weeks.

Figure 4.6 *Test-Retest Score Distributions*

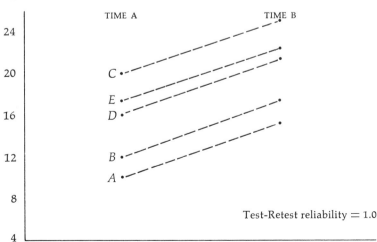

Equivalent forms reliability coefficient.   The equivalent forms reliability coefficient is quite different from test-retest reliability. Equivalent forms reliability provides an index of consistency, but the consistency is between two equivalent forms of a test. The type of consistency reported is an index of the students' consistency on the traits being measured by the two forms of the test.

The equivalent forms reliability coefficient is determined by obtaining a correlation coefficient between the test scores obtained on the two equivalent forms of the test. Usually the forms are given at very short intervals, of less than one week, to prevent change with regard to the trait in the individual being tested. The important issue for this type of reliability is the development of equivalent forms of a test to measure a specific trait. Basically the equivalent forms of a test are intended to measure the same traits or attributes, but the items on the test are different. The major publishing houses do an excellent job of writing equivalent forms of a test.

The equivalent forms reliability coefficient is quite helpful to individuals selecting a test if they are concerned with assessing a student more than once on the same trait. If an assessment is going to be made a second time by a different test, it is important to know whether the two tests (or two forms of the same test) measure the same traits or attributes. The equivalent forms reliability coefficient is an indication of the consistency with which the two tests measure the same trait. If a potential user is concerned with only the selection of a single external measuring device for a single assessment of a student, the equivalent forms reliability coefficient is not important to the decision.

Internal consistency reliability index.   Internal consistency is reported for tests in which items are intended to measure the same trait. The items are divided into two groups and a correlation between the responses on the two groups is determined. If the correlation is high, the test is reported to have internal consistency. In most cases, measures of internal consistency provide good estimates of equivalent forms reliability.

In selecting an appropriate externally developed test, educators must be concerned with both the validity and the reliability of the test. In most educational settings the most important aspect of the test is its content validity. Once this has been established, the test selectors can consider the appropriate reliability indices. These vary according to the situation. If a test does not possess content validity, as determined by the potential user, it cannot be used as an effective evaluation instrument.

The foregoing discussion has presupposed that the externally developed test measures a stable trait. If the trait being assessed is not stable, the concept of test-retest reliability is meaningless. For example, tests developed to assess a particular attitude may have content validity but very low test-retest reliability. The reason for the low correlation between the two testing periods may be a function of the fact that the attitude being measured is not stable. The attitude an individual has toward something may change very quickly, and if it does, he will not show consistent scores on a test designed to measure that attitude on two different occasions. In this case, a more important reliability index would be that of internal consistency, because this helps determine whether the test gives consistent results at any one point in time.

Usability of Test Scores

The validity of a test is of utmost importance. It is probably worse to have a test that actually measures something other than what it purports to measure than it is to have no test at all. Yet it is conceivable that a test be perfectly valid and its results unusable. Suppose, for example, that a new test is administered in a particular school system to measure vocabulary. Scores reported as 43 or 24 or some other such number, have no meaning. They must be interpretable if the test is to provide usable results, or they must provide meaningful information about the students' performance. If test scores are to be usable, the reference system for interpretation must be available. Moreover, the reference system must be appropriate for the objectives that the particular school has established for using the test. Validity certainly is an important criterion for judging tests but tests must be more than valid; they must provide usable results.

Tests of supposedly stable characteristics, such as intelligence, should also provide reliable results, but these must be stable too. Recall, for example, the meaning of test-retest reliability. This implies the degree to which each student maintains the same relative position in the score distributions that result from two separate administrations of a test, but test-retest reliability does not require that each student receive the same score on both administrations of the test. The conditions for test-retest reliability would be met if each student's score increased or decreased by some constant amount from the first testing session to the second. As a phenomenon this has been demonstrated with intelligence tests on many different occasions by many different researchers.

We must question the usability of scores that result from tests when we know that the score will change upon repeated testing. How does an educator choose the cut-off score to be used in deciding who should be considered as gifted, if he knows that a given student's scores will all go up or down upon repeated testing? How can IQ scores be used for grouping students for instruction? How can students be assigned to instructional tracks on the basis of IQ scores when the scores are known to change upon repeated testing? This is not to say that IQ scores are not valid or that they are not reliable. What we have questioned is the usability of scores. When tests of stable traits are being considered, usability should imply that test scores remain constant, within reasonable limits, over repeated testing with the same instrument.

A usable score is one that is interpretable and one that remains constant (when a stable trait is being measured), but we must expect all test scores to vary somewhat upon repeated testing. Theoretically, every test score is somewhat in error. A student may receive a score of 25 on a test when she really should have received a 24. The next time the student takes the test she may receive a 22 when she really should have received a 24. These differences between what a student actually scores on a test and what she really should have received are called measurement errors.

Measurement errors have a number of different causes. A test question may be stated in such a way that it causes a student to respond incorrectly when actually she knew the correct answer or, on the other hand, caused her to respond correctly when she did not actually know the answer. The room may be too hot for one individual to work well while it is just right for another. Some students may be overtired at the time of the exam. And, of course, there is always guessing. A student may guess the answer to a question correctly at one time and incorrectly at another. It is generally felt by measurement experts that every test score contains a certain amount of error and does not reflect a student's "true score."

A true score is defined as a measure of the knowledge that a student actually possesses or the score that the student would have received on a test if there were no measurement error. In other words, a student's true score is the score he obtained on the test plus or minus the error of measurement present in that score. This relationship between true scores, obtained scores, and error scores is generally expressed as

$$\text{True score} = \text{Obtained score} \pm \text{Error score}$$

It is further assumed by measurement experts that if a student took the same test over a number of times, there would be just as many obtained scores larger than the true score as there would be obtained scores smaller than the true score. That is, one half of the error scores would be positive and one half of the error scores would be negative. The greatest number of error scores would be small scores, with fewer and fewer numbers of error scores occurring as the size of the error score increased. Measurement theory suggests that a frequency distribution of error scores would appear as in Figure 4.7. Error scores are assumed to be normally distributed.

If it were possible to calculate the standard deviation of the error scores that a student obtained upon repeated testings with the same test, we would have the standard deviation of a normal distribution of error scores. This standard deviation of error scores is called the *standard error of measurement*. We are concerned here not with how the standard error of measurement is calculated but rather with the information that it provides. Suppose you were choosing an external measuring device for your school system. In studying the technical manual for a particular test, you might find that the standard error of measurement reported is 4. What this value tells you is that, if this test is used, the true score of 68 percent of the students tested will be within four score points of their obtained score. In other words, you

Figure 4.7 *Normal Distribution (Percentages)*

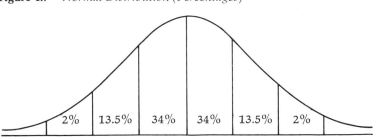

know that 68 percent of the students will actually possess true scores somewhere between four points below their obtained score and four points above their obtained score. Of the students tested 95 percent will actually have true scores between eight points (two standard errors of measurement) below and eight points above their obtained scores. It is extremely important to notice that we do not know which students we are talking about when we say that 68 percent of the students have a true score within ±1 standard error of measurement of their obtained score. We know only that of all the students tested, 68 percent will have a true score within that range.

It is clear that the standard error of measurement provides no information about how accurate an individual student's test score is. It is generally accepted, however, as an index of how accurate or reliable a test is for an entire group of students. For example, if a teacher were forced to make a choice between two standardized tests, the standard error of measurement would be very helpful. If test 1 had a reported standard error of measurement of four while test 2 had a reported standard error measurement of eight, which test would you choose? Assuming all other things about the tests to be equal, you would probably choose test 1, because you know that test 1 will provide for the majority of people obtained scores that will contain smaller error scores than will test 2. In other words, test 1 will yield more reliable results.

In addition to being valid and reliable, a test must provide usable results. To be usable, the results must be interpretable. In addition, if the results of tests of stable traits are to be usable, they must remain constant within reasonable limits. By reasonable limits is meant that the standard error of measurement should be relatively small.

Summary

In this chapter, we have shown that the staff of a school have a number of factors to consider when attempting to choose an external measuring device. The objectives for choosing the test—or, in other words, what the test is supposed to measure—must first be established. Once these objectives are known, the staff must check the tests from which the choice is to be made to be sure that they are in agreement with the established objectives. There should be information available from the test publisher that indicates that the test possesses a type of validity in agreement with the purpose for which it is to be used. There should also be evidence that the test is reliable. When achievement and aptitude tests are being considered, one would probably look for the tests to possess test-retest reliability. If an attitude measure is being considered, one would be most concerned about its showing internal consistency.

In addition to being in agreement with objectives, valid, and reliable, the test must provide usable results. The test publisher must provide appropriate norms so that the scores can be interpreted. If seniors at Hawkville High School are to be tested but norms are available only for juniors, then the test cannot be considered usable for Hawkville because appropriate norms are not available. In connection with usability, there should also be an indication as to how much students' scores can be expected to change upon repeated testing. This will provide the staff with some basis for interpretation of scores if the test is administered on more than one occasion.

The staff should also evaluate the tests for availability of forms. If the test is to be administered to a large group or if it is to be administered on more than a single occasion, it may be advisable to use two or three equivalent forms of the test. The testing company should indicate whether more than one form is available and should provide information as to degree of equivalent forms reliability.

Finally, one must consider the monetary cost of tests. Suppose that the Hawkville staff had found that two different tests were equivalent in all the criteria listed above. The only basis for distinguishing between the two tests, then, might be that one is less expensive than the other. Educators must be careful when comparing costs of tests to make sure that the services and materials are equivalent. The proper use of an external measure requires technical reports, administration manuals, test booklets, answer sheets, scoring, and reporting of scores. All these items must be taken into consideration when one is computing the cost. Cost should be the last criterion to consider when attempting to choose between tests, however. One should never sacrifice any of the other criteria for judging an external measure merely in order to save money. It is better to test less frequently with more costly but appropriate tests than to test more frequently with less costly and inappropriate tests.

Reflections

1. External measuring devices are tests developed by individuals outside the setting in which the tests are to be used, and they are commonly called standardized tests.
2. Externally developed tests to assess aptitude, achievement, and attitude are often standardized tests. Each is designed to measure a different aspect of a student's mental characteristics.
3. The content of an externally developed test must be closely related to the objectives or behavior to be evaluated.
4. The requirements to review before selecting an external measuring device are its validity, reliability, and usability.
5. A test is valid if it is measuring what it purports to measure.
6. Four different types of validity are content, construct, predictive, and concurrent validity.
7. A test is reliable if the test consistently measures whatever it is measuring.
8. Three different indices of reliability are: test-retest reliability, equivalent forms reliability, and internal consistency.
9. The reliability of an instrument that is measuring an unstable trait should be expected to be low.
10. The usability of a test implies that the scores are interpretable and that when the trait being measured is stable the test scores are reliable.
11. The standard error of measurement is the standard deviation of a normal distribution of error scores.
12. Students' scores on a given test can be expected to rise upon repeated testing even though the test may possess a high degree of test-retest reliability.
13. A student's true score is the score the student would have received if there were no measurement error.

Exercises

1. For each objective that you have previously suggested, determine the types of measure (aptitude, attitude, achievement) that are needed to evaluate that objective.
2. Using Oscar K. Buros' *Mental Measurement Yearbook* (7th ed., New Jersey: Gryphon Press, 1972) determine whether

there are external measures available that could be used in your evaluation.

3. Select a standardized test and review it for potential users. Use the format that is used in Buros' *Mental Measurement Year book*.
4. Given the two sets of scores 9, 7, 5, 4, 2, and 3, 3, 8, 1, 5, arrange them so that there is (a) a positive correlation between them and (b) a negative correlation between them.
5. The test-retest reliability of an attitude measure is almost always lower than the reliability of an achievement test. Develop a one-page position paper presenting your rationale for this observation.

Selected References

VALIDITY

Ebel, R. L. *Essentials of Educational Measurement.* Englewood Cliffs, N. J.: Prentice-Hall, 1972. Pp. 435–48. This chapter is devoted to a general discussion of the problems, purposes, and characteristics of test validity.

Green, J. A. *Introduction to Measurement and Evaluation.* New York: Dodd, Mead, 1970. Pp. 64–71. Different classifications of validity are briefly introduced. Then the four types of validity (construct, content, concurrent, and predictive) are presented, along with a clear explanation of their purposes.

Nunnally, J. C. *Educational Measurement and Evaluation.* New York: McGraw-Hill, 1972. Pp. 21–37. The author explains validity as it is related to the three major functions of testing: prediction, assessment, and trait measurement.

Remmers, H. H., N. L. Gage, and J. F. Rummel. *A Practical Introduction to Measurement and Evaluation.* New York: Harper & Row, 1965. Pp. 119–21. This is a very short presentation of the definitions of construct, concurrent, predictive, and content validity.

RELIABILITY

Bartz, A. E. *Elementary Statistical Methods for Educational Measurement.* Minneapolis: Burgess, 1968. Pp. 51–56. The determination of test reliability is discussed and the split-halves method is illustrated, utilizing a small number of scores.

Durost, W. N., and G. A. Prescott. *Essentials of Measurement for*

Teachers. New York: Harcourt Brace Jovanovich, 1962. Pp. 14–19. Presents methods of determining reliability and the factors that affect it.

Eichelberger, R. T. "Practice Effects of Repeated IQ Testing and the Relationship Between IQ Change Scores and Selected Individual Characteristics." Ph.D. dissertation, Southern Illinois University, Carbondale, Illinois, 1970. This research study documents the effects of several different variables on student performance on repeated testings.

Green, J. A. *Introduction to Measurement and Evaluation.* New York: Dodd, Mead, 1970. Pp. 71–80. Here is an elementary statistical explanation of reliability determined through the methods of test-retest, alternate forms, and split halves.

Lewis, E. L. "The Effects of Practice and Specific Item Learning on Verbal and Nonverbal Ability Assessment." Ph.D. dissertation, Southern Illinois University, Carbondale, Illinois, 1971. This research study investigates the nature of score increases that occur upon repeated testing.

Stanley, J. C., and K. D. Hopkins. *Educational and Psychological Measurement and Evaluation.* Englewood Cliffs, N. J.: Prentice-Hall, 1972. Pp. 114–17. The authors unfold the concept of test reliability through the medium of a consistent and easily comprehensible example.

CORRELATION COEFFICIENTS: CALCULATION
AND INTERPRETATION

Bartz, A. E. *Elementary Statistical Methods for Educational Measurement.* Minneapolis: Burgess, 1968. Pp. 39–50. Illustrations of perfect correlations are given and short. examples of calculating correlation coefficients are presented.

Noll, V. H., and D. P. Scannell. *Introduction to Educational Measurement.* Boston: Houghton Mifflin, 1972. Pp. 81–92. The authors give a good presentation of interpreting and calculating correlation coefficients.

Stanley, J. C., and K. D. Hopkins. *Educational and Psychological Measurement and Evaluation.* Englewood Cliffs, N. J.: Prentice-Hall, 1972. Pp. 58–68. This section begins with clear discussion of correlation and then proceeds with different statistical procedures for calculating Pearson's r.

5

Standardized Achievement Tests

CONCERNS

1. What is a standardized test?
2. How does an achievement test differ from other types of test?
3. How is a standardized achievement test developed?
4. What should the potential test user expect of materials that help him select tests?
5. In what ways can standardized achievement tests be used in the school?

What Is a Standardized Achievement Test?

In Chapter 4, standardized tests were described as externally prepared measuring instruments that measure concepts and skills generally accepted as appropriate at a particular point in a student's educational experience. Because standardized tests are used by different schools in different areas of the country and because they are generally administered less often than internal measures are, the objectives measured by standardized tests are usually less specific than those assessed by internal measures. Standardized tests are generally longer, also, and assess a broader range of content and skills than internal measures do. Standardized tests are so called not because of the results but because the administration procedures—directions, time limits, test booklets, answer sheets, and so on—are standard.

A standardized achievement test has a quite different purpose from that of aptitude and attitude tests. Achievement tests concentrate on what a student is supposed already to have learned at the time the test is administered. Aptitude tests concentrate on what a student can be expected to achieve in the future. Attitude tests concentrate on affective measurements, on what a student feels or thinks about things. In practice, there is considerable overlap, at least of achievement and aptitude tests, in what the various types of test actually measure. In theory, however, they are supposed to assess certain quite different attributes. Achievement tests measure a student's past success, whereas aptitude tests attempt to measure a student's potential for success in the future. We shall concentrate in this chapter on standardized achievement tests.

Construction of Standardized Achievement Tests

To best understand a standardized achievement test, the teacher should be aware of the procedures used in developing it. Publishers generally provide such information but there is no definite format that determines what or how information is provided. This section of this chapter describes a procedure for developing a standardized achievement test, in order to clarify for the potential teacher the extensive work involved in the development of such tests.

Determining Content Area

Initially, the developers of an achievement test must determine the appropriate content area to be covered and the nature of the group for whom the test is intended. Until recently, test groups have been defined according to grade level. This has seemed appropriate because almost all schools were organized into grades. Today, however, many schools have adopted nongraded structures in the belief that instruction should be individualized. Consequently test publishers have reconsidered the groups for whom they develop tests, which are now directed more toward students who have a common set of experiences rather than a common grade. Schools that prefer grade-level testing may still use it, but in comprehending the experiences of the students for whom a test was initially intended, the teacher can make professional decisions about the most appropriate way to evaluate particular students in particular schools.

After defining the group of children to be evaluated, the test developer must define the content areas to be assessed. Because curriculum patterns vary within schools, test developers try to determine the most common content for defined groups and levels of children. This is made difficult by the fact that many school systems have not carefully considered their objectives and, as a result, cannot clearly define the subject content to which their students are exposed. Therefore, test developers usually depend on reviews of the most commonly used classroom textbooks in order to determine content areas rather than looking to schools for this information. Once content to be included in tests has been determined, the relative importance of each area must be properly weighted. The content areas most heavily emphasized in the textbooks are considered most important; those less heavily emphasized are considered less important.

Constructing Test Items

Once the content of a test has been defined, developers construct potential test items. Specialists in the subject areas tested prepare test items, usually in a multiple choice format, because this is generally regarded as easily and objectively scored. The item writer prepares questions that he judges possess content validity from the specialist's point of view. A number of items may assess the same trait. Each item must undergo vigorous field testing before it is included in a final test.

The item writer is concerned not only with content validity but also with different types of cognitive functioning. Many educators and test developers define cognitive functioning as B. S. Bloom *et al.* did in *Taxonomy of Educational Objectives* published in 1956. In the handbook titled *Cognitive Domain,* the following levels were defined: knowledge, comprehension, application, analysis, synthesis, and evaluation. In order to be certain that items are developed at different cognitive levels, a table of specifications is sometimes generated such as the one in Table 5.1. The item

Table 5.1 *Cognitive Specifications*

		CONTENT AREA *Reading*	
COGNITIVE LEVEL	*Vocabulary*	*Comprehension*	*Spelling*
Knowledge			
Comprehension			
Application			
Analysis			
Synthesis			
Evaluation			

writers attempt to prepare items at each cognitive level for each content area and test items appropriate for particular levels of previous experience. If levels of previous experience are defined as school grade levels, a table of specification is constructed for each level. Writing a number of items for each cell consumes time but is essential if generalized achievement tests are to assess all content areas at all levels of cognitive functioning.

Field testing.   Field testing begins after a group of items has been pooled. The items are administered to groups of children with past experiences defined as prerequisites for the test. The items are also administered to individuals with more and less than the prescribed level of past experience. This procedure allows the test developer to determine whether a test item is actually appropriate for the grade level for which it was developed.

Item analysis. Once the results of the field testing have been received by the test developer, the process of analyzing each item begins. Item-difficulty and item-discrimination indices are determined for each grade level in which the item was administered. (The procedures for developing these indices are discussed in detail in Chapter 9.) The item-difficulty index gives the percentage of students who responded to the item correctly. The larger is the percentage of students who respond correctly to the item, the less difficult the item is.

The item-discrimination index is more difficult to interpret. It is found by identifying two groups of students, one that scores low and one that scores high on general achievement tests. The results of the two groups are compared. If the results are similar, the item being evaluated has a poor item-discrimination index. If the results are not similar, the item has a good discrimination index and it is either positive or negative. A positive index indicates that the high-scoring group did better than the low-scoring group on the test item, while the reverse is true if the index is negative.

The test developer is interested in how item indices vary between grade levels. The expectation is that an item becomes less difficult and discriminates more poorly as the previous experiences of the students increase. But experience ultimately is subjective, and there are no set guidelines appropriate for all standardized tests. The levels of difficulty and discrimination required before an item is included on a test are generally decided subjectively by each test developer.

After the items have been analyzed, some are rejected as not useful for further consideration. Others are included in a new item pool. This is different from the previous pool in that the data for each item now provide additional empirical evidence about its assessment potential. Finally, from the new item pool, the test developer determines which items will be included in the final test.

Testing Procedures

The test developer must determine time limits for tests. They should not be too long and yet must adequately cover the topics of concern. The table of specifications allows the test developer to determine the percentage of items that assess particular traits at particular cognitive levels and to determine whether that percentage accurately reflects the importance of that content area and level of functioning in the textbook under review. For example, in developing a mathematics achievement test for third graders, it may be found that approximately 10 percent of the content of all third-grade mathematics textbooks is devoted to multiplication of one two-digit number by another two-digit number. About 10 percent of the items on the mathematics achievement test should therefore assess the students' ability to multiply two two-digit numbers. A look at the table of specifications allows the test developer to determine whether the percentage of items measuring the students' ability to multiply two-digit numbers is sufficient. Items not included in the test may then be reviewed for the development of a second form of the exam. The criteria for the selection of items for a second form of the test are identical to the criteria for the first. The rigorous procedure discussed above results in two tests developed from a pool of carefully defined items that have been evaluated subjectively and empirically. The test developer has confidence that the items will accomplish the intent of the test.

The standard procedures to be employed in administering the test are then developed. The time limits for each component of the test can be established, and the procedures for distributing materials and providing instructions to the students are written. Norms must also be developed. The test developers must define the populations for which the test was developed and define the subpopulations that might require separate sets of norms. Random samples must be selected for the norm population and the test must be administered to students. Once the results have been obtained, the raw scores are converted to meaningful scaled scores such as percentile ranks, grade equivalents, and stanines. The process must be repeated for both forms of the exam.

The Test Manual and Associated Aids

The work of the test developer does not end when the test has been developed and the norms obtained. Test manuals and associated aids for test users must be prepared so that the users have information sufficient to determine whether the test is appropriate for their purposes and the results can be used correctly. In preparing the manuals and associated aids, the publishers closely follow the standards set by the American Psychological Association in *Standards for Educational and Psychological Tests and Manuals.* This set of standards should be known by test users as well.

All tests should be accompanied by test manuals that provide information about interpretation, validity, and reliability, directions for administering and scoring the test, and scales and norms appropriate for the test. The manual is the primary information source for the test user who needs specific information about a test. For this reason, it must be up to date and complete.

Test interpretation. The material that a publisher prepares to accompany a test should provide score scales that minimize the risk of incorrect interpretation. In cases in which incorrect interpretation might occur—with, for instance, grade equivalents— the publisher develops examples of proper interpretation according to the scale score provided. For achievement tests, the publisher provides an accurate description of the content covered by the test. Some publishers report the table of specifications as well. Finally, the test publisher must provide information about what scores can be interpreted. Most achievement tests have subscores, and the interpretation of these is more meaningful than an interpretation of the total score. For instance, if subscores are available for reading, vocabulary skills, spelling, and arithmetic, a single total score would provide the teacher with much less information than would be obtained from interpreting the four subscores individually.

Validity. The manual prepared by the test publisher must contain information about the test's validity. In the case of an achievement test, the manual must be precise with respect to the content that is sampled and evaluated. If the test requires an outside validity criterion the publisher must completely and accurately describe the outside criterion.

Concurrent validity and predictive validity both require outside criteria. To establish the concurrent validity of a test, the developer finds the correlation between the test and, usually, some other test purported to measure the same trait. The correlation has no meaning to the potential user unless he is aware of the characteristics of the outside test, and the developer has the responsibility of providing this awareness. Predictive validity requires that the test be correlated with some future observation.

It may be reported to predict success in college, for instance. If this is important to the test user, he must know how the test developer defines success in college. Success could mean first-year grade-point average or graduation within four years or any of many other possible definitions. The test developer must define carefully the terms of the variable being predicted.

When the test publisher decides to prepare two or more manuals, the first is for administrators, supervisors, and teachers and provides information in a form that has meaning for individuals who are not testing experts or statisticians. This manual should be written in such a way that measurement terminology is well defined for the reader. The second type of manual is technical and provides information, including statistical information, for individuals who are prepared to study the test in depth. This manual should contain the details of the statistical analyses that provide supporting evidence for the utility of the test. The two types of manual are prepared for different audiences, but both are necessary for standardized achievement test users.

Reliability.   The test publisher must be sure that reliability is covered in the test manuals too. The test publisher must provide evidence that the test is dependable and consistent in discriminating among the students being evaluated. Reliability estimates must be determined and reported for every score that the manual has indicated can be interpreted. Evidence that subtest scores are reliable must be provided. The total reliability of the test does not necessarily provide evidence that the subtests are reliable, but this can be determined in the same manner as the reliability of the total test.

When more than one form of a test has been published, the developer provides evidence of the equivalent forms reliability for the test and for each subtest. In almost all cases, the publishers also provide evidence concerning the internal consistency of the test and of test-retest reliability. The manuals should be accurate and precise about the time intervals employed in the test-retest study and evidence should be provided about the similarity of the scores in addition to the correlation between the scores.

Manuals that accompany the test must discuss the potential error that can be expected with one test score. The concept of standard error of measurement must be discussed and reported. The test publisher must be explicit in defining the characteristics of the population for which the standard error of measurement was calculated. This is extremely important to the potential user because of the fact that error of measurement may be greater for one group of students than for another; it might be greater for poor achieving students than for high achieving students, for example. Test users must seek tests that have as little error as possible for the particular group they wish to assess. Therefore, the groups for which the standard error of measurement was computed must be identified.

Directions for measuring and scoring. The manuals accompanying the test must contain very precise procedures for administering the test. This is crucial for standardized tests. The directions should tell the student what he is required to do and if a definite time limit is required, it should be stated. If the student is to be discouraged from guessing, he should be told the appropriateness and effect of guessing on the test. The directions for scoring should also be explicit and the scale scores available from the test must be explained carefully. If the directions for administering and scoring are not precise and are not followed, the test is not a standardized achievement test.

Information about norms. Finally, the materials accompanying a test must provide information about its norms and the score scales available for interpretive purposes. The norm groups must be precisely defined and the time of year when the norms data were collected must be reported. Most test publishers provide norms for two or three different time periods during the school year, but the students in the norm groups may have taken the test at one specific time. The norms obtained at the time of year when the user expects to administer the test are the most appropriate norms. Norms provided for time periods other than that in which the user anticipates using the test are subject to errors of interpolation and extrapolation. These are a function of the assumption that must be made about the pattern of student learning throughout the year. The assumption is usually that students gain in achievement at a uniform rate throughout the year. D. L. Beggs and A. N. Hieronymus (see the references at the end of this chapter) were unable to support empirically a uniform gain in achievement over the year. Thus the assumption that norms gathered at one time period during the year are appropriate for another time period may not be true. Therefore, the potential test user should have confidence only in norms that are reported for an actual testing date and should attempt to choose a test that has norms established for the time of year when he expects to administer the test.

Only after all these tasks have been completed is the test publisher prepared to present a test to potential users. The amount of work required in the development of a standardized achievement test is tremendous. The expertise of the item writers is only the initial factor, and the quantity and quality of material included in the manuals accompanying a test provide a sufficient indication that no teacher or group of teachers within a school district can afford the time or expertise necessary to develop a test in this manner. Standardized achievement tests are therefore desirable if they assess the traits considered important by teachers in a particular learning environment. Standardized achievement tests should not be used simply because they exist or because most schools use them. If the objectives of the school system are such that no standardized achievement test can be found that would adequately assess those objectives, then the school should not use a standardized achievement test.

Use of Achievement Test Results

Once a school system has decided that a particular achievement test is appropriate, the results of the test can be put to use in many different ways. Before the various uses for test results can be reviewed, however, it is important to understand what scores are available from standardized achievement tests.

Subtest Scores

A general standardized achievement test can be viewed as a combination of several smaller, specific achievement tests. For example, the Iowa Tests of Basic Skills has subtests for each of the following content areas:
1. Vocabulary
2. Reading comprehension
3. Language skills
    a. Spelling

    b. Capitalization

    c. Punctuation

    d. Usage

4. Work study skills

    a. Reading maps

    b. Reading graphs and tables

    c. Using reference materials

5. Arithmetic skills

    a. Concepts

    b. Problem solving

Each subtest of the Iowa Tests of Basic Skills is designed to assess a particular set of behavior. The combination of all subtests constitutes the entire general achievement test. Test scores can be obtained for each of the subtests as can a composite score for the total test. In addition, validity, reliability, and normative data are available for the subtests and for the total test.

It can be argued that the most meaningful scores from a standardized achievement test are the subtest scores because these are related directly to particular behavior from a specific content area. Composite scores from standardized achievement tests, on the other hand, generally represent some type of average of the subtest scores. As such they present information neither about a student's particular strengths and weaknesses nor about strengths and weaknesses of the curriculum. Composite scores present a description of the average performance of the students across different content areas Consider a particular school that had determined that the arithmetic skills subtests of the Iowa Tests of Basic Skills were inappropriate for its purposes. The composite scores would include scores from subtests that had already been deemed inappropriate. This school system would be better advised to look only at subtests appropriate for its purposes. The remainder of this section will emphasize uses of subtest rather than composite scores.

There are many ways in which standardized achievement test results can be used in a school system. The six general uses of subtest scores in such results to be discussed in this chapter are:

 1. Criteria that enable the teacher to check on content emphasis

2. Information for curriculum review by the staff and the individual teacher

3. Criteria for determining the academic progress of the individual student

4. Information for comparing various subject matter abilities of the student
5. Information to help diagnose the strengths and limitations of the individual student
6. Information for the selection and placement of students in academic areas

Content Emphasis Check

One major use of standardized achievement tests is the teacher's check on the emphasis placed on content. For example, a teacher might place major emphasis on vocabulary. If this teacher plans to emphasize knowledge of vocabulary words, then a review of standardized achievement tests would help determine which test would be most appropriate for the level being taught. The Comprehensive Test of Basic Skills and the Iowa Tests of Basic Skills might be appropriate for this teacher. The vocabulary lists in them are not the same, however. Discovering this, the teacher must decide which of the two subtests more appropriately fits the needs of the particular class evaluation. The results of the test can then be reviewed to determine whether the emphasis placed on vocabulary is actually evident in the performance of the students as evidenced by the test results.

Figure 5.1 presents a profile chart with which a teacher could record the average performances of a class as the percentile achieved on each of the subtests of an achievement test.

The Comprehensive Test of Basic Skills and the Iowa Tests of Basic Skills provide reading comprehension subtests as well as vocabulary subtests. A teacher who has been emphasizing vocabulary rather than reading comprehension should reasonably expect to see students do better on the vocabulary test than the reading comprehension test, regardless of which standardized test is chosen. Although all teachers would hope that students would do well on both subtests, because content is interrelated, nevertheless if the teacher finds that students perform better on reading comprehension than on vocabulary, the teacher must consider that the actual emphasis may not have been the one the teacher thought was being achieved. It may be that this teacher would be satisfied to find that the students were doing better in reading comprehension than in vocabulary, but this remains a subjective choice. The important point is that the results of the

Figure 5.1   *Class Averages Profile Chart*

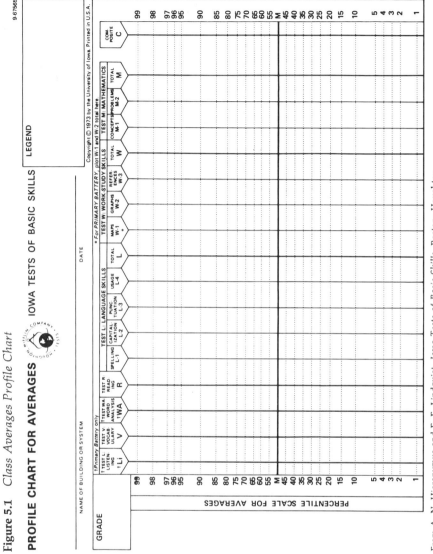

From A. N. Hieronymus and E. F. Lindquist, *Iowa Tests of Basic Skills*. Boston: Houghton Mifflin, 1973. Reprinted by permission of the publisher.

subtests can help the teacher determine what the past emphases in class have actually been and what future emphases should be.

Test results can be useful only if the teacher has had the opportunity before administering a test to review the subtests and determine that they assess areas of content appropriate for the specific class. If this decision has been made, then the teacher must examine the intended emphasis to discover why anticipated results are or are not consistent with the actual results.

The Comprehensive Test of Basic Skills provides a composite score of the reading comprehension and vocabulary subtest scores that indicates a student's total reading score. The composite reading score may be used to examine the status of a group of students in reading generally. The Iowa Tests of Basic Skills, on the other hand, recommends that the test user *not* combine the two subtest scores for a composite score for reading ability. The reasoning behind this recommendation is probably quite similar to the arguments we have already presented against the use of composite scores. Before the administration of the test, the teacher can review the Comprehensive Test of Basic Skills and the Iowa Tests of Basic Skills to determine which more closely fits the specific philosophical position of the class or curriculum with respect to reading. Once this decision has been made, the results can be applied meaningfully to determine whether intended emphasis is being achieved. The teacher may not be satisfied with the reading subtests available in generalized standardized achievement test batteries. The *Seventh Mental Measurements Yearbook* by Oscar Buros reviews over one hundred reading achievement tests. There is a wide variety of tests, from which one is almost certain to fit any given philosophical position with respect to reading.

Another area in which content and emphasis may differ is arithmetic. If we compare the Comprehensive Test of Basic Skills and the Iowa Tests of Basic Skills to decide which of the two tests might be most appropriate for a particular teacher, we shall find that the Iowa Tests of Basic Skills provides test scores for arithmetic concepts as well as for arithmetic problem solving. The results of these can be summed to get a composite score interpretable as an arithmetic skills score. The Comprehensive Test of Basic Skills, on the other hand, provides three subtests: computation, concepts, and application. As with the Iowa Tests of Basic Skills, a composite arithmetic score can be obtained. The teacher here too must review the content of both standardized achievement tests to determine which most closely approximates the emphasis on content that has been placed on arithmetic in the classroom. Once the decision has been made, the teacher can review the results of actual teaching. This check on emphasis within the content area of arithmetic requires that the teacher look at subtest scores, not at composite scores.

A teacher in the classroom of today has the opportunity to go in many different directions when covering a concept. Most teachers like to find checkpoints that help determine whether they are teaching information that is beneficial to the students and whether they are helping them toward competence in a particular content area. Standardized test results aid in the effective assessment of the teacher's achievement in particular areas. The tests should be used not to evaluate the teacher's technique but to provide information as to whether emphasis placed on specific components of a content area is being communicated to the students. Selection of tests and subtests of achievement in specific content can be an effective aid to the teacher, but the use of tests that the teacher feels are inappropriate for what is attempted in the classroom has little utility for a teacher who wishes to examine the product of classroom teaching.

Curriculum Review

To assess the effect of curriculum on students in a school system in general, educators responsible for curriculum review should determine which tests most closely approximate the behavior considered most important by that school system. Only in this way can test results be used in curriculum evaluation. Two achievement tests that might be so reviewed are the SRA Achievement Test Battery and the California Achievement Test.

With the SRA Achievement Battery, subtest scores can be obtained for social studies, science, language arts, arithmetic, and reading. With the California Achievement Test, subtest scores can be obtained for vocabulary, reading comprehension, mathematics, and language. These tests measure different aspects of the curriculum of a school system but, in the assessment of the same general content areas the emphasis of the two tests is somewhat different. Individuals responsible for curriculum review must review the two tests and decide which most closely fits the curriculum and provides subtest scores that can be used most effectively in that school. Once this has been done, the staff must establish guidelines for interpreting the results.

All too often educators establish the criterion that test results must be equal to or better than those of half the schools in the norm-reference sample. Because only 50 percent of the schools in any group can be in the top half of any score distribution, it seems much more realistic to establish, based on the particular curriculum being employed in the school system, criteria that will indicate success in the various content areas to be tested before the data are actually obtained. This will require that the school district carefully review its curriculum to determine what phases of it are emphasized at each grade level. It should then be established what is to be expected at each grade level. The advantage of this procedure is that it indicates the confidence of the school district in the curriculum that it has and that the educators are trying to assess the degree to which their curriculum is successful.

Assume, for example, that the Hawkville school system has selected the SRA Achievement Battery, that the test has been administered, and grade-level norms have been reported to the schools. For grade 5, the following comparisons were observed as a change over last year's results. Social studies increased 0.8 grade equivalents; science increased 0.7 grade equivalents; language arts increased 1.2, arithmetic 0.6, reading 1.0. Given these results, the individuals responsible for reviewing the curriculum can see very quickly that the major gains were accomplished in language arts and reading. If the curriculum review committee had earlier determined that in grade 5 the major emphasis should be on language arts and reading, then these results would indicate that the curriculum had achieved the emphases intended. On the other hand, if the intent of the curriculum had been to concentrate on arithmetic, social studies, and science, then the gains that the students achieved would appear to indicate that the desired emphases do not coincide with the actual effects.

Such test results should not be used as a basis for criticizing particular teachers. They should be used as information in the evaluation of the general curriculum of the school district. The same type of evaluation should take place at all grade levels, but the results may or may not be expected to be the same across all of them. The most important step in the process of analyzing test results for curriculum review should be to establish that a test actually covers the tasks that the educators in a school system believe are important and that the criteria for success have been established before administration of the tests.

Individual Academic Progress Criterion

A third important use for standardized achievement test results is to help determine how well particular students are progressing in academic areas covered by the test. This is the use to which standardized achievement test results are most frequently applied. Under no circumstances should a teacher interpret the progress of a student by test results alone, however. As discussed in previous chapters, there are so many variables that can affect a single test observation that a teacher can place total confidence neither in the test scores nor in the changes that occur from one score to another. Test results can be used with other observations to help compose a good picture in which the teacher, student, and parent can observe how well the student is moving through the school environment. Figure 5.2 presents a profile sheet for recording a student's test results for nine different administrations of the Iowa Tests of Basic Skills. Such cumulative information can be extremely valuable in evaluating a student's progress.

Test results might be used to evaluate a student's movement through the curriculum as follows. Suppose a school system has decided to use the Stanford Achievement Test. Part of the rationale for selecting this test might have been that it makes available ten separate subtest scores. These are: word meaning, paragraph meaning, spelling, work study skills, language, arithmetic computation, arithmetic concepts, arithmetic application, social studies, and science. The teachers and other individuals who review the curriculum may have determined that these ten subtests are most appropriate for an evaluation of the students' abilities in this particular school system. The decision to select the Stanford Achievement Test must be based on the assumption that the content that is covered by the test is relevant to the academic program of the school.

Figure 5.3 is an achievement profile for hypothetical student J.J. His scores are reported for all ten subtests, taken when he was in grades 5 and 6. J.J.'s tests were taken at the beginning of the year, and the middle or median score on the test for the fifth grade is 5.1, while the middle or median score for the sixth grade is 6.1.

Figure 5.2   *Cumulative Profile Chart*

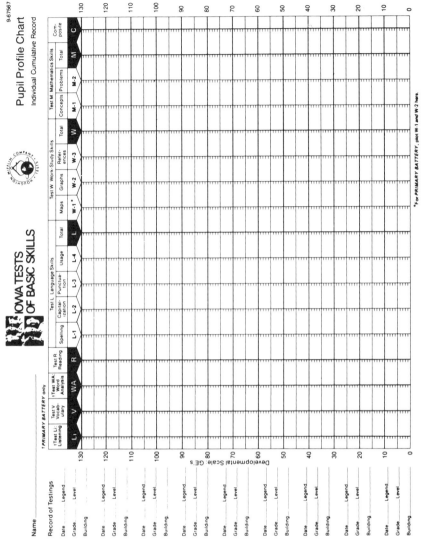

From A. N. Hieronymus and E. F. Lindquist, *Iowa Tests of Basic Skills*. Boston: Houghton Mifflin, 1973. Reprinted by permission of the publisher.

Figure 5.3 *Hypothetical Achievement Profile*

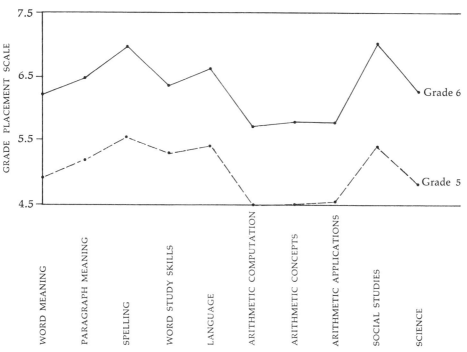

J.J.'s profile indicates the progress he made between the beginning of the fifth grade and the beginning of the sixth grade in the
ten content areas covered on the Stanford Achievement Test. J.J.
has progressed more in some areas than in others, but it is obvious
that he has made fairly consistent progress in all the areas covered
by the test. Looking at J.J.'s achievement profile, we can see that
he was above the median value in the same areas in grade 5 as he
was in grade 6. Where J.J. was below the median in grade 5, he
was also below the median in grade 6. However, he has shown
progress even in areas in which he was below the median of the
norm group to which he is being compared. J.J.'s profile should be
encouraging to a teacher concerned with J.J.'s progress with respect to content areas covered on the Stanford Achievement Test.
This profile could be interpreted by the classroom teacher to mean
that J.J. is making progress and will be able to hold his own with
respect to the norm group in all the content areas measured by the
Stanford Achievement Test.

Caution should be used in attempting to assess the academic

progress of students from an achievement profile. In general, an achievement profile with scores at the median of the score distribution indicates future growth of approximately one grade equivalent during the year. This may cause us to expect that the student who is above average will grow more than one grade equivalent and that the student who is below average will increase less than one grade equivalent. The teacher must not expect all students to grow at a uniform rate, however. It is not unusual for students who score quite high as fifth graders to show an increase of less than one grade equivalent as sixth graders. Sometimes this is attributable to error of measurement. Other factors, such as a maximum possible score (referred to as a ceiling), also limit the amount of growth that a student's score can indicate. Therefore, the teacher must always be careful to interpret a student's achievement profile with reference to the student's performance the last time the test was administered.

Measure of Comparative Ability

Another use of test results is comparison of the abilities of students in various content areas. Figure 5.4 shows a class record sheet for recording the performance of each of several students in the Iowa Tests of Basic Skills. Comparison of students' performances between subtest areas enables the teacher to determine the strengths and weaknesses of students. In J.J.'s profile, for example, such comparison reveals that he does best in social studies. His weaknesses appear to be in arithmetic and science. Given this information, the teacher might initiate some type of program that would help J.J. do better in arithmetic and science and might additionally enrich his program in social studies and other cognitive areas requiring a high degree of verbal skill. In some areas J.J. may need enrichment and in others he may need remedial programs to help him acquire some of the basics that he has missed along the way. In other words, the teacher can use J.J.'s profile to assist him to get the most out of his education. The comparison of results across the subtests must be made by the teacher who keeps in mind that an average performance on the test means only an average for a particular norm group. If the norm group is not appropriate for J.J., then the grade equivalent scale scores will have little or no meaning.

A teacher can analyze subtest scores with respect to items

Figure 5.4 *Comparative Performance Record*

CLASS RECORD SHEET

Grade _____ Teacher _____ Date Tested _____

Building _____ City, or District _____

IOWA TESTS OF BASIC SKILLS
PRIMARY BATTERY
BASIC EDITION

Form _____ Level(s) _____

9 67596

Names of Pupils	Sex (B or G)	Age Yrs./ Mos.	Level	Test V Vocabulary		Test WA Word Analysis		Test R Reading		Test L-1 Spelling		Test M-1 Math Concepts		Test M-2 Math Problems		Total M Math Total		C Composite	
				GE	PR	GE	PR	GE	PR	GE	PR	GE	PR	GE	PR	GE	PR	GE	PR

From A. N. Hieronymus and E. F. Lindquist, *Iowa Tests of Basic Skills*. Boston: Houghton Mifflin, 1972. Reprinted by permission of the publisher.

answered correctly and incorrectly. For instance, if J.J. achieved a relatively poor score in arithmetic computation, the teacher might look for the items that he missed. It might be that J.J. missed several items that were covering the same concept. For instance, J.J. may be able to multiply numbers of no higher than one digit. His multiplications of two-digit numbers indicate that he failed to realize that multiplying two-digit numbers is different from multiplying one-digit numbers. This type of analysis can occur only when the teacher has access to the items to which the individual student responded. Examination of the characteristics of the items students miss may indicate weaknesses that can be corrected through remedial work. General comparison across subject matter areas is less painstaking than is looking at particular items to see the nature of correct responses. The latter procedure, using test results for diagnostic purposes, requires of the teacher a great deal of analysis of test results. An analysis of this type has merit only when the teacher believes that the test items measure the content that it is thought should be measured.

Placement Criterion

Standardized achievement test results can be used with the selection and placement of students in academic areas related to the test results. The SRA High School Placement Test is one of the most commonly used tests for entrance into high school. It provides scores in educational ability, reading, language arts, arithmetic or modern mathematics, social studies, and science methodology, and it is designed to measure the amount of information a student has in each of these areas upon entrance to high school. Many high schools, especially some that group students by cognitive ability, use the results from this test in order to place students in appropriate groups. The test user must be cautious in using test results in this way, because any test is only as good as the content that it covers. Test users must be sure that the various subtests on the SRA High School Placement Test do in fact cover the skills required for proper placement in the high school curriculum.

Teachers and counselors must be aware too that test results are not always accurate and that they are a function not only of cognitive ability but of other extraneous variables that may cause scores to fluctuate from exam to exam. If a student's test results are inconsistent with previous achievement results, especially as rated by previous teachers, either the test should be readministered at another time or the results of that test observation should be considered lightly. Curriculum organization should be such that a student can shift from one class to another if his performance in the classroom shows that achievement test results have not provided a good indication of his abilities. The major criticism voiced against using tests for placement is that placement tends toward locking a student into that section for the rest of his academic career. Curricula must provide sufficient flexibility for movement of students to avoid this fault. If standardized achievement tests frequently misplace students, the curriculum must allow for movement of students to correct this error.

Use of standardized tests must be preceded by thorough evaluation of their content area before the test is administered. This includes determination of the test's content validity for the environment in which the test is to be administered. Once the content validity has been established, then the teacher can use the test in many different ways. It may be used as a check on classroom teaching emphasis or as a review of the curriculum to determine how well students in various classes are doing. In addition, the standardized test can facilitate individual student evaluations that will allow for more individual instruction or at least modification of the learning environment so that the students can derive more from their education. A teacher must be willing to commit a great deal of time to selection of appropriate tests and to thorough analysis of the results of tests so that the students' time and program costs are made worthwhile.

Use of Standardized Items in Criterion-Referenced Tests

Items from standardized achievement tests can be used as criterion-referenced items. The teacher determines which items evaluate a particular skill and, if the student can answer the items, the ability to perform that skill has been demonstrated. If the student cannot answer the items, the skill has not been learned. Using standardized achievement test results in this way obviates the use of norms provided by the test publisher. The teacher must establish the criteria for success. Student failure of items demonstrates clearly that the student does not know the concept and that more work must be done in that area.

Teachers should seriously consider using the items on a standardized achievement test as criterion-referenced items. Because they have been extensively reviewed before being included in the tests, there is every reason to believe that such test items are important to cognitive areas. Therefore, it may be valuable to evaluate the responses to each item on a test rather than compiling composite scores or even subtest scores. Analysis of individual items should provide the teacher with the most information that can be received from a standardized achievement test.

An example may help illustrate how standardized test results can be used in both norm-referenced and criterion-referenced systems of interpretation. Consider the report for the seventh grade of Shakerag Elementary School presented in Figure 5.5. It presents two scores that allow comparison of a student to the national group for the Iowa Tests of Basic Skills and one score that allows comparison of that student to other students in Shakerag Elementary. It can be seen in this report that Billi Klub obtained a grade equivalent of 9.3 on the vocabulary subtest, which converts to a percentile rank of 90. It can be concluded that Billi scored as well on the vocabulary subtest as the student who scored at the median of students in the national norm group who were in the third month of the ninth grade. In addition, Billi scored higher than 90 percent of students in the national norm group who took the vocabulary subtest. This list report also indicates that Billi Klub scored higher than 89 percent of students who took the vocabulary subtest in the local school. This norm-referenced information can be extremely valuable, but it does not indicate what Billi Klub knows or what skills he possesses.

Figure 5.6 presents a listing of Billi's responses to each item on the M-1 subtest of the Iowa Tests of Basic Skills. This individual student response analysis reveals the number of each item in the subtest, the difficulty level of the item, and the fact of whether the student answered the item correctly (+) or incorrectly (−) or left the item blank (0). The percentage of items answered correctly, the percentage answered incorrectly, and the percentage of items omitted are also presented for each subtest. Finally, the grade equivalent and percentile rank for each subtest are included.

Concern for Billi Klub's mathematics achievement could stimulate reference to his individual student response analysis,

Figure 5.5 *Hypothetical List Report of Seventh-Grade Students for Performance on Level 13, Form 5 of the Iowa Tests of Basic Skills.*

LIST REPORT PUPIL GRADE EQUIVALENT SCORES
WITH PERCENTILE RANKS

IOWA TESTS OF BASIC SKILLS
LEVELS EDITION

SCORES REPORTED: GRADE EQUIVALENT — NATL / LOCAL PAGE

SHAKERAG ELEMENTARY GRADE 7 FORM 5 SCHOOL CODE DATE TESTED 09/73 FALL PROCESS NO 0-0034-0

	LEVEL SEX	TEST V VOCABULARY V	TEST R READING R	TEST L: LANGUAGE SKILLS SPELLING L-1	CAPITALIZATION L-2	PUNCTUATION L-3	USAGE L-4	TOTAL L	TEST W: WORK-STUDY SKILLS MAPS W-1	GRAPHS W-2	REFERENCES W-3	TOTAL W	TEST M: MATHEMATICS SKILLS CONCEPTS M-1	PROBLEMS M-2	TOTAL M	COMPOSITE C	CODED INFORMATION 1 2 3 4 5 6 7 8 9 10 11 12 13 14
STUDENT NAME		GEPR	GEPR	GEPR	GEPR	GEPR	GEPR	GEPR	GEPR	GEPR	GEPR	GEPR	GEPR	GEPR	GEPR	GEPR	
FOSDICK, R F	13	7456	8985	8574	6338	7759	8774	7864	7965	9187	7353	8172	6127	7458	6845	7868	
11/11	B	45	84	73	38	60	73	83	61	86	50	70	23	55	40	65	
KLUB, BILLI	13	9390	7967	10495	9280	10999	9384	10094	7150	10196	9490	8986	8171	7868	8072	8886	
12/02	G	89	66	96	84	99	83	95	45	96	90	84	71	67	72	85	
TEEN, ERNEST	13	8478	8985	6337	7658	9384	7962	7864	8170	9187	8475	8580	7865	7663	7766	8378	
12/02	B	71	84	33	61	85	57	63	66	86	73	77	64	61	63	75	
MOU, JOHN	13	5825	6233	4007	6642	7150	6439	6032	6131	7865	7558	7153	4302	6129	5210	6130	
13/02	B	15	28	5	43	50	32	28	26	62	54	47	3	28	9	23	
RUCKER, TUCKER	13	8579	8477	6337	5626	7963	8267	7050	8374	8171	7864	8172	8579	9595	9090	8276	
12/11	B	75	76	33	25	64	63	47	71	68	61	70	80	96	91	73	
WALDESTA, KAZ B	13	8884	8681	8269	3403	6134	8267	6541	7456	7559	7966	7663	7559	7663	7664	7868	
12/09	B	81	80	68	3	34	63	37	51	57	65	59	56	61	60	65	
RICHTER, CHAUNCY T	13	8884	6946	8269	7658	8268	7962	8067	9692	9187	8678	9189	9290	8584	8887	8378	
12/00	B	81	43	68	61	68	57	67	92	86	76	87	91	85	88	75	
TROY, COY	13	7865	7150	7658	7962	7963	8267	7985	8374	7354	8881	8172	8986	7868	8481	7970	
12/03	B	55	46	59	65	64	63	65	71	59	79	70	87	67	81	68	
LEAVES, REAVES	13	7968	6742	5424	5422	4019	4110	4710	4710	5420	6029	4406	5314	5210	5413	6028	
12/00	B	59	38	19	21	8	7	8	8	15	27	6	12	9	11	21	
WOOH, BRENT	13	6028	6334	5018	4410	5729	6845	5523	6436	7559	5114	6336	5413	6945	6230	6130	
12/11	B	18	30	14	10	29	38	20	32	57	13	30	11	41	25	23	
WOOH, PAM R	13	7354	7661	6540	7962	7963	5527	7050	9995	9187	9490	9593	9795	8279	9090	8174	
12/08	B	42	58	38	65	64	21	47	94	86	90	93	96	77	91	72	
WHISKERS, JODY	13	6741	7661	7048	5422	6134	7962	6643	7456	6537	6742	6949	7559	7868	7664	7152	
12/00	B	29	58	46	21	34	57	38	51	34	40	43	56	67	60	46	
WHISKERS, JULIE	13	9087	7355	7252	6134	7759	7251	7050	7456	8984	7660	8071	8274	7252	7766	7868	
12/01	G	84	50	50	34	60	45	47	51	82	58	68	75	49	68	65	
O'SHEA, RICK	13	8274	7967	7862	8470	8572	6845	7966	9289	8680	7558	8478	7865	6945	7459	8072	
13/00	B	68	66	62	73	72	38	65	87	78	54	76	64	41	56	70	
SER, LANCE	13	8884	8375	9587	9483	9789	9384	9539	8374	6945	8169	7867	8069	8074	8072	8581	
12/04	G	81	73	89	87	90	83	91	71	41	68	64	68	72	72	79	
CALLEY, CALVIN	13	3403	4810	5424	5422	3304	5932	5015	5826	4915	6131	5621	5413	7252	6332	5028	
13/02	B	2	8	19	21	3	27	12	21	12	28	17	11	49	28	7	
LISTER, JOYCE	13	6334	6233	6540	5422	4919	7251	6032	6844	5522	5114	5825	5922	6129	6025	6130	
13/03	G	22	28	38	21	17	45	28	38	19	13	20	18	28	21	23	
REA, DOE A	13	9794	10599	8980	7962	8978	8774	8677	7761	7865	8271	7969	8065	8074	8072	8987	
13/00	G	94	99	81	65	79	73	77	56	62	71	68	68	72	72	87	
OLIVER, SHIRLEY	13	7354	6233	7658	7650	7963	5527	7253	6131	5522	7253	6336	6842	7458	7152	6846	
12/11	G	48	21	59	61	64	21	51	26	19	50	30	37	55	48	38	
KELLY, HOLLY	13	8477	7763	8472	6338	6541	6439	6942	6844	6537	6742	5745	5977	5722	5820	7152	
12/04	G	67	60	73	52	59	45	36	69	71	57	64	74	63	54	65	

From A. N. Hieronymus and E. F. Lindquist, *Iowa Tests of Basic Skills*. Boston: Houghton Mifflin, 1973. Reprinted by permission of the publisher.

Figure 5.6 *Hypothetical Individual Student Item Response Report for Level 13, Form 5 of the Iowa Tests of Basic Skills.*

Test M-1		% correct= 31	% incorrect= 69		% not answered=	
Mathematics Concepts	Item Number	7898009788990810798190018127908900111790071819187				
	Response	3267030848291505933244981706820167146758436 97595				
G	Difficulty Level	---+-+++-++--+--------------------+-++-++-+---++				
E 61	Skill	5445434635243532624345424325454634344753624 36364				
		DDDDDDDEEEEE FFFFFFFGGGGGGGGGGMMNNNNNNNNNNNPRRSSWWWW				
PR 27		1223456 233455223333456673555555566 1345				

From A. N. Hieronymus and E. F. Lindquist, *Iowa Tests of Basic Skills.* Boston: Houghton Mifflin, 1973. Reprinted by permission of the publisher.

Figure 5.7 *Skills Classification Table for Test M-1, Iowa Tests of Basic Skills.*

TEST M-1 MATHEMATICS CONCEPTS

Skills Classification

C—Currency
    C-1 Reading and writing amounts
    C-2 Relative values of coins

D—Decimals
    D-1 Reading and writing
    D-2 Relative values
    D-3 Rounding
    D-4 Fraction, decimal, per cent equivalents
    D-5 Fundamental operations: ways to perform
    D-6 Fundamental operations: estimating results

E—Equations, Inequalities, and Number Sentences

F—Fractions
    F-1 Part of a whole and partitioning of a set
    F-2 Relative values
    F-3 Equivalence
    F-4 Terms
    F-5 Fundamental operations: ways to perform
    F-6 Fundamental operations: estimating results

G—Geometry
    G-1 Points, lines, and planes
    G-2 Recognizing kinds and parts of geometric figures
    G-3 Angles and triangles
    G-4 Dimensions, perimeters, and areas of polygons
    G-5 Parts and areas of circles
    G-6 Surface area and volume of solids

M—Measurement
    M-1 Quantity
    M-2 Time
    M-3 Temperature
    M-4 Weight
    M-5 Length
    M-6 Area and volume
    M-7 Liquid and dry capacity
    M-8 Precision of measurement

N—Numeration and Number Systems
    N-1 Counting
    N-2 Ordinals
    N-3 Place value and expanded notation
    N-4 Numeration systems other than base ten
    N-5 Properties of numeration and number systems
    N-6 Special subsets of the real numbers

P—Per Cents: Meaning and Use

R—Ratio and Proportion

S—Sets

W—Whole Numbers
    W-1 Reading and writing
    W-2 Relative values
    W-3 Rounding
    W-4 Partition and measurement: average
    W-5 Fundamental operations: terms
    W-6 Fundamental operations: number facts
    W-7 Fundamental operations: ways to perform
    W-8 Fundamental operations: estimating results

From A. N. Hieronymus and E. F. Lindquist, *Teacher's Guide for Administration, Interpretation, and Use: Iowa Tests of Basic Skills.* Boston: Houghton Mifflin, 1971. Reprinted by permission of the publisher.

Figure 5.8   *Items 82 and 96 of Test M-1, the Iowa Tests of Basic Skills.*

---

82. Which of these numerals represents the greatest number?

    1) .307   3) **3.07**

    2) **.730**   4) **3.7**

96. Which of the following is greater in value than .761?

    1) **.8**   3) **.7603**

    2) **.699**   4) **.716**

From A. N. Hieronymus and E. F. Lindquist, *Iowa Tests of Basic Skills, Form 5, Level 13.* Boston: Houghton Mifflin, 1971. Reprinted by permission of the publisher.

and the teacher could determine that Billi achieved a grade equivalent of 8.1 on the M-1 subtest and 7.8 on the M-2 subtest. By looking at the item responses it is possible to get an idea of the skills Billi Klub actually possesses. For example, Billi missed items 82 and 96, both of which measure skill D-2. By looking at the skills classification table in Figure 5.7 (included in the administrator's manual for the Iowa Tests of Basic Skills) one can determine that the skill measured by items 82 and 96 is related to the relative values of decimals. For further information about the skill involved in these two items, reference could be made to the actual test. Figure 5.8 reproduces items 82 and 96 from Level 13, Form 5, of the Iowa Tests of Basic Skills. Following this examination procedure for each student and each subtest allows teachers to determine which skills students possess and which still need work. This is the way that standardized test results facilitate use of a criterion-referenced interpretation system.

Reflections

1. A test is standardized when the directions, time limits, test booklets, answer sheets, and other conditions relating to the test administration are identical for each administration of the test.

2. Standardized achievement tests are developed for the purpose of assessing what a student has learned. Aptitude tests assess a student's capability to achieve in the future. Attitude tests concentrate on what a student feels or thinks about specific things.
3. The procedure for developing a standardized achievement test includes the following steps:
   a. Define the content area to be assessed
   b. Establish a table of specifications
   c. Construct potential items to be included in the test
   d. Test the items in the field
   e. Analyze the field-test results
   f. Construct the test
   g. Determine its validity and reliability
   h. Establish standard procedures for administration
   i. Develop the test manuals
4. To select an appropriate standardized test, a potential test user should consult the manuals that provide information about test interpretation, validity, reliability, directions for administering and scoring, and scales and norms.
5. Standardized achievement test results can be used as
   a. Criteria that enable the teacher to check on content emphasis
   b. Information for curriculum review by the staff and the individual teacher
   c. Criteria for determining the academic progress of the individual student
   d. Information for comparing various subject matter abilities of the student
   e. Information to help diagnose the strengths annd limitations of the individual student
   f. Information for the selection and placement of students in academic areas

Exercises

1. Select any standardized test. List the elements of the test or the test environment that are to be standardized. Discuss the effects on the test results of not meeting each of the standards set forth by the test publisher.

2. Using the A.P.A. *Standards for Educational and Psychological Tests and Manuals,* assess the merits of a standardized test.
3. Review the standards set forth in *Standards for Educational and Psychological Tests and Manuals* and place each standard in one of three categories for selecting a test: (a) absolutely necessary, (b) good but not necessary, (c) not necessary.

Selected References

STANDARDIZED ACHIEVEMENT TESTS

American Psychological Association, *Standards for Educational and Psychological Tests and Manuals.* Washington, D. C.: APA, 1966. This details standards for standardized tests and their manuals.

Anastasi, A. *Psychological Testing.* New York: Macmillan, 1968. Pp. 390–412. The nature and use of achievement tests are explored and actual test items are included.

Beggs, D. L., and A. N. Hieronymus. "Uniformity of Growth in the Basic Skills Throughout the School Year and During the Summer." *Journal of Educational Measurement,* 5 (1968), 91–98. Description of a study of the achievement growth of students over the school year and during the summer using standardized achievement test scores as the measure of growth.

Bloom, B. S., et al. *Taxonomy of Educational Objectives.* Handbook I. *Cognitive Domain.* New York: McKay, 1956. Detailed discussion of the problem of identifying levels of psychological functioning and classifying educational objectives accordingly.

Buros, O. K. *The Seventh Mental Measurements Yearbook.* Highland Park, N. J.: Syphon Press, 1972. Presents information about tests such as publishers, number of forms, number of levels, and general purposes. Critiques of the tests are also presented. To find a particular test, especially older ones, it may be necessary to check previous yearbooks.

Gronlund, N. E. *Measurement and Evaluation in Teaching.* New York: Macmillan, 1971. Pp. 263–95. Chapter 12 is a thorough discussion of standardized achievement tests and their construction and use.

Lindvall, C. M. *Measuring Pupil Achievement and Aptitude.* New York: Harcourt Brace Jovanovich, 1967. Pp. 116–42. Chapter 7 describes a few tests and explains the development, selection, and use of standardized achievement tests.

Mehrens, W. A. and Lehmann, I. J. *Standardized Tests in Education.*

New York: Holt, Rinehart and Winston, 1969. Pp. 129–200. In Chapter 3 the authors discuss the purpose and classifications of standardized achievement tests in comparison with teacher made tests. Examples of available standardized achievement tests are analyzed and frequently asked questions are answered.

TYPES OF SCALED SCORES

See the references in Chapter 3.

STANDARD ERROR OF MEASUREMENT

Bartz, A. E. *Elementary Statistical Methods for Educational Measurement.* Minneapolis: Burgess, 1968. Pp. 56–58. Gives a definition of the standard error of measurement and a short example of its calculation.

6

Standardized Aptitude Tests

CONCERNS

1. What is an aptitude test?
2. How does an aptitude test differ from other tests?
3. How is a standardized aptitude test developed?
4. What materials should help the potential test user select a test?
5. In what ways can standardized aptitude tests be used in the school?

Standardized aptitude tests attempt to measure a student's potential or capability for future success in a particular area. In this chapter, we shall discuss the characteristics and possible uses of a number of different types of standardized aptitude test. The term "aptitude" does not necessarily mean that a student already has the skill being assessed. It implies either that the student has a particular skill now or has the potential for its development with the appropriate learning opportunities. In a broad definition of aptitude such as this, standardized achievement tests and standardized aptitude tests are quite similar. The achievement test measures how much has been learned at a particular time; the aptitude test determines where the student is at the time the test is taken and where he can go in the future. The use of an aptitude test as a predictor is the factor that distinguishes aptitude from achievement tests.

[Achievement tests are not designed to provide an indication of future success, but frequently they are found to be as good for predicting success as aptitude tests because of the considerable overlap in the content of the two.] A great deal of confusion arises in trying to differentiate achievement and aptitude tests. Items prepared for the one are quite similar to items prepared for the other. In theory, an aptitude test should do the better job of predicting future success. In actual practice, achievement tests may serve as well as aptitude tests because the two measure many of the same concepts.

Aptitudes are defined either as very general concepts relating to general capabilities of individuals or as an individual's capability to perform a specific task. For example, the measure of an individual's general scholastic aptitude is intended to be an indication of how successful that individual will be in school in general. A measure of musical aptitude, on the other hand, is an indication of an individual's capability to sound out rhythms, to hear tones, and so on. In this case, aptitude relates to the very specific content area of music, and it may or may not be related to other content areas. Another specific aptitude is manual dexterity, the individual's ability to manipulate material with his hands. This aptitude may be related to several content areas but it is related primarily to eye-hand coordination. There are as many aptitudes as there are skills that an individual could conceivably possess and there are tests to assess a large number of these aptitudes. Reference to the results of an aptitude test must very carefully indicate the general or specific aptitude assessed.

Development of Standardized Aptitude Measures

Our primary purpose in explaining how standardized aptitude measures are developed is to indicate the subjective decisions that are entailed. This should help the test user understand the limitations of such tests.

Initially, the test developer must determine the aptitude or aptitudes to be measured. This is made difficult in the fact that in most cases aptitudes may be assessed in more than one way, and in many cases the components of an aptitude may be as important as, if not more important than, the aptitude itself. The next responsibility for the test developer is to determine the method of assessment. He must decide whether speed, for example, is an important factor in the aptitude. In many cases, it should not be, and the developer may decide it is appropriate to develop a test in which the factor of speed is all but totally eliminated. This might be accomplished by setting time limits for the exam such that almost everyone could finish. Because from practical experience we know that some individuals will take three hours to complete an exam that most people can finish in thirty minutes, the test developer must consider carefully how to set appropriate time limits for aptitude measurement.

How the test will be administered must also be considered. Will the test be administered to a group or to individuals and will this be done by a testing specialist or by a teacher trained in the area of test administration? The developer must answer these questions. The primary difference between group tests and individual tests is that the person administering an individual test has the opportunity to incorporate in his evaluation observations of each student as he completes the individual test. In a group test it is neither practical nor appropriate to record observations of individuals.

The test developer must then decide the format in which the test will appear. It may be a multiple-choice test, a true-false test, or a test requiring something other than written responses. Some aptitudes can be measured by a paper and pencil test; others cannot. A test of a student's ability to distinguish certain sounds must provide items that determine his ability to distinguish those sounds. Records or tape recordings, rather than written items, might be used in such assessment. Items other than written ones present the additional problem for test developers of determining how to standardize the administration of tape recordings, for example, so that they can be used repeatedly in an identical manner.

   The question of the effect on the aptitude test score of individual reading ability has arisen recently because of a concern that many aptitude tests do not provide accurate indications of aptitude when students have reading difficulties. In other words, the question is whether students score low on an aptitude test because they have had little potential in the area being tested or because they cannot read the test questions. The problem is obviated when scholastic achievement is being measured, because poor reading ability is clearly a severe limitation on scholastic aptitude. In other areas of special aptitude, it may not be so important that students be able to read. It may be more important to follow verbal directions or a pictorial model in the form of a diagram. The test developer must therefore consider the reading ability of the individuals or groups responding to the test, and if it is found irrelevant to the aptitude being measured, then the developer must eliminate the factor of reading ability. Directions can be read to the students. Students taking a test can be allowed to ask any questions before the administration of the test. They can be shown where to respond on an answer sheet, and some test items can be designed in a format that requires no reading at all.

   The development of actual items for a standardized aptitude test is then quite similar to the process for standardized achievement tests. Once the items or tasks have been defined, the test instrument is administered to several different groups in order to develop norms. In the remainder of this section, we will discuss the importance of norms to three different aptitude tests.

The Scholastic Aptitude Test

The scholastic aptitude test is the most commonly used aptitude test in the public schools today. It measures the ability of students to do well in school. This scholastic aptitude test is sometimes called an intelligence test, but this term is too broad because an intelligence test tries to measure aptitude without reference to school performance.

   In the example we shall discuss, the test developer has decided to develop a group test and that speed is only a small factor in scholastic aptitude. Even though he is aware that the test must have some time limit, he has decided that time should not be a major element in the score a student receives on the test. He will, therefore, establish a time limit in which most students can reasonably be expected to attempt all the items on the test.

Our test publisher has also decided that his scholastic aptitude test will have two subtests and that scores will be provided for each. The two subtests will be described as verbal and nonverbal subtests. The verbal subtests will include items that require reading ability and a knowledge of words drawn from the student's vocabulary. The verbal subtest score will depend on the student's ability to read, because the test developer has decided that reading is a vital component of scholastic success. The nonverbal subtest will require minimal ability to read.

A formula that corrects for guessing will be applied in score determination. The exact formula is to be published in the test manual; it will be designed to reduce a student's score by subtracting from his total number of right answers the number of items he may have guessed correctly. The purpose of the application of a formula for correction of guessing is to discourage random guessing. The philosophy is that the student should respond to all items to which he thinks he knows the answer but not to those items for which he has no idea of the correct answer. The directions for a test that has such formula applied to the scoring process should make clear to the students that they are not to guess at items they do not know. Failure to inform the students completely destroys whatever value the correction for guessing procedure may have.

The test developer in our example has decided that the scholastic aptitude test should consist of verbal and nonverbal subtests, but some students will do quite well on one subtest and not on the other. Thus the developer should prepare norms for both subtests. Most testing experts would recommend that a composite score not be used when the subtest scores are available, but our test publisher will prepare norms for composite scores in order to make his test more marketable. The manual to accompany the test must emphasize the interpretation of the subtest scores and point out that the composite scores may mask meaningful differences.

The test developer then selects a norm group. For scholastic aptitude, he may search for groups of individuals of approximately the same chronological age. Since the test developer expects the test results to improve as age increases, he will administer the same test to several different age groups. He will then determine average scores for each age group. The average score is converted to a score called "mental age," defined as the average score of a particular chronological age group on a particular test. For example, if a group of eight hundred students who are ten years old took an aptitude test and averaged a raw score of 18, then the mental age for the raw score of 18 would be 10. Thus interpretation of the raw score of 18 on this test reveals that it is the average obtained by the norm group of ten-year-old students. Similarly, students ten years and six months old averaging 20 would yield the data that the mental age conversion score for 20 is 10–6. That is, the raw score of 20 is the average score obtained by the norm group of students of age ten years and six months.

The concept of mental age has been closely associated with intelligence testing for quite some time. The intelligence quotient (IQ) or intelligence score used in the schools today is defined as mental age divided by chronological age times 100. This equation should indicate that an individual with an intelligence test score of 100 is doing average work compared to other individuals of his chronological age. In other words, an intelligence quotient of 100 implies that mental age equals chronological age. An IQ score greater than 100 indicates that mental age is greater than chronological age. An individual who had obtained such a score would be chronologically the same but mentally older than students taking the exam who obtain an IQ of 100. Conversely, a score less than 100 would indicate a test score equivalent to the average score of a group mentally younger than the individual taking the score though they may be chronologically of the same age. But the concept of IQ has been expanded to mean a great deal more than this to many people. It has come to be thought of as an indication of innate ability rather than aptitude, how well a student may be expected to do in school in comparison with others who have taken the same test. This confusion in IQ interpretation has caused IQ scores to be severely criticized. Indeed criticisms of the interpretations of IQ scores are warranted and should be heeded, but nevertheless, if the IQ score is interpreted strictly as an indication of how a student performed in comparison to the norm group, at a particular point in time, on a test designed to measure concepts necessary for success in school, then the IQ score can provide valuable information.

An effort to counteract confused interpretation of scholastic aptitude scores is evidenced by a large number of educators who advocate the use of deviation scores. The deviation score is defined as the score of the individual minus the average score of the individual's chronological age group divided by the standard error of the test. It provides for the test interpreter an indication as to whether the individual is above or below the average score for his age group. A deviation score of 0 would indicate that the student is doing as well as other individuals in the norm group of his chronological age. A positive deviation score would indicate that the individual is doing better than the norm group, a negative score that he is not doing as well as the others. Even so, one must be careful in interpreting deviation scores, because the nature of the distribution demands that half the individuals will necessarily have a negative deviation score. Because our society always pushes for individuals to do better than others, the effect will be to elevate the average score of a group but 50 percent of the individuals will still do less than average work. Therefore, the test user will have to use caution when interpreting deviation scores. Nevertheless, the deviation score is less susceptible of error in interpretation, and all the information of the IQ score is included in the deviation score. The tendency to consider the deviation score as something more than what it is seems not to be as great as the same tendency with regard to IQ scores. Moreover, IQ scores have been so grossly misinterpreted for so long that it seems unlikely that we will soon be able to correct the misconception people have about them. It seems advisable to look to deviation scores for tests of scholastic aptitude, and to avoid use of the term "IQ." The only other alternative seems to be to eliminate scholastic aptitude tests completely.

It is the responsibility of the test developer to provide norms both for IQ scores and deviation scores. Norms must be provided, and the test publisher must be specific in defining norm groups. The process of collecting this information requires item analysis, and this in turn may cause revisions in the test or elimination of some of the test items. During this stage of test development, too, the test developer will have the opportunity to determine whether the time limits that he has imposed on the test are realistic.

Once the aptitude test has been developed, evidence of the predictive validity of the aptitude measure must be given. Predictive validity of the test is of utmost concern with aptitude tests because the test is designed to determine future capability. The test developer must describe to what degree he believes his test predicts future accomplishment in the area that the test is designed to measure. If predictive validity coefficients are not provided by the test developer, then one must question whether the test can measure capability.

A major criticism of scholastic aptitude tests is that they are culturally biased—that is, not fair to individuals from a particular culture or subculture—and, as a result, the test does not adequately predict how well they will do in a school composed of members culturally different from them. Some test publishers show that characteristics of culture or subculture do not interfere with the predictability of their aptitude tests and that cultural bias is not a function of their tests. Cultural bias may be a function of the school system. If a scholastic aptitude test predicts with great accuracy that students will or will not be successful in school, then the test is doing what it is designed to do. Individuals who wish to be critical of the cultural bias of a particular test should turn their attention not only to the test but also to that which they are trying to predict.

The Manual Dexterity Test

The purpose of a manual dexterity test is to determine ability to manipulate objects by hand. For example, a student might be required to move a peg from one place on a pegboard to another or he might be required to place the pegs in a particular color arrangement. The test developer must define the task that is appropriate to some known criterion—that is, the task to be performed must be related to future activity that the test developer hopes to predict. A test of manual dexterity to be used to select individuals with an aptitude for dental hygiene must test skills that are required of a dental technician. A test for selecting assembly-line workers must test manual dexterity on an assembly line.

The test developer has the responsibility of providing instructions for individual testing sessions and guidelines for observation during administration. The test manual should provide specific details of what the test administrator should observe and how to report on his observations. Scoring procedures for the test must also be described.

In a test of manual dexterity, the test developer must decide what roles speed and reading performance should play. It is probably important for the test developer to place major emphasis on speed in a manual dexterity task. The effect of speed should be to require individuals to show better eye-hand coordination. Therefore, time limits on the test tasks should allow the evaluators to differentiate among individuals who can and cannot perform particular tasks with reasonable speed. In most cases, the aptitude of manual dexterity should not be affected by an individual's ability to read, however. Test directions should therefore be given orally, and pictures of the required manipulations should be presented to reduce the requisite reading element.

Once these decisions have been made, then the test is administered to norm groups that have shown varying degrees of ability with respect to manual dexterity. The scores of a norm group of dental technicians could be evaluated as percentile rank. The test developer must then publish the norm groups for the test so that potential users will be able to determine which are comparable to the individuals they hope to test. Definition of norm groups by skill groups for a manual dexterity test is of course, different from the establishment of age norms for scholastic aptitude tests.

It is also important for the developer of a manual dexterity test to determine the effect of repeated testing on the defined tasks. It could be that an individual with sufficient practice with the pegboard would eventually develop skill with the pegboard but not do well on some other task. The effect of practice should be described and explained in detail in the test manual. The test user can then determine whether an individual with previous experience of a particular task should be administered that task or, at least, test results of such a person can be compared to a norm group with similar previous experience. The most important aspect of the manual dexterity aptitude test is its predictive validity. It is the responsibility of the test publisher to state to the test user what norm groups are relevant for particular settings and what the level of predictive validity is for them.

The Musical Aptitude Test

The format of a musical aptitude test is important to the manner of its administration. For instance, aptitude with rhythm and tone must be tested by the production of some musical sounds within the test administration. Consistency of sound presentation, with either a tape recording or a carefully designed record, should allow the individual being tested to hear a sound and respond to it in a controlled time sequence. As with the manual dexterity test, reading ability is probably not important when measuring musical aptitude, and therefore the requirement of reading should be placed at a minimum.

The number of times an individual may hear a sound must be standardized in a musical aptitude test. The test developer must inform the potential test user about what to do if extraneous sounds, such as a bell ringing should interrupt the testing session. The test administrator must have an established standardized format to indicate how he should deal with such interruption. If this information is not available, then the test cannot be considered a standardized test.

Norms for the musical aptitude test should be gathered from various age groups and, as with the scholastic aptitude test, an average score should be determined for them. The musical aptitude score should indicate the individual's amount of musical aptitude as measured by a particular age group and should not be restricted to specifically defined groups such as musicians and nonmusicians, as would be the case if norm groups were defined by skills. The norm group established for a musical aptitude profile should be similar to norms for a scholastic aptitude test rather than similar to norms for dexterity tests.

Reporting Information About Standardized Aptitude Tests

A test developer has the same responsibilities for reporting information about standardized aptitude tests as he does for reporting on standardized achievement tests. Therefore, we shall only briefly review the six basic things that the test developer must provide with standardized tests. They are: (1) the test manual, (2) information to assist in the interpretation of the test results, (3) information about the validity of the test and, for an aptitude test, its predictive validity, (4) statements as to the reliability of the test, (5) specific directions for the administration of the test, and (6) the norms with very precise descriptions of the various norm groups. It seems to the authors that if any of the six pieces of this minimal list of information were not available, the test user should not try to reach the decision to use that test. If a test publisher does not provide all the above information about his test, the test user should not use that test.

The potential test user should now realize the amount of work required in the development of a standardized test. It seems impossible that any particular school district could devote so much time to the development of testing instruments. Therefore, school districts should carefully consider the use of standardized aptitude tests and their appropriateness for the tasks they wish to measure.

Aptitude Tests in the School

The reading readiness test is one of the most common uses of an aptitude test to determine when a student is ready to move on to new activities. It is important for the potential test user to determine whether students have reached the point in their educational development when they can successfully begin to read. Reading readiness scores provide information primarily about knowledge of words and the students' ability to put words together. There are many reading readiness tests on the market, and educators should select the test that most closely approximates the manner in which reading will be taught in their school.

The scholastic aptitude test is also often used for grouping individuals. David A. Goslin, in *Teacher and Testing*, reviewed 714 elementary schools; of these 40 percent used scholastic aptitude tests for grouping children and about 30 percent used individual tests. Schools that place children in special classrooms may choose individual tests to get more precise measures of behavior. Grouping does occur with respect to scholastic aptitude tests, and their use along with other indicators such as achievement, interest, motivation, personality, and teacher assessment seems appropriate.

Children should not be grouped solely on the basis of scholastic aptitude scores, however, because they are subject to as much error and perhaps more error than any other test.

The most widely accepted use of aptitude tests is by vocational and educational counselors. When aptitude tests are administered by a counselor for purposes of advising a student about his career, then it is the responsibility of the counselor to be sure that the student interprets the results properly. The student must be made aware of norm groups and what the aptitude measures mean. Final decisions about vocational and educational aspirations should not be based totally on the aptitude measures, however. For a student in a state of confusion about his future, it is appropriate to use aptitude tests to help the student in his attempt to assess his own aptitudes and abilities. The aptitude test can give a student confirmation as to his ability or lack of ability in particular areas that may seem important to him.

Limitations of Aptitude Measures

In our discussion of the development of the aptitude tests, there were several indications of definite limitations to standardized aptitude measures. Such limitations from the standpoint of the potential test user pertain when he attempts to prepare, select, administer, and interpret aptitude tests. The first question that the user of an aptitude test should ask is: "What do I have when I get the results from an aptitude test?" Because the aptitude test is an attempt to assess the capability of individuals to perform prescribed tasks, these tasks must be very firmly established in the mind of the user before tests of that capability are used or interpreted. Scholastic aptitude tests provide no information of use outside the school setting. Scholastic aptitude is related only to school success and should not be interpreted as a measure of general innate ability.

A second question should be "To what are the scores related in the real world?" If one is concerned to predict success on an assembly line, the manual dexterity test must differentiate the ability of the people to perform on an assembly line. A test that does not do this should not be used. It is the responsibility of the test user to make sure that the task to be measured does relate to the intended criteria of the test.

The test user should also be concerned with the effect of reading ability on the aptitude measure. If the aptitude measure eliminates the general factor of reading, then the task being predicted must also eliminate the factor of reading. For example, if a manual dexterity test requires the ability to read directions, then the test user should have some notion of the student's ability to read. The same is true for speed; if speed is not a factor in the job or the criterion that the test is designed to predict, then the test should not be affected by speed.

It is almost a constant criticism that scholastic aptitude tests (or intelligence tests) are culturally biased toward individuals with certain cultural characteristics. This criticism has been directed at the tests themselves and it is our opinion that the test user should be quite cautious with this criticism. If the test has been shown to have predictive validity for the classroom setting for groups from all cultures, then it is not the test that has cultural bias. One should be cautious in criticizing a test for cultural bias if it has predictive validity. If it does not have predictive validity, one of the reasons it may not is that it is biased culturally. It is the responsibility of the test developer to try to determine what cultural bias may exist within his instrument, but if the test user has been informed that the test possesses predictive validity, then the test user must assume that it is not the test but the criteria that has the cultural bias.

Repeated research with scholastic aptitude tests indicates that there is a considerable increase in test scores from a first testing period to a second testing period, although the phenomenon has not been found to persist over relatively long intervals between testing sessions. This increase in scores from a first to a second administration can also be seen in other types of aptitude tests. The unique format of a test—for instance, the requirement of listening to a tape recording or a record—may enhance a student's ability to do better on it a second time. In other words, previous experience with tests could cause scores to be higher if the students have had previous experience with them. Most test publishers attempt to compensate for this effect by providing more than one form of a test. It would seem appropriate that the students be given an opportunity to respond to sample questions before the actual administration of the test to help compensate for the effect of practice. Since the practice effect has been found to prevail in aptitude measures, it should be described in the test manual so that the interpreters will realize the magnitude of the effect and, as a result, more appropriately interpret the results.

Reflections

1. An aptitude test is an attempt to measure a student's potential or capability for future success in a particular area.
2. Aptitude tests are developed to assess a student's capability to achieve in the future in a particular area, while other tests are developed primarily to assess the current status of a student with respect to cognitive or affective abilities.
3. The procedure for developing a standardized aptitude test includes the following steps:
   a. Determine the aptitude to be measured
   b. Determine the way in which the aptitude measure is to be administered to the student
   c. Develop the items or tasks
   d. Test the aptitude measure in the field
   e. Determine validity and reliability
   f. Establish standard procedures for administration
   g. Develop the aptitude measure manual
4. A potential test user should have a manual that provides information about the potential use of the test results, validity, and reliability of the aptitude measure, directions for administering and scoring the measure, and norms that are appropriate for the user.
5. Standardized aptitude measures may be used to do the following things in a school setting:
   a. Determine when a student is ready to move on to new activities
   b. Group students within the classroom
   c. Counsel educationally and vocationally career-minded students.

Exercises

1. Define a specific aptitude that you wish to assess.
2. Develop an assessment of the aptitude you have defined. Limit the time for assessment to ten minutes.
3. Determine what procedures and environments are to be standard for the assessment.

4. Administer the aptitude measure that you have developed to at least ten individuals.
5. Assess the results of your measurement effort. Do you believe you are measuring what you intended to measure? Do you need to modify some of your testing procedures?
6. Prepare a position paper on the topic, "Intelligence Tests: What Do They Measure"?

Selected References

STANDARDIZED APTITUDE TESTS

Goslin, D. A. *Teacher and Testing.* New York: Russell Sage Foundation, 1967. The author discusses uses of standardized test results in the schools.

Gronlund, N. E. *Measurement and Evaluation in Teaching.* New York: Macmillan, 1971. Pp. 296–338. In Chapter 13 the author uses real test items to illustrate the different types of standardized aptitude tests.

Mehrens, W. A., and I. J. Lehmann. *Standardized Tests in Education.* New York: Holt, Rinehart and Winston, 1969. Pp. 65–126. The authors discuss aptitude tests and evaluate various tests that are presently available.

Nunnally, J. C. *Educational Measurement and Evaluation.* New York: McGraw-Hill, 1972. Pp. 392–416. Gives examples of aptitude tests that measure special abilities.

SCHOLASTIC APTITUDE TESTS

Brim, O. G., Jr., et al. *American Beliefs and Attitudes About Intelligence.* New York: Russell Sage Foundation, 1969. This volume covers some of the results of a series of studies on the perceived social consequences of standardized testing in the United States.

McClelland, D. C. "Testing for Competence Rather than Intelligence." *American Psychologist,* 28 (1973) 1–14. The author criticizes the traditional intelligence testing movement and offers an alternative, based on criterion sampling.

Noll, V. H. and D. P. Scannell. *Introduction to Educational Measurement.* Boston: Houghton Mifflin, 1972. Pp. 362–67. The topics discussed are the influences of heredity and environment on IQ and testing the culturally disadvantaged.

McNemar, Q. "Lost: Our Intelligence? Why?" *American Psychologist,* (1964), 871–82. The author believes that the concept of general intelligence still has a rightful place in the study of psychology. In the development of his paper, he includes brief discussions of many psychological studies.

Remmers, H. H., N. L. Gage, and J. F. Rummel. *A Practical Introduction to Measurement and Evaluation.* New York: Harper & Row, 1965. Pp. 123–24. Gives some examples of cultural influences on IQ scores.

STABILITY DEFINED

Gerberich, J. R., H. A. Greene, and A. N. Jorgensen. *Measurement and Evaluation in the Modern School.* New York: McKay, 1962. P. 61. Gives a short explanation of the concept of stability.

Mehrens, W. A., and I. J. Lehmann. *Standardized Tests in Education.* New York: Holt, Rinehart and Winston, 1969. P. 36. Gives a short discussion of the measure of stability used to estimate reliability.

Part Three

Internal
Measuring
Devices

7

Types
of Internal
Measures

CONCERNS

1. What is the purpose of developing internal measuring devices?
2. How is criterion-referenced testing employed in an internal testing program?
3. How is norm-referenced testing employed in an internal testing program?
4. What are the limitations of internal measuring devices?
5. How are local norms established for any test, external or internal?
6. What are the major problems in developing an internal measuring device to evaluate attitudes related to the schools?
7. What roles do classroom observations play in an educational evaluation?
8. How can observation data be collected in the schools?
9. What are the different types of test developed for internal testing programs?
10. What are the advantages and limitations of the various types of test developed for internal testing programs?

Although standardized tests are used widely throughout the United States and the world, they are not the tests most commonly used in the schools. The majority of tests used in schools are developed by the classroom teacher. We have defined such tests as internal measuring devices because they are tests that are developed by individuals within the environment in which the test is going to be administered. Standardized tests, on the other hand, are developed to be used across a wide variety of curricula and school systems. A standardized test assesses generally accepted concepts and skills rather than the specific cognitive concepts dealt with in daily instruction.

The classroom teacher must develop measuring instruments relevant to particular environments. For example, a teacher might wish to determine whether the students in a classroom can spell a specific set of twenty-five words. Because there is probably no standardized test available that includes the specific twenty-five words the teacher wants to assess, the teacher must develop a test specifically for those words. Such teacher-made tests are not standardized and probably will not be normed over a large number of students.

When a teacher or a group of teachers within a school system decide that an internal measuring device must be developed to assess a specific set of skills, they must make a number of decisions about the characteristics of the test to be developed. The purpose of this chapter is to discuss such decisions.

Reference Systems with Internally Developed Tests

Criterion-Referenced System

One of the first decisions in writing a test for a specific purpose relates to the reference system to be used for interpretation of the results. If the test is to assess whether individual students possess required skills at a particular point in time and whether those skills can be identified, then a criterion-referenced test should be developed. If, on the other hand, the test is primarily to assess the status of students relative to some identified group, then a norm-referenced test should be developed.

The criterion-reference system is commonly used with internally developed tests. For example, a spelling exam such as discussed above would usually require each student to spell the twenty-five words. The teacher's interpretation of the results is based on whether each student correctly spells each of the twenty-five words. In this example each individual word represents a criterion. The student who spells a word correctly has met a criterion successfully. The student who misspells a word has not yet achieved the criterion. In many cases like this, the teacher can describe specifically what is expected of each student. After this a test can be developed that allows determination of the students' ability to perform particular tasks. In tests of this type, the items themselves are the criteria and the student is assessed according to whether he responds correctly to each item.

Consider also the example of a teacher who is just completing a unit on multiplication by single-digit numbers. Students must know how to multiply single-digit numbers before they can learn to divide them. If the teacher has determined that this ability to multiply is important before beginning the study of division, a criterion-referenced test may be chosen to examine students on the skills necessary to move to that unit of instruction. A test consisting of several items would be designed so that each assesses whether a student possesses the ability to multiply by a given single-digit number. For example the test may include:

$$
\begin{array}{cccccc}
3 & 4 & 5 & 6 & 7 & 6 \\
\times 2 & \times 4 & \times 5 & \times 3 & \times 8 & \times 9 \\
\hline
\end{array}
$$

in addition to other items. If a student gets all the items correct, he is ready to move into division. If a student were to miss

$$
\begin{array}{c}
6 \\
\times 9 \\
\hline
\end{array}
$$

then the teacher would conclude that that particular student needs more practice with multiplication by 9. In other words, the teacher can determine whether a student is ready to move into division, needs more work with multiplication of particular numbers, or needs more work with multiplication by all single-digit numbers.

While this type of criterion-referenced testing is commonly employed in classrooms, it is not so frequently employed across departments or schools. Considerable interest today in the nongraded school, for example, calls for instruction on the basis of abilities or capabilities rather than age, as in traditionally graded schools. In a nongraded school, criterion-referenced tests are essential for assignment of students to groups for instruction. That is, a student who answers certain items on a test correctly is judged to possess certain skills and thus ready for a particular unit of instruction, whereas another student may be assigned to a different unit of instruction because he has demonstrated different skills on the test. Certainly teachers' judgments and other assessments would also enter into the final assignment of a student to a group for instruction, but the criterion-referenced test has an important role in individualizing instruction.

A number of programs use cut-off scores for predetermining the level of activities a student will pursue. For example, the Individually Prescribed Instruction (IPI) program of the Research and Development Center of the University of Pittsburgh has employed cut-off scores on a test for assigning a student his next unit of instruction. If in this program a student is studying a unit in mathematics, he takes a test upon completion of a unit. If he responds successfully, he is assigned to the next unit of instruction. If he does not get the required percentage of items correct, he is assigned activities designed to further his understanding of the concepts in the original unit of instruction.

The validity of tests used for placement is of utmost concern. Criterion-referenced tests require only content validity, a criterion of whether the items on a test actually assess the skills or concepts intended for assessment. As we discussed in Chapter 4, the content validity of any measuring device must be determined by the individual who plans to use the test. Therefore, the teacher who plans to use the test he develops must decide whether the test items are successful as assessors. The teacher can, and probably should, seek the opinion of colleagues, but in the final analysis the decision about content validity is personal.

Reliability is of little concern in relation to criterion-referenced tests for use in the individual classroom. One type of reliability is called test-retest reliability, and it indicates the degree to which students tend to score the same on two separate administrations of the same test. When a teacher develops a criterion-referenced test for a classroom, the purpose is for making decisions as to what instructional activities should be pursued with individual students. If a student misses certain items on an administration of the test, the teacher will concentrate on the concepts measured by those items. A teacher would neither expect nor want a student to score the same on the test if he were to take it a second time. We do not judge test-retest reliability to be appropriate for criterion-referenced tests used in the classroom.

Internal consistency reliability implies that students should demonstrate consistent responses throughout the test. Because in a criterion-referenced test each item is defined as the criterion for a particular skill or concept being assessed, a student may respond to items in what would appear to be an inconsistent way because the items assess different concepts rather than because the test is not good. We judge internal-consistency reliability as inappropriate for criterion-referenced tests.

Equivalent forms reliability seems to be of little value with respect to classroom tests because it is concerned with two different forms of a test giving consistent results. Most classroom teachers are lucky to find enough time to develop one good test to assess a particular set of skills, let alone time to develop two tests to measure the same set of skills. Consequently, few develop parallel forms of the same test and, as a result, equivalent forms reliability has no meaning for them.

A further reason for our statement that reliability has little meaning with respect to criterion-referenced tests rests with the purpose for which the items on a test are developed. Criterion-referenced tests include items developed to determine whether an individual possesses certain skills or concepts. If an item possesses content validity (assesses what it is designed to assess) and all students get the item correct, the test item is still a good item for a criterion-referenced test. But measures of reliability are based on a philosophy of testing that considers an item poor to which all students respond correctly. In this more traditional testing approach, a test is designed to separate people who know more from people who know less about a subject. As a result, some test items are judged to be good only if some students in the group being tested answer them incorrectly. We feel that measures of reliability developed for tests that require that there be a certain proportion of wrong responses to each test item cannot be applied to tests in which an item can be included even if all students answer it correctly or all students answer it incorrectly. Consequently, we recommend that the teacher be concerned only with being certain that each item on a criterion-referenced test possesses content validity. If the test has appropriate content validity, reliability will take care of itself.

A major problem with criterion-referenced tests is that there is a tendency to oversimplify; the item may be so specific as to be unrealistic or unrelated to what the teacher actually hopes to assess. This may be a function of oversimplification of objectives in an effort to make them specific, or it may be a reflection of specific instructional objectives in oversimplified items. At any rate, the teacher who is developing a criterion-referenced test must guard against writing items that do not assess real objectives because they are too narrowly defined.

Norm-Referenced System

A teacher or school system may wish to use norm-referenced in addition to using criterion-referenced tests. Norm-referenced tests may be particularly useful in assessing affective characteristics. For example, to determine attitudes toward required physical education teachers may develop a questionnaire to be administered to all children in a school district. In addition to this overall assessment, the school district might be interested in how attitudes toward required physical education vary from school to school within the district. The results from the entire school system might be considered norms against which the results of individual schools could be compared. It might be, for instance, that 75 percent of the children in the entire school system favor required physical education whereas 95 percent of the students in Logan School favor it. The conclusion can be reached that a greater proportion of students in Logan School favor required physical education than in the remainder of the school system.

In the Logan School example, local norms were established. In establishing local norms, it is important that the characteristics of the norm group be described. In most cases, this is quite easy to do since most individuals within a district are familiar with it. The most common definition of norm groups for local norms is by grade level. For instance, in the physical education example, it might have been appropriate to provide norms for each grade level, since it could be that the response pattern to the questionnaire would differ for children in the lower and upper grades.

The procedure for developing local norms is time consuming

and requires that internally developed tests be administered to appropriate groups of students across the entire school system. The results of the testing must then be gathered and analyzed, and the norms must be established and distributed to all the schools or classroom teachers that might be interested in them. In addition, each school or classroom must have its data analyzed so that the activity of each classroom can be described. A school district will probably not want often to develop local norms on internally developed tests, but when it is necessary the same rigor must be maintained as is expected from external test developers.

Criterion-referenced and norm-referenced systems have a place in the internally developed testing program of schools. The criterion-referenced system is probably the most widely used, but the norm-referenced system, especially when an instrument has been developed for district-wide use, has its place in the internal program. Each system has peculiar advantages and limitations. It is the responsibility of the individuals who will be using the test results to determine which reference system will be most helpful in improving the learning opportunities of the child.

Attitude Measures

The current emphasis on affective attitudes in the schools has made teachers aware of the need to assess attitudes in the classroom. Unfortunately classroom teachers find that most standardized instruments measure attitudes toward fairly general topics and in many cases this type of attitude measurement is not appropriate for particular classrooms. For instance, most tests that attempt to assess particular attitudes toward a school were not developed for any particular school. Instruments standardized on a national level are intended to be used in any school setting, but there are characteristics that set each school apart from every other school. A student's attitude toward a particular school may be considerably different from his attitude toward school in general. In other words, teachers who wish to know how children feel about specific things within a particular school setting frequently find either a standardized instrument that assesses very general attitudes or no standardized instrument at all. When a teacher is unable to find an appropriate standardized attitude measure, one must be developed. The first and most important thing to define is the specific attitude to be assessed. This definition must be precise and communicate to others the specific nature of the attitude being measured.

*A major limitation in the development of attitude measures is that students in particular and people in general tend to respond to paper and pencil attitude measures as though they were tests. Because one's response to a test is generally a response in the way one thinks he is expected to respond, an attitude measure may not reflect actual attitudes toward the topic in question. As a result, we never really know whether the results of a paper and pencil attitude measure reflect the actual attitudes of the individuals responding. This has caused many educators to conclude that the paper and pencil format is inappropriate for assessing attitudes. One alternative may be for the teacher to develop observational techniques that could be used in the classroom, on the playground, or in group or individual activities. Observational techniques are time consuming, both in the planning and in the interpreting. The time must be considered well spent, however, if the observation leads to identification of attitudes or other conditions that cause students to act in a particular way.

The first step in developing observational techniques is to identify the specific attitudes of concern and the behavior believed to be related to those attitudes. For example, in defining specific attitudes toward a particular school, one might say that fighting in the classroom indicates a poor attitude toward school. But most teachers have control over their classrooms, so that fighting is not likely to be observed. Moreover, fighting is such gross behavior that measures of it are not really appropriate. More subtle things such as not listening to other students recite and not paying attention to assigned tasks are the types of behavior more likely to be observed in the classroom as indicators of poor attitudes toward school.

Once the behavior to be observed has been defined, it is the responsibility of the teacher to determine how observations are to be made. The teacher must be able to continue in the role of teacher while observation is in progress. Therefore the method of researchers who come into the classroom, observe and record data and then afterwards check the reliability and validity of their assessments is not an appropriate procedure for a classroom teacher who has simultaneously the responsibility of guiding the learning experiences of the students in the classroom.

One possible observation schedule for a teacher concerned about a student who seems not to be responding to activity in the class is to look for behavior that distracts the student or for the types of behavior that the student does express in response to particular stimuli. A systematic procedure for collecting such information would be to spend five minutes each hour observing without obviously isolating the student. By doing this, the teacher is not keeping the student under direct observation all the time and so still has the opportunity to remain the leader in the classroom. During the five minute segment in which the student is observed, the teacher should have available a tally sheet on which to indicate types of response and stimuli that seem to cause them. If the child does nothing in the face of various stimuli, this too should be recorded by the teacher. A week of such observation should result in a fairly significant amount of information about what does and does not seem to stimulate the student. This data may enable the teacher to identify actions that will make the student more involved in the classroom. This observation technique should also provide the teacher with concrete information to which to refer when trying to determine how to help the student relate better with the environment.

A classroom teacher could follow this observational procedure when no assistance is available. In more affluent school districts, where aides are available, the teacher could define terms and procedures and ask an aide to observe a student according to them. The teacher would then be wholly free to attend to classroom responsibilities. In any case, the observation technique must be planned ahead of time, material must be made available for the teacher's response, and the results of observation must be summarized at the end of each time segment.

It is not uncommon for students, or anyone else for that matter, to perform differently when they know they are functioning under close scrutiny. Therefore, the student should be unaware that he is being observed. The observation procedure is an attempt to get a better assessment of how a child feels or reacts in a particular setting and to describe reactions to various stimuli in various environments. The assessment will be much more precise if the procedure for observation allows the student to be observed in situations as similar to the actual environment as possible.

Advantages and Limitations of Test-Item Types

There are several different test-item formats with which to compose tests. In this section we shall discuss six types of test question. Any test may include one or more item types, depending on the purpose of the test. In Chapter 8 we shall provide several examples of each type of item along with more detailed guidelines for distinguishing good items from bad ones.

Multiple Choice

One commonly used form of test item is the multiple-choice question. This is written as a stem to which the student is to respond by completing a sentence, answering a question, or solving a problem. The distinguishing attribute of a multiple-choice question is that the stem is followed by a number of alternatives from which the student must choose the most appropriate response. An example of a multiple-choice test item is:

The type of validity of major concern to the developer of criterion-referenced internal measuring instruments is:
1. predictive
2. content
3. construct
4. concurrent

The individual responding to this item would be expected to select alternative 2 as the most appropriate completion of the sentence begun in the stem.

In multiple-choice items, the stem must be explicit and provide sufficient information to allow the individual who is responding to understand what is expected. The correct response must be presented as one of the possible choices. There can be as few as two alternatives or as many as a teacher can invent. Usually multiple-choice items present four or five alternatives. This type of item is found in the majority of externally developed tests.

It is usually extremely difficult to develop a good multiple-choice question. The three, four or more incorrect alternatives (called foils) that must be provided must definitely look like possible alternatives to the correct response. Multiple-choice items often have alternatives that anyone would recognize to be incorrect even if he knew little about the content being tested. Such alternatives are worthless because they do not require the respondent to think. In developing the multiple-choice item, the teacher must decide on the question and not only the correct response but also meaningful alternatives to the correct response.

The multiple-choice test item is extremely easy to score because the correct response has already been designated. All the teacher must do is look to see whether the correct response has been chosen. Another advantage to the multiple-choice format is that with it content sampling is usually not limited by time. Items can be developed to sample several different aspects of content at once, and a large number of items can be administered in a relatively short time period.

In preparing for a multiple-choice exam, a student can be expected to concentrate on specifics. This is a real limitation on the value of multiple-choice tests if one is concerned that the students demonstrate ability to analyze or synthesize. Multiple-choice tests that require students to analyze and synthesize can be developed, but the amount of time required to do this is extremely lengthy. All cognitive levels can be assessed with multiple-choice items but, in general, they lend themselves most readily to recall of factual information. Another important limitation of the multiple-choice item is that the student's response gives no evidence of his originality or ability to respond without being given a choice of responses. This format is also subject to student guessing, which means that a scoring system that corrects guessing may have to be applied. If such a system is not employed, the score that is obtained is quite likely to be subject to error.

Completion

The completion item is sometimes called a fill-in-the-blank item. This provides the individual with a sentence or a statement from which a word or phrase is missing that he must supply. For example, a student might be asked to supply the missing term in the following completion item:

A test developed by a teacher for use within the classroom is called a(n) _____ measuring device.

In this item, the student would be expected to fill in the word "internal."

Completion items differ from multiple-choice items in that the individual does not have a number of stated responses from which to choose. Extreme care must be taken to indicate clearly what is expected; completion items often elicit incorrect responses not because students do not know the material but because the statement is so vague that they have to infer too much of the teacher's expectation.

The completion item is usually easy to develop because the test writer has only to compose a sentence from which some term can be omitted. It is important that the item be written sufficiently clearly that the student can determine what question is being asked and what term is to be supplied. A serious shortcoming of this type of item is that it encourages the item writer to take sentences out of context from textbooks, and most sentences in textbooks depend on contextual information. The completion item, however, must be based on a sentence that is complete in and of itself.

Completion items are relatively easy to score because there is only one correct response. If it is possible for the student to use more than one of several synonymous terms, the scorer must then decide which terms best match the keyed response. Another problem is the legibility of the student's handwriting.

The content area that can be covered by completion items is extremely large. In fact, there seems to be very little if any restriction on the area that can be covered by this type of test. In general, the student prepares to answer very specific responses because completion items require recall of factual information. Completion items are not conducive to determining an individual's ability to synthesize and analyze information. An advantage of this type of item is that it limits guessing in that the student must supply the correct response. However, since completion items require single-word or short-phrase responses, there is little opportunity to assess originality.

Short Answer

A short-answer question is one in which the individual is asked to provide a relatively short response to a particular question, summarize a particular set of material that has been discussed, or indicate similarity between two or more things. The short-answer item itself is very precise. The individual responding to the item must originate the response, but to be correct the response must be related directly to the question. The short-answer question usually requires a response of two or three sentences or at most a short paragraph or it may ask the student to list a number of factors, as, for example,

List five (5) ways in which the results of a standardized achievement test may appropriately be used by a school system.

The student would, of course, be expected to provide five of the six uses discussed in Chapter 6 of this text.

Short-answer items are usually quite easy to prepare. Each item requires a specific response, of course, but the test writer has only to provide the question, not alternatives for the answer. A real difficulty with short-answer questions is that in many cases they are difficult to score, because there may be more than one way to indicate a correct response, and the individual grading the test must be aware of the various ways in which the correct response can be communicated and also be willing to give credit where credit is due.

Short-answer questions usually allow ample sampling of content area. Severe time limits may decrease the breadth of sampling, but this would be likely to occur only in unique circumstances. An important attribute of the short-answer format is that it can be used either to ask for specifics or to encourage individuals to put several ideas together, and to synthesize, to formulate generalities. In preparing for a short-answer exam, the student must study specific factual matter and general concepts. Short-answer questions generate original responses and eliminate almost totally the problem of student guessing. Scoring original responses allows the teacher to gain a great deal of information other than just quantitative information. This can be extremely helpful in determining areas of concentration in subsequent instruction.

True-False

A test item commonly used is one in which the individual is asked to determine whether a particular statement is true or false. For example:

Criterion-referenced interpretations may be made of items included in a norm-referenced test.

The obvious response is that this is a true statement. The true-false and short-answer formats are frequently combined. If the student first decides that a statement is false, he must then provide the reason in a short answer that states why he thinks it is false. Such combination permits the evaluator to determine why a student believes a statement to be true or false.

The true-false item can be extremely difficult to prepare because the test writer must make sure that the item communicates the idea of concern. This type of item is, like the completion item, often developed by taking sentences directly from a textbook and, as in the completion item, this procedure is not a good one. The true-false item must communicate a particular idea that can be judged true or false solely on the basis of conditions set forth within the item itself. The true-false test is of course extremely easy to score because there is only one correct answer.

True-false items allow for a large sampling of content area in a short time. Students study very specific factual information, because true-false items are built on very specific information and, in general, are best used to measure recall. Probably the most unfortunate limitation of the true-false item is that it promotes guessing. A student has a 50–50 chance of being correct in his response, whether or not he has any idea as to whether the item is true or false. Therefore, a correction for guessing should be used in scoring. One effort to overcome this limitation is to ask the student to justify his response if he judges the item false. This modification in the true-false format can largely eliminate guessing in a true-false test.

Matching

A matching item requires the student to match a stem or stimulus to the appropriate response or alternative. An example is on page 163. The respondent would be expected to place the letter "b" next to number 1, "c" next to number 2, and "d" next to number 3.

The matching item is very difficult to write because there must be provided several stimuli or stems and several responses to match any of the stems. The problem is the same as that in developing a multiple-choice item, but it is more complex. In a

Figure 7.1 *Example of a Matching Item*

For each item in the lefthand column choose the phrase in the right-hand column that best completes it. Place the letter of the correct completion in the blank beside the term.

_____ 1. Test-retest reliability
_____ 2. Internal consistency reliability
_____ 3. Equivalent forms reliability

a. provides adequate measures of a theoretical underlying construct
b. provides consistent results over repeated administration
c. provides consistent results throughout the test
d. provides consistent results in parallel tests
e. provides adequate indication of future behavior

multiple-choice item, the foils need be appropriate for only one stem. In a matching item, the stem and the foils must all be related to a particular area, and all the responses must seem appropriate for each stem. The content area is limited because all the stems must be related and all the responses must be related to those stems.

It is extremely easy to score. The student usually studies specifics for this type of exam much in the way that he would study for a multiple-choice exam. In most cases matching questions call for knowledge at the level of recall and no original responses are demanded in the matching format. Matching is subject to guessing but not to the same degree as with the multiple-choice exam, because an incorrect guess may cause the student to miss more than one response.

Essay

In an essay item the student is asked to provide an original, written response to a stimulus. Usually he is asked to provide detailed information and to relate its specifics in a meaningful answer to a rather general question. The essay question differs from the short-answer question in that it requires a much more lengthy and much more integrated response to a much more general statement.

The essay question requires interrelation of many facts and opinions. An essay question in a test of basic measurement concepts might be:

Describe the role of measurement in the evaluation of a school system.

Usually educators find the essay item quite easy to write. It is easier than other types because the writer need not be concerned with providing correct responses and foils, but the essay item must be stated in such a way that the individual who responds knows what question is being asked.

The essay item is extremely difficult to score because it results in the incorporation of many ideas into an individual writing style, and the scorer is forced to be cognizant not only of the correct response but also of many of the different ways in which that response can be expressed. Suppose, for example, that a teacher asked the following essay question on a measurement test:

Identify the term *percentile.*

A student could respond by saying that a percentile is one of the 99 scores in a distribution of scores which divide the distribution into 100 equal parts, or he could say that it is a score point below which a given percentage of the scores in a distribution fall. Either response would have to be considered correct.

Essay items can severely limit the sampling of content area because of the time required to supply an appropriate response. The instructor may cover all levels and types of objectives and knowledge, and as a result the student must prepare both specifics and generalities. Guessing is effectively eliminated. Another problem of this format, however, is that students may develop a facility for including in their answers a great deal of superfluous information. The scorer must be aware that the presence in one answer of four or five different types of response to one question implies that the individual might be guessing. If the person reading the exam is not aware of this, guessing could occur within an essay exam just as it occurs within a multiple-choice format.

There is an interesting pattern to item formats and their criteria. Tests that are relatively easy to prepare are hard to score, and tests that are hard to prepare are relatively easy to score. To resolve this dilemma, it would seem appropriate to indicate that internal tests require a great deal of work. An educator may spend much time developing items that can be scored rapidly. On the other hand, one could spend less time preparing items but more time grading and interpreting their answers. In any case, if a teacher or a school system is going to develop its own cognitive or affective tests, it is the responsibility of the system to realize that preparation and execution of evaluative instruments is very time consuming. Tests require a great deal of time and effort from the test developer as well as from the students being tested. This can be justified only if the information gathered can be used to help improve the learning environment of the students.

Criteria for Assessing Item Types

How does a teacher determine which item is most appropriate for a particular internal test? At least six criteria must be considered: (1) difficulty in preparing the item, (2) difficulty in scoring, (3) sampling the content area, (4) student preparation, (5) type of knowledge to be assessed, (6) type of response to be made.

Difficulty of Preparation

An item must be prepared in such a way that it communicates to the respondent the type of response desired, no matter how easy or difficult the material that is being assessed. This particular criterion relates to how much work and time it takes to write a question such that the respondent is aware of what question is being asked and the manner in which he is expected to respond. The primary concern in preparing any test item is that it communicate to the respondent the question that is being asked.

Difficulty of Scoring

One aspect of the difficulty of scoring is the objectivity of the scoring process. It may be that the item has no clearly defined correct answer and that the test scores must therefore be subjectively determined. Subjectivity may also be a factor when there are variables such as legibility that could affect an individual's score. Another difficulty in scoring a test is the length of time it takes to read and interpret the response. If there is a simple right or wrong answer and quick observation can determine whether the student has written or marked the correct response, then this difficulty is minimized. On the other hand, if the student has written a great deal, more effort and time may be required to score the item. Thus several different factors add to the problem of obtaining a result that is meaningful and interpretable.

Sampling of Content Area

Some item formats allow sampling of several different segments of content area within a short time period; others severely restrict the amount of content sampling that can occur in a given time period. This limitation is related directly to the amount of time educators have for administering tests. Given infinite time, any test item format would be appropriate and all the content area that is desired could be examined. One must realize, however, that only limited time can be used from the school calendar for assessment and evaluation. Teachers preparing a test must determine precisely how much content area is to be assessed, the amount of time available, and how they wish to sample the content area in their testing procedures.

Student's Study Procedure

Another criterion in determining which item type to use is the procedure that students will be expected to use in preparing for exams. In most classes the student should do more than memorize specific facts. Since students seem to study differently for different types of test item, the teacher must consider that the types of item will affect the way students prepare for an exam. If more than memorization of facts is wanted, the teacher will have to use test items that require the student to synthesize material.

Type of Knowledge to Be Assessed

What knowledge can be assessed by a particular format is an important criterion in assessing the type of item to be employed. Some types are more appropriate than others in finding out whether the student has recall or can select specific responses. The ability to analyze, synthesize, and evaluate, requires other types of format. We are not saying that all levels of knowledge cannot be assessed by all six types of questions. But teachers have a tendency to use a particular type of item for particular cognitive levels. To fall into a pattern of always using the same item type is to have a strong tendency always to assess the same cognitive level. It is crucial that a teacher not fall into such a pattern if the teacher is to be able to assess more than one level of cognitive ability.

Type of Response Desired

In many instances the teacher may consider it important to determine whether the individual can originate responses and therefore should determine which item type best requires the student to provide an original response. If originality is not a concern, then the best item may be one that merely allows the student to choose a correct response. But because such items may result in guessing, questions requiring only that a student choose between alternatives may not be appropriate.

Reflections

1. Internally developed tests must be developed to assess the things in the school environment that are specific to that system or curriculum.
2. Criterion-referenced tests are employed in an internal testing program if the teacher wishes to know whether a student possesses a particular set of skills.
3. Norm-referenced tests are employed when a student's performance is to be compared with that of other pupils.

4. Some internally developed tests tend to be oversimplified and not directly related to the total learning environment.

5. The process in establishing local norms is identical to the process for standardized tests, with the exception that the norm group is the group of students in the local school district.

6. Two major problems in developing internal tests to evaluate attitudes are:

    a. A tremendous amount of time is spent in developing the instrument

    b. Many individuals respond to items in a way that they think they are expected to respond rather than the way they actually think or feel.

7. Classroom observation procedures are an alternative method to paper and pencil measures of attitudes for obtaining indications of attitudes.

8. Observation data can be collected unobtrusively by the teacher who has developed a systematic way of tallying observed activities during a short time period in the school day.

9. The types of item format available to the teacher are:

    a. Multiple choice
    b. Completion
    c. Short answer
    d. True-false
    e. Matching
    f. Essay

10. The six criteria to employ in assessing the advantages and limitations of item types are:

    a. Difficulty of preparation
    b. Difficulty of scoring
    c. Sampling of content area
    d. Procedure student will use in preparing for exam
    e. Type of knowledge that can be assessed
    f. Type of response that can be made to the item.

Exercises

1. Review the objectives for the class in which this textbook is being used. Determine which objectives require a measure that cannot be obtained from an external measuring device.

2. For objectives that require an internal measuring instrument,

what types of reference system are required to provide sufficient information for assessment?

3. Review the objectives that require the assessment of some attitude. Precisely describe the attitude that needs to be assessed.
What are the components of the attitude to be assessed?
Should these be added together to form an overall attitude or should each component be assessed and interpreted independently?

4. For each internal measuring device that needs to be developed,
review the various item formats and determine which are
appropriate for each measuring instrument.

Selected References

GRADED–NONGRADED CLASSROOMS
See the references in Chapter 2.

LEVELS OF COGNITIVE FUNCTIONING
Bloom, B. S., ed. *Taxonomy of Educational Objectives.* Handbook I.
Cognitive Domain. New York: McKay, 1956. Pp. 201–07. The
different levels of cognitive functioning are defined and discussed.
Stanley, J. C., and K. D. Hopkins. *Educational and Psychological
Measurement and Evaluation.* Englewood Cliffs, N. J.: Prentice-
Hall, 1972. Pp. 173–82. Bloom's six-level classification of the
cognitive domain and other classifications are illustrated by means
of test items at each level.
Thorndike, R. L., ed. *Educational Measurement.* Washington, D.C.:
American Council on Education, 1971. Pp. 28–31. Gives a brief
description of the major categories in both Bloom's taxonomy and
Gagne's learning hierarchy.

ATTITUDE MEASUREMENT
Anastasi, A. *Psychological Testing.* New York: Macmillan, 1968.
Pp. 479–87. Presents attitude measurement, its applications,
methodological problems, and scaling samples.
Mehrens, W. A., and I. J. Lehmann. *Standardized Tests in Education.*
New York: Holt, Rinehart and Winston, 1969. Pp. 255–64. The
authors attempt to demonstrate a need for attitude measurement,

relate attitude to learning, and describe techniques used currently in attitude measurement.

Noll, V. H. and D. P. Scannell. *Introduction to Educational Measurement.* Boston: Houghton Mifflin, 1972. Pp. 435–39. Gives a short presentation of attitude measurement in which special emphasis is placed on the method of equal-appearing intervals and the Likert method.

8

Constructing Internal Measures

CONCERNS

1. What are the criteria to consider in determining whether an individual has the potential to develop a good internal measuring device?
2. What are some general guidelines for writing good test items?
3. What clues help students answer multiple-choice questions without their knowing the correct responses?
4. What is the most important thing to do in constructing a classroom observation scale?
5. What are the guidelines for constructing a test of several different item formats?
6. What is the primary criterion for the utility of an internal measuring device?

Test-Item Criteria

The process of constructing an internal measure is complex and time consuming if the test writer wishes to acquire data useful in helping a student gain as much as he can from his education. The less aware the test developer is of how effectively to use test results, the less difficult this process is. Unfortunately many individuals see the process of developing internal measures as trivial and requiring few, if any, skills. In this chapter we shall demonstrate why the process of developing an instrument of internal measure requires careful planning and thinking if the results of evaluation are to be meaningful.

The importance of constructing a good item for a test is most evident in a criterion-referenced test. The test item is the criterion. All conscientious teachers want evaluative criteria to be meaningful and relevant to the students' classroom experiences. When the criterion is the test item, the individual who interprets test scores must be assured that the student's response is a response to the criterion and not a response to poor item writing or to guessing. To ensure that student responses are meaningful, the test writer must be sure that each item communicates the question being asked and that it does not provide inadvertent or unnecessary clues to the appropriate response.

The individual test writer himself should meet certain criteria also. The first requirement is thorough knowledge of the material to be assessed. This should not be a problem when the test writer is the teacher developing a test to be used within her classroom, but it may be a criterion difficult to meet if a group of teachers is developing a test to be used by other teachers in a school-wide testing program. The chemistry teacher should not prepare social science examinations, nor should English teachers prepare chemistry exams.

The item writer must also know the educational and psychological characteristics of the individual students for whom the test is intended. For example, a test designed to assess fourth-grade students' ability to spell should not be prepared by an eighth-grade teacher. The eighth-grade teacher is probably not as aware of the learning experiences and curriculum expectations of fourth-graders as is the fourth-grade teacher. This means not that the fourth-grade teacher will develop an easier test than the eighth-grade teacher will, but rather that the fourth-grade teacher will develop a test more relevant or applicable to the fourth-grade student.

A good test developer must be able to state and describe specific objectives for the measuring instrument. If the teacher has this skill, the items written will precisely reflect the objectives. When the test developer cannot or does not develop specific objectives for a test, inclusion of some items may be haphazard, and the result may be that interpretations of student responses will not be meaningful. Interpretations of responses are generally more meaningful when the specific objectives defined by teacher precede the decision as to which items to include on a test. The results obtained from such tests can thus be interpreted as they relate to specific objectives.

Another criterion of the good item writer is the ability to communicate effectively in writing. A major concern for any item writer is whether the respondent is answering the question that the item writer intended to ask. For example, if a teacher wanted to discover whether a student knows what preparations John Wilkes Booth made before assassinating Abraham Lincoln, the following question might be asked: "How did John Wilkes Booth kill Mr. Lincoln?" If the student were to respond "with a gun", he would have answered the question but the teacher would have failed to inform him of the response expected. The response "with a gun" answers the question correctly, but it is not a question demanding knowledge of the preparations Booth made. The item developer must not assume that the respondent can interpret the questioner's intent. The item must fully communicate that intent. To be sure that it does this, the item developer may be required to define several terms or indicate a specific format for the response. In the Booth example, the teacher might instead have used the following question: "Outline in sequential order the known activities of John Wilkes Booth during the five days before he killed Mr. Lincoln." In this format the teacher has better communicated the intention of her question and the student knows the type of response that is expected.

Finally, the individual developing a test must be able to use different formats to collect information from students. As discussed in the previous chapter, a variety of formats allows the teacher to solicit different types of information. If the writer uses only one format, the levels of knowledge that are assessed may be limited. Moreover, the student will study not for knowledge but for particular types of test questions. The teacher who has the ability to ask questions using different item formats will be better able to obtain the type of information desired and better able to encourage students to study content.

Preparing Test Items

The next sections of this chapter are intended to assist the test developer to prepare various types of item format. They should help the teacher to be better prepared for asking specific questions that will elicit useful and meaningful information.

Multiple Choice

By far the most commonly used item format for standardized achievement tests is the multiple-choice question. A major reason seems to be that multiple-choice items can be scored objectively. Moreover, test publishers employ outstanding item writers capable of writing items for all levels of knowledge in this format. Internal testing programs also require multiple-choice items, though in general the use of multiple-choice items in internal testing programs is not as great as in external tests because teachers do not have the necessary time to develop good items. A teacher might want to spend the time necessary to develop a good item that could be included in an item pool and used periodically every year or every semester, but if the test item is to be used once only, the time element makes it inefficient.

In a multiple-choice test item, the stem of the question should present a single problem. We shall use an item developed in Chapter 7 as an example:

The type of validity of major concern to the developer of criterion-referenced internal measuring instruments is:
1. predictive
2. content
3. construct
4. concurrent

In this item the respondent is presented with a single problem. The stem is rather long, but it is important that the item communicate the conditions that must be known to answer the problem. The student must know that the question relates to a criterion-referenced internally developed test. If this information is not known, then the question is too vague and the respondent might defend other responses.

The stem of the question is only part of the concern of the item writer. The item writer must also consider the alternatives from which the respondent is to choose his response. The correct response must be included. The foils or incorrect responses must be meaningful. That is, it must appear that each foil could possibly be the correct response. The easy phase of writing the responses is the preparation of the correct response. The foils are more difficult because they must be meaningful and yet not provide inadvertent clues to the correct response.

A number of factors can make a foil seem unreasonable. One error that occasionally occurs in poor items is that while the correct response is grammatically correct the foils are not grammatically correct with respect to the stem of the item. This may be readily observed by the respondent and, as a result, he can answer the question by selecting the grammatically correct response without knowing it is correct. Suppose the item presented on page 174 had been written as follows:

The type of validity of major concern to the developer of criterion-referenced internal measuring instruments is:
1. predictive and concurrent
2. content
3. construct and content
4. predictive and construct

Since the item asks for the *type* of validity, a student could eliminate responses 1, 3, and 4 because they include more than one type. It is unusual to find an item in which all foils can be eliminated because of grammar, but it is not at all unusual to find items in which one or two foils can be so eliminated.

Another cue to the correct response in the example above lies in the poor set of responses. If the student had not detected the grammatical problem, he might have selected response 2 because all the other responses are of similar length and much longer than the correct response. Novice item writers tend instead to supply a correct response that is longer than the foils. A good guideline is to make all seemingly possible responses approximately equal in length.

Another error frequently made in developing foils is to write all the incorrect responses so that they mean the same thing. This happens often when the item writer is trying to use a specific number of foils. Suppose the responses available to the multiple-choice question on page 175 had been:

1. predictive
2. content
3. empirical
4. numerical

The respondent who knows that alternatives 1, 3, and 4 are all names for the same type of validity might have correctly chosen alternative 2 because it is the only one that means something different. Each foil must be distinct and provide a unique response to the problem presented in the stem.

A fourth clue to the correct response lies in the use of such absolute qualifiers as "All," "Never," "Always," and "None." Students have learned that the inclusion of such qualifiers in a response usually makes it incorrect. As a result, they tend to avoid such responses, and the teacher should not include them in the foils.

That students can and do look for such clues was demonstrated in a study by M. J. Slakter and R. A. Koehler (1969). In their research, they attempted to teach students to look for such clues in responding to multiple-choice items. They found that students who were aware of clues to the correct response were able to score higher on a test consisting of nonsense items than students who were unaware of the clues. It is generally believed and has been demonstrated that students learn these clues by themselves just by taking tests. Thus, if teachers are to gain meaningful information from multiple-choice items, they must attempt to eliminate clues that could allow students to respond correctly without knowing the material being tested.

A multiple-choice item is not judged by the number of responses available to the respondent. There is no need for all the items in a multiple-choice test to have the same number of foils. The merit of the response set of the item is determined by the number of meaningful foils available to the student. If the item writer believes there are only two meaningful foils to a stem, it is better to list only those two foils than to write additional foils that are not meaningful.

There are several other specific guidelines that could be suggested for preparing multiple-choice items, but they can all be summarized under the general category of communicating with the respondent. At no time should the item writer lose sight of the attempt to gain specific information from the student. If the student is unaware of the information being sought, it is unlikely that the response will be meaningful, whether the response is right or wrong.

Completion

Completion items are generally considered easy to develop and easy to grade. This is true as long as there is only one correct response and the item writer provides sufficient information in the statement for the respondent to know the limitations of the problem presented. In Chapter 7 the following item was presented:

A test developed by a teacher for use within the classroom is called a(n) _____ measuring device.

There is only one acceptable word that can be inserted in the blank. Once the limitation that the test is developed by the teacher for use within the classroom has been stated in the sentence the respondent has the necessary information to adequately respond to the problem presented.

Suppose the following question had been intended to discover whether a student knows who is responsible for developing a test to be used in a specific classroom: "An internal measuring device is developed by _____." Given the intention, this is not a good completion item because there is more than one correct response —for example, "the teacher," "some teachers in the system," "any teacher in the school system," and so on. The item is not specific enough to indicate exactly what question the item writer had in mind.

Completion items should not be taken directly from textbook statements since most textbook sentences, taken out of context, do not contain sufficient information to stand alone. In completion items, the statement must contain all information necessary to describe the conditions of the problem.

Short Answer

Two short-answer questions introduced in Chapter 7 are:

List five (5) ways in which the results of a standardized achievement test may appropriately be used by a school system.

and

Outline in sequential order the known activities of John Wilkes Booth during the five days before he killed Mr. Lincoln.

In each question a specific parameter is defined in the statement of the problem. In the first question, the student is asked to list a precise number of things. The reader will notice that in this textbook we have listed six possible uses of the results of standardized achievement tests. The question has asked the respondent to list only five. This is much better than asking the respondent to list all ways because the word "all" places a new dimension on the question. The respondent must first ask whether the word "all" means the six as defined by this text or the total number that the respondent can think about? Such qualitative words can cause the respondent immense difficulty when they cause him to be uncertain of the intent of the question.

In the second question a different type of parameter is defined. The respondent is told to *outline* the activities of a five-day period. This information is important to the student because it informs him of the expected format of the response. Thus the item writer has communicated the intent of the question.

Short-answer questions must present a very specific description of the problem to be solved. The description of the problem must define all necessary parameters in terms that are descriptive and meaningful to the respondent. In many instances this type of question should provide the respondent with an idea as to the type of response that is expected. When these guidelines are taken into consideration, item writers may find that the development of this type of item is not as simple as appears.

True-False

The true-false format is like the completion format in that the completion format asks for a response that makes a statement true. The guidelines apropriate for the completion format are therefore also appropriate for the true-false format.

The key guideline for the true-false format is the requirement that the statement can stand alone. There must be in the statement information sufficient for the respondent to know the parameters surrounding it. If the statement uses specific terminology and is precise, then the true-false item should communicate to the respondent.

In a true-false question there is usually a key word that causes the statement to be true or false. In some cases it is important to underline these key words. For example it would seem appropriate to underline a word that converts a positive statement into a negative one. In Chapter 7 we gave this example: "Criterion-referenced interpretations may be made of items included in a norm-referenced test." To meet the same objective, an item might have been developed as follows: "Criterion-referenced interpretations may *not* be made of items included in a norm-referenced test." In this example it is important for the respondent to see the word "not" because the item writer wants the individual to respond to the statement as it is presented. The item writer should not try to mask the negative element of the question with some intent of trying to trick or fool the student. The purpose is to find out whether the student has specific information.

As with multiple-choice items, absolute qualifiers such as "All" and "Never" should be avoided in true-false items. Students sense that qualifiers such as these usually make an item false. As a result, the inclusion of such qualifiers causes the item to measure something other than what was intended.

Matching

The guidelines for developing matching items are basically the same as those for the multiple-choice format. The matching format of a test item can be considered a special case of the multiple-choice item because in the matching format several stems share the same listing of possible responses. This places a special burden on the item developer because it can be difficult to find several stems that can be grouped together. In addition, the correct response for one stem must be a good foil for the other stems. This requires that the content of the stems be homogeneous; otherwise the correct responses would be poor foils for the other stems.

In Chapter 7 the following example of a matching item was given:

_____ 1. Test-retest reliability	a. provides adequate measures of a theoretical underlying construct
_____ 2. Internal consistency reliability	
_____ 3. Equivalent forms reliability	
	b. provides consistent results over repeated administrations

c. provides consistent results throughout the
test
d. provides consistent results in parallel tests
e. provides adequate indication of future behav-
ior

An important guideline for preparing matching items is to provide more responses than stems. This prevents the student from guessing the correct response by eliminating the response that he knows and providing him with only one possible response to the unknown stem. Suppose the stem had appeared as follows:

_____ 1. Test-retest reliability
_____ 2. Internal consistency reliability
_____ 3. Equivalent forms reliability

a. provides consistent results over repeated ad-
ministrations
b. provides consistent results throughout the
test
c. provides consistent results in parallel tests

If a student knew that "a" is the correct response for "1" and "b" is the correct response for "2," he would automatically know that "c" is the correct response for "3" because it is the only one left. Teachers sometimes try to overcome this problem by indicating that a response may be used more than once. We feel, however, that it is better to have a different response for each stem and, as a result, one must provide more responses than stems.

Essay

The naive item writer is usually of the opinion that the essay question is the easiest to develop. This is far from true if the item developer wants to obtain information that can be interpreted. The essay is intended to allow the student to synthesize or analyze a set of information in a meaningful and original response. The essay question is less restrictive than the short-answer question but contains certain limitations nonetheless. An example of an essay question is:

Describe the role of measurement in the evaluation of a school system.

This question is general, but there are limitations placed on the problem. The question limits the response to the evaluation of a school system.

A less-effective essay question dealing with the same objective would be: "Describe the role of measurement in evaluation." This statement of the problem is too vague because the respondent could answer the question in terms of student evaluations, teacher evaluations, or system evaluations. As in all the previous formats discussed, the item writer is concerned with asking the student to respond to a specific problem; if the student does not understand the problem as presented, the results are meaningless.

Classroom Observation

During the last several years there has been an increased interest in systematically obtaining information by observing students in the classroom. In obtaining such information, educators believe they are better able to determine how students will react to given conditions in the classroom. Paper and pencil measuring devices are unable to simulate actual classroom conditions, but collection of observational data from the classroom requires that a system must be established. The first thing that must be considered is the type of behavior to be observed. It might be fighting, daydreaming, or constructive or interruptive verbalizing. The teacher must define specifically what actions will constitute observable behavior.

Were a teacher specifically to define this as fighting, for example, the behavior to be observed might be actual participation in physical contact with other students that is intended as harm. Observation of daydreaming might observe students who are awake but unaware of the activities occurring around them. Constructive verbalizing might be understood as talking to others and responding to questions, generating questions, or taking part in discussions related to the objectives of the class. Interruptive verbalizing might be observed as refusal to allow others to complete their responses or questions. Such reference points for collecting information help define specific activities that either the teacher or some other educator is to observe.

Next the teacher must determine a systematic schedule for observing and recording observations. It might be decided to observe each day in an unobtrusive manner the behavior of one child for five minutes in the morning and five minutes in the afternoon. The teacher may collect information during a free discussion period when the students are allowed to work on or discuss a topic of interest to them. The teacher must also decide with what frequency (for example, every thirty seconds) during the five-minute time period observed activities should be recorded. Here is an example of a record made by one teacher during a school day.

Student Pat _____

Date _____

Time 30-second intervals

    0 = No defined behavior
    1 = Fighting
    2 = Daydreaming
    3 = Constructive verbalizing
    4 = Interruptive verbalizing

Interval	1	2	3	4	5	6	7	8	9	10
Morning	0	2	2	0	4	3	3	4	1	1
Afternoon	0	0	0	0	2	2	2	3	3	3

The key to gaining meaningful information from classroom observations is adequately defining the relevant behavior to be observed. If the behavior is specifically defined, the data collected is more likely to be valid and the interpretation of the results can be more meaningful.

Organizing an Internal Test

Before organizing a test, the developer must establish specific objectives. It may be that each item is to assess a specific objective or that several items are to assess a single objective. It is the test developer's responsibility to determine which items are to be included in the test.

Next he must decide the order in which the exam questions will be given. One guideline for this decision is to group the items according to format: all the multiple-choice items together, matching questions together, and so on. This allows the student to establish a continuity in his method of response and helps him with efficiency of time. If the item formats are interchanged, the student will generally require more time to complete the exam.

Within the groupings of items, the teacher should group items according to the objectives they are written for. If there is a single question for each objective, then items similar in content should be grouped together. If there are several items for each objective, these should be grouped together. The rationale for the grouping of the items is similar to the rationale for the grouping with respect to item format. Usually it is best to place at the beginning of the exam the questions that require a minimum of response. Multiple-choice or true-false questions, for example, should appear early in the exam. Similarly, the easier items should appear at the beginning of the test. In this way the student can begin gradually to use his mental processes. As he moves into the exam, he has a tendency to relax and organize his thoughts better. Consequently, the questions requiring him to formulate his own response should appear toward the end of the test, because he is likely to perform better with them then. This method of organization also assists the student in monitoring his time. Students have a tendency to over-respond to questions requiring original formulation of response, especially when they feel sure that they know the correct response.

Each item must be presented completely on one page. The stem of a multiple-choice item should not appear on the bottom of one page with the alternative responses on the top of the next page. Turning pages back and forth breaks thought patterns, and if the student responds incorrectly to an item, it may be because of the way in which it was presented. This type of error renders results meaningless and can always be avoided by an aware teacher.

Before the exam is administered, the teacher must decide whether the items are to be weighted differentially. This means that the teacher must assign score points to each item. Because in a criterion-referenced system the item is the criterion, the student either meets the criterion or does not, and the number of score points for answering correctly is of little consequence. If the score on the exam is to be an accumulation of points from each of the exam questions, then the teacher must determine subjectively the weight for each item. The teacher may review the relative merits of each objective and in many cases will find that one objective is more important than another. Having determined the weighting of the items, the teacher must communicate the differential weightings to the students taking the test.

Before administering the test, the teacher should prepare a key of the correct responses. The teacher can thus ensure that the items communicate properly to the reader. Typing errors that may have occurred during the final preparation of the test can be corrected in the review required to compose the key, and for the short-answer and essay items the teacher can identify errors that may cause a student to lose points because of lack of clarity or content difficulty. The teacher should consider this time well spent because of the merits of one final check on how well the test items have been constructed.

Multiple-choice, true-false, and matching items are often called objective items because they can be scored objectively. That is, the teacher simply looks at the student's choice to see if it matches the keyed response. If it does, it is correct. If it does not, it is wrong. In other words, with an answer key, the teacher can determine on a purely objective basis whether a student has responded correctly.

Essay and short-answer items, on the other hand, require original responses. Since the same thing can be said in many ways, the teacher must decide subjectively whether each response is correct. A number of factors can influence a subjective decision and the teacher should attempt to guard against these influences. For example, the tendency to judge a response according to the character of the student should be guarded against. A teacher may decide that John's response is correct because of personal favor whereas Keith's response, which may be essentially the same as John's, is judged wrong. A teacher would certainly not intentionally allow this to occur, but attitudes may unconsciously influence scoring. Thus the teacher should score essay items without knowledge of whose paper is being scored. The teacher should also guard against letting handwriting, spelling, punctuation, sentence structure, and writing style influence scoring, unless these factors are part of what the test is designed to measure.

Since short-answer and essay items usually have a number of different points that must be made in the response, the teacher must decide how to weight the subparts. In a response that included six different points, the teacher must decide whether each is of the same importance or one is to be weighted more heavily than the other. This decision must be made before the scoring begins and adhered to for each response scored if it is to be certain that the same weighting is applied for each student.

The teacher should next determine the appropriate time limit for the test. As we indicated earlier, most internally developed tests are not speed tests and therefore the time limit should be sufficiently long to allow all individuals to respond to each item. If the time limit is too brief, students can be allowed additional time to respond. This can be done in an internally developed test because there is no standard administration procedure to follow. The time limit is a subjective decision made by the teacher who is going to use the results.

The final step must provide detailed directions for the students taking the test. If multiple-choice items or true-false items are included and a correction for guessing is to be made, then the directions should inform the student that a formula that corrects for guessing is to be used. One such formula is to subtract the number of wrong responses from the number of correct responses. This is a fairly severe correction for guessing, certainly more severe than is suggested in most measurement textbooks. We feel that this severity can be justified because the purpose of correcting for guessing is to discourage guessing in order to be able to assume that a student's response reflects what he knows and not how well he can guess. The correction "score = rights — wrongs" imposes a strong penalty for guessing items incorrectly and should be more effective in discouraging guessing than less severe corrections. Whatever correction formula is used, it must be communicated in the directions so that the respondent will know the risks of guessing. When a correction for guessing formula is used, the directions should state explicitly that an item should be answered only if the student knows the correct response.

Some teachers have made a practice of allowing students to select the items to which they choose to respond from a number of items provided. The use of optional questions seems to imply either that the given and the optional items all measure the same objective or that the teacher has not determined specific objectives for the exam. We encourage the teacher to include items that everyone should attempt to answer and to eliminate the choice of optional items from tests.

If there are several different item formats in the test, the teacher should provide separate instructions for each type. This ensures that the student knows the intention of the problems being presented or questions asked.

All the information in this chapter is intended to assist the potential teacher in developing internal tests that render usable and meaningful results. Even after all these guidelines have been followed and the test is technically correct, the internally developed measuring device is only as good as the information that is used. If the results are not used to help the student, then the teacher should reconsider the reasons why the test was developed and administered.

Reflections

1. The criteria for a good item writer include
   a. A thorough knowledge of the material to be assessed
   b. The ability to develop specific objectives for a test
   c. Knowledge of the individuals taking the exam
   d. Ability to communicate in writing
   e. Ability to use different item formats to gain information about a student's knowledge
2. Some general guidelines for writing good test items are:
   a. The item should be precise and specify all necessary conditions.
   b. Absolute or qualitative terms should be used cautiously.
   c. Key words in the problem should be underlined.
   d. The respondent should be provided with information about the format of the response.
   e. Be sure that the items are grammatically correct.
3. In developing multiple-choice items the item writer should be cautious about providing the following cues to the respondent:
   a. The correct response is a different length from the other responses.
   b. The subjects annd verbs do not agree.
   c. The foils all have the same meaning.
   d. The foils contain qualitative terms such as *never, always, all,* and *none.*

4. For an observational scale to provide meaningful data, the behavior must be explicitly defined for the observer or observers.
5. If a test has more than one type of item format among the items, the following guidelines should be observed:
   a. The items should be grouped according to item format.
   b. Within the item formats, items developed to assess similar ideas should be grouped together.
   c. Directions should be provided for each item format.
   d. When differential weighting of the items is necessary, this should be communicated to the students in the directions.
6. An internally developed measuring device is effective if the results are used to improve the learning environment for the student.

Exercises

1. Construct a measuring device that will provide the necessary information to assess an objective for this course.
2. Organize your measuring device and seek a critical review from at least two of your colleagues. Revise the instrument as you feel necessary.
3. Prepare the written directions and administer the instrument to a sample from the class.
4. Determine the results of your measuring device and then review the objectives for which the device was developed. Be sure that you have obtained the information that you believe is necessary.

Selected References

CONSTRUCTING TEST ITEMS

Thorndike, R. L., ed. *Educational Measurement.* Washington, D.C.: American Council on Education, 1971. Pp. 81–129. Chapter 4 deals with writing short-answer, alternate-choice, multiple-choice, matching, and context-dependent test items.

McFarland, S. J., and C. F. Hereford, eds. *Statistics and Measurement in the Classroom.* Dubuque: Brown, 1971. Pp. 87–114. Very practical suggestions are given to help teachers make better tests.

Storey, A. G. *The Measurement of Classroom Learning.* Chicago: Science Research Associates, 1970. Pp. 46–75. Chapters 4 and 5 deal with oral, essay, completion, multiple-choice, matching, and true-false items. Guides, criticisms, use, and examples of each type are included.

Thorndike, R. L., and E. Hagen. *Measurement and Evaluation in Psychology and Education.* New York: Wiley, 1961. Pp. 27–59. Essay and objective tests and their advantages, limitations, and effective use are presented with good examples.

CLASSROOM OBSERVATION

Green, J. A. *Introduction to Measurement and Evaluation.* New York: Dodd, Mead, 1970. Pp. 296–99. An illustration and description of the checklist method of observation is given, in addition to anecdotal records, a log book, and case studies.

Sawin, E. I. *Evaluation and the Work of the Teacher.* Belmont, Calif.: Wadsworth, 1969. Pp. 75–86. Gives instructions for making informal observations and anecdotal records.

Noll, V. H., and D. P. Scannell. *Introduction to Educational Measurement.* Boston: Houghton Mifflin, 1972. Pp. 442–65. The observational techniques described and illustrated are rating scales, anecdotal records, systematic observation, and sociometric methods. The advantages, limitations, and effective use of each method are discussed.

TEST-WISENESS

Slakter, M. J., and R. A. Keohler. *Test Wiseness: Final Technical Report.* Fredonia, New York: Teacher Education Research Center, State University College at Fredonia, 1969. The authors present a detailed discussion of the results of research involving the training of students in the principles of test-wiseness. The work includes a description of general test-wiseness principles and clues that may be built into specific items.

9

Standards for Judging Internal Measures

CONCERNS

1. How are items selected for an internally developed test?
2. What type of validity is of most concern to the developers of an internally developed test?
3. What types of reliability can be obtained for internally developed measures?
4. What item-analysis procedures are appropriate for tests developed to discriminate among students?
5. What item-analysis procedures are appropriate for criterion-referenced tests?
6. How can consistency of observation data be checked?

Internally developed tests assess the degree to which students possess certain traits that have been concentrated on in classrooms. Because internal measures relate to specific information that has been taught within the classroom, they are the most commonly used tests. The teacher must build and judge the quality of these tests. The purpose of this chapter is to present a discussion of several criteria the teacher can employ in such evaluation. It is also important to judge the quality of the instruments of observation before using their results. Standards similar to those for external measures must be applied to such instruments and these will be discussed in this chapter too.

Four standards that should be used in judging internal measures are its validity, reliability, and usability, and the results of item analyses. Validity is determined by assessing how well the test measures what it is supposed to measure. Reliability is assessed by determining how consistently the test measures what it is supposed to measure. Usability is primarily concerned with the interpretation of results in the context in which the test is administered. Item-analysis procedures emphasize the various ways in which the classroom teacher can assess the items within a test to determine what items should be included.

Norm-referenced Tests

Norm-referenced tests developed for use in a classroom are almost always used to determine differential levels of student knowledge. They are not used to determine if a student possesses a particular skill.

Validity

There are different types of validity that might be appropriate for a test. For the internally developed test, there seem to be two of primary importance. One is the content validity of the internally developed test and the other is concurrent validity. As you may recall from Chapter 4, content validity is determined by the individual who uses the test by reviewing the items of the test and making a subjective decision as to whether the items assess the traits that the teacher wants assessed. Tests developed by classroom teachers who should know the traits they want to assess should have content validity because the teachers themselves develop the tests. In using this standard for judgment, the teacher is primarily concerned with reviewing the test to make sure that she has covered all the important topics that have been covered. Once a teacher is satisfied of a test's content validity, the judgment can be checked with other teachers who teach the same content. If they agree that the test assesses properly, the teacher can be confident that it possesses a high degree of content validity. Of course, it is important that the teacher communicate clearly to colleagues what the test is designed to measure.

The concurrent validity of the test is not as easy to assess as content validity. Concurrent validity is determined by finding the relationship between the internally developed test and some other criterion that occurs at about the same time the test is to be administered. This criterion may be another test or it may be observations made by a teacher. Two criteria that might be appropriate for assessing concurrent validity of an internally developed test might help clarify this standard. An internally developed test may be intended to determine how well students can multiply by two-digit numbers, for example. A second test or some exercise may be administered within the class being assessed in its ability to multiply two-digit numbers. If the results from the work activity within the class and the responses to the test are similar, then the test should be judged to have concurrent validity.

Another criterion for assessing concurrent validity might be related to the world outside the classroom. For example, the teacher might measure the respect of children in the class toward others' property. The test may be intended to differentiate levels of respect. The teacher may obtain the results from the test and add to them an independent rating of the teacher's own, or of an aide, as to the respect that each child shows for others' property. Such rating is a subjective decision based on the actual activities of students within the classroom. This type of assessment is different from a paper-pencil test developed to assess attitude. The teacher might very well try to determine the concurrent validity of an attitude test by comparing the test results to observations of the environment in which the child actually shows his respect toward others' property. If the results of the test and the observations are closely related, then the test could be judged to possess concurrent validity.

Reliability

Reliability indicates a test's ability to measure consistently whatever it measures. Consistency may mean how consistent test results are from one test administration to another or it may mean how consistent results are within the test instrument itself. These two different forms of reliability are called test-retest reliability and split-halves (or internal consistency) reliability. The test-retest form of reliability determines whether an individual's score maintains the same relative position in the distribution of test scores from one test period to another. Split-halves reliability determines the tendency of an individual to perform the same on one half of an exam as on the other half of the exam.

The test-retest reliability coefficient is determined by finding the correlation between the test results observed between two administrations of a test. Table 9.1 shows how the test-retest reliability coefficient is obtained. Data has been collected on five students who took the same test twice. The correlation coefficient between the two sets of test scores is +1.0. This correlation coefficient indicates that each student had the same relative position on the results of both administrations of the test.

Since the test-retest reliability coefficient is really a correlation coefficient, it can have values ranging from −1 to +1. An r of +1 indicates that each student had the same relative position in both score distributions. An r of −1 would mean that each student was the same distance from the average score on the distribution on both administrations of the test but on one administration was above the mean while on the other was below the mean. An r of 0 would indicate no tendency for students to have the same relative position in the two score distributions. Since test-retest reliability indicates the tendency to maintain the same relative position, an r of +1 is the best possible value. If consistency from one administration of a test to another is important, one would not want to use a test that yielded a negative reliability coefficient, because this would indicate a tendency for students who scored high the first time to score low the second, and vice versa. One would also not want to use a test with a reliability coefficient close to 0. While one would not expect to find an r of +1, it is not unusual to find a reliability coefficient of between +.70 and + .90. We cannot provide definite guidelines as to a cutoff value for deciding whether a test possesses sufficient test-retest reliability. That decision must be made by the teacher for each

Table 9.1 *Test-Retest Reliability Coefficient*

	COLUMN 1	COLUMN 2	COLUMN 3	COLUMN 4	COLUMN 5
	Test Administration 1	*Test Administration 2*	*Column 1 × Column 2*	*Column 1²*	*Column 2²*
Jodi	10	15	150	100	225
Brent	12	17	204	144	289
Julie	20	25	500	400	625
Pam	16	21	336	256	441
Mike	17	22	374	289	484
	75	100	1564	1189	2064

Reliability coefficient =

$$\frac{(\text{number of subjects} \times \text{sum of column 3}) - (\text{sum of column 1} \times \text{sum of column 2})}{\sqrt{[(\text{number of subjects}) \times (\text{sum of column 4}) - (\text{sum of column 1}^2)] \times [(\text{number of subjects}) \times (\text{sum of column 5}) - (\text{sum of column 2}^2)]}}$$

$$= \frac{(5 \times 1564) - (75 \times 100)}{\sqrt{[(5 \times 1189) - (75)^2] \times [(5 \times 2064) - (100)^2]}}$$

$$= \frac{7820 - 7500}{\sqrt{(5945 - 5625) \times (10320 - 10000)}}$$

$$= \frac{320}{\sqrt{(320)(320)}}$$

$$= \frac{320}{\sqrt{(320)^2}}$$

$$= \frac{320}{320}$$

$$= +1$$

If X = a score in Column 1
Y = a score in Column 2
N = the number of students
Σ = the sum of a set of scores, then
the equation for the test-retest reliability coefficient is:

$$\text{reliability coefficient} = \frac{N \Sigma X - \Sigma X \Sigma Y}{\sqrt{[N \Sigma X^2 - (\Sigma X)^2] [N \Sigma Y^2 - (\Sigma Y)^2]}}$$

test. We can say that the closer the test-retest reliability is to + 1, the more consistent the results will be. The closer the test-retest reliability coefficient is to 0, the more inconsistent the results will be.

Split-halves reliability provides evidence as to whether individual students maintain their same relative rank when the test is divided into two approximately equal parts. To assess the split-halves reliability of a test, the content of the test items must be divisible into two parts each intended to measure the same thing. This is often accomplished by separating items according to their number on the test, the even-numbered items in one group, the odd-numbered items in another. Computation of a split-halves reliability coefficient is similar to the computation of the test-retest reliability coefficient. The only real difference between the two is in the nature of the scores. In the test-retest reliability coefficient, a student receives two scores, one each from two administrations of the same test. In the split-halves reliability coefficient, the student also receives two scores but the first represents the number of even-numbered items answered correctly on a single administration of the test and the second score represents the number of odd-numbered items answered correctly on the same test. The split-halves reliability coefficient provides information as to whether the individual has maintained the same relative rank within a particular test. The limits on the split-halves reliability coefficient are the same as for the test-retest reliability coefficient. The major difference between the two reliability coefficients is that the test-retest reliability measures consistency of test results over time while the split-halves measures consistency of responding within a given test.

Usability

Usability reflects concern with whether scores can be interpreted as scores or only in terms of how each student scores with respect to other students. If the tests are to be usable, then the teacher should be able to use the test results by themselves and interpret the test results for a particular student without referring to other students in the class. In reviewing the data presented in Table 9.1, a teacher would be concerned with the fact that the mean of the test given at Administration 1 is 15 while the mean of the same test given at Administration 2 is 20. There has been a substantial increase in the test scores from the one administration to the other. It would be extremely difficult to determine which result is more meaningful for, or more representative of, an individual student. Remember that the norm-referenced test is developed for the purpose of differentiating among individuals and the results for any one individual may be interpretable only by comparing that score to the scores of other individuals. If this is the primary purpose of the test, then usability is not as important as reliability. If the teacher plans to use the test results to indicate what the individual can do as compared against some criterion other than how others do in the class, then the concept of usability becomes a much more important factor.

Item Analysis

Item analysis procedures are used to determine whether an item is functioning properly in a particular exam. In the norm-referenced system a test is intended to differentiate among the students with respect to the knowledge that they have on the topic being assessed. Therefore, a very important criterion to be met in any test item is that it discriminates among students who know more about the topic being assessed and those who know less. The two item-analysis indices most important are the item-difficulty index and the item-discrimination index.

An item-difficulty index is determined to find out how difficult an item is for individuals responding to the item. Item difficulty can be defined as the proportion of individuals who respond correctly to an item. That is, the item-difficulty index is the number of people who respond correctly to an item divided by the total number of people responding to the item.

$$\text{Item-difficulty} = \frac{\text{number of individuals responding correctly}}{(\text{total number responding incorrectly}) + (\text{total number responding correctly})}$$

Using this definition, the maximum value that the item-difficulty index can attain is $+1$ and the minimum value is 0. The closer the item index is to 0, the more difficult the item is. As the difficulty index approaches 0, a larger proportion of the individuals incorrectly responded to the item. One would assume that this means that the item is more difficult. As the ratio approaches $+1$, very few of the individuals missed the item. This would lead one to assume that the item is not very difficult. There are no

cut-off values in terms of how large or small an item-difficulty index should be to be included in the test. In a test intended to differentiate among the students, it would seem to be a waste of time to
include an item with a difficulty index of $+1$. This would mean
that the item is not difficult for any of the students and that it does
not help differentiate among the various levels of knowledge
present in the group. If the item-difficulty index is 0, the test is
not differentiating among the ability of the individuals because
no one can respond correctly to the item. Therefore, the difficulty
index of an item included on a test should be greater than 0 and
less than $+1$. Any given test should include items of varying
difficulty levels and most of the items should have a difficulty
index of around $+.5$, which means that one-half of the students
respond incorrectly.

The second item-analysis index important in the norm-
referenced test is the item-discrimination index, determined to
find out which items do the best job of differentiating among the
individuals who score highest and those who score lowest on a
test. To determine this index, the teacher must identify the high-
scoring groups and the low-scoring groups on the total exam.
Usually a teacher will attempt to determine the upper 27 percent
and the lower 27 percent of the students and use these two groups
to define the high scores and low scores on the exam. Thus the
test results from the individuals who scored in the middle 46
percent of the group are not used. The rationale behind this elimination of individuals is usually that the test does not do a good
job of differentiating among the individuals in the middle of the
distribution, and the differences in scores found among the middle
46 percent may be due to errors in measurement.

The item-discrimination index is defined as the number of individuals correctly responding in the upper 27 percent minus the
number of individuals correctly responding in the lower 27 percent. This quantity is divided by the number of individuals in
either the upper or the lower 27 percent of the group. The discrimination index calculated for an item can have a value somewhere between $+1$ and -1. If the discrimination index is $+1$, the
item does a perfect job of discriminating between high scorers and
low scorers. That is, all the students in the upper 27 percent got
the item correct and none of the students in the lower 27 percent
got the item correct. As long as the discrimination index is positive,
more people in the upper 27 percent than in the lower 27 percent
got the item correct. If the discrimination index is 0, then the same

number of people in both groups got the item correct or, in other words, the item does not discriminate between people who score higher and people who score lower. If the sign of the discrimination index is negative, the item is called a negative discriminator. That is, more people in the lower 27 percent than in the upper 27 percent got the item correct. If the discrimination index is −1, then all the people in the lower 27 percent got the item correct while no one in the upper 27 percent got the item correct.

Since a norm-referenced test is developed to discriminate among individuals who know more about a topic and individuals who know less, the discrimination index should not be 0. Likewise, the item should not be a negative discriminator. If the sign of the discrimination index is negative, the item is weighted in favor of the lower group. As with the difficulty index, it is not possible to set exact cut-off values that the discrimination index should achieve before an item is included in a test. However, the discrimination index of all items should be positive and most items should have a value of somewhere between +.3 and +.7.

$$\text{Item discrimination} = \frac{\begin{array}{l}\text{(number of correct responses in upper 27} \\ \text{percent)} - \text{(number of correct responses} \\ \text{in lower 27 percent)}\end{array}}{\text{number of people in upper 27 percent}}$$

Table 9.2 presents an example of how item-difficulty and discrimination indices could be calculated for six different test items. The test items themselves are not presented.

Criterion-referenced Tests

A criterion-referenced test is developed to determine whether the particular student can respond correctly to a particular item or task. Each student is compared with the task that is required of him by test item rather than with persons taking the test. The ability of a criterion-referenced test to discriminate between individuals knowing more and individuals knowing less is not important. The important issue is to determine whether the test item assesses what the teacher wants to have assessed. Although it may be important to have information about the overall general area, each individual item is important because each is a criterion. In the norm-referenced system it is important to study the individual items but overall it is most important for the entire test to be able to discriminate in the manner that the teacher wants it to

Table 9.2 *Item-Difficulty and Item-Discrimination Indices*

	TEST ITEM					
	1	2	3	4	5	6
Total number of responses to item	100	100	100	100	100	100
Number of individuals in						
Upper 27 percent	27	27	27	27	27	27
Lower 27 percent	27	27	27	27	27	27
Middle 46 percent	46	46	46	46	46	46
Number of correct responses in						
Upper 27 percent	27	13	27	14	12	20
Lower 27 percent	0	27	27	14	6	10
Middle 46 percent	0	40	46	4	8	25
Number of incorrect responses	73	20	0	68	74	45
Item-discrimination index: $\dfrac{\text{correct upper 27\% } - \text{ correct lower 27\%}}{\text{number in upper 27\%}}$	$\dfrac{27-0}{27}=1.0$	$\dfrac{13-27}{27}=-.52$	$\dfrac{27-27}{27}=0$	$\dfrac{14-14}{27}=0$	$\dfrac{12-6}{27}=.22$	$\dfrac{20-10}{27}=.37$
Item-difficulty index: $\dfrac{\text{number correct}}{\text{total number of responses}}$	$\dfrac{27}{100}=.27$	$\dfrac{80}{100}=.80$	$\dfrac{100}{100}=1.0$	$\dfrac{32}{100}=.32$	$\dfrac{26}{100}=.26$	$\dfrac{55}{100}=.55$

differentiate. With respect to criterion-referenced tests, the standards for judging a test are related primarily to judging the individual item.

Validity

The first standard for the criterion-referenced test is the validity of the item. This is by far the most important standard with which the teacher should be concerned. For the criterion-referenced test to have real meaning in the classroom, each item must possess content validity, and this can be determined only by the individual who is going to use the test results.

It is also important for the teacher to attempt to assess the concurrent validity of the paper and pencil measure that she has developed. For example, in an attitude test in which the individual is asked to express his attitude toward drugs, one question might ask the student what he would do if he knew of a fellow student who was using drugs. A student asked this particular question would undoubtedly be given the opportunity to respond in any manner that he felt appropriate. The hope might be that the individual would indicate in his response how he would act if he were in an environment in which one of his friends was using drugs. If after judging subjectively from observation the teacher decides that individuals are responding to the item in a manner different from how they would behave in a real environment, then the test item has no real value. This form of concurrent validity places a great deal of responsibility on the teacher, but the teacher has daily contact with the students and is able to observe them in a variety of settings. The primary purpose of the criterion-referenced test is to assess how an individual would respond in real life. If the responses to an item are not similar to actual observed behavior, then we should not accept the results from that single item given at a single time under a single set of circumstances.

Reliability

Split-halves reliability and test-retest reliability seem to have no place in the criterion-referenced system, because they are concerned with a student having the same relative position in two different distributions of scores. This type of reliability implies comparing the individuals against each other. In the criterion-referenced system, students are compared not against each other but only against the test item itself. Therefore, the idea of maintaining the same relative rank with respect to some known group has no meaning in the criterion-referenced system. The only type of reliability or consistency measure that may be of major importance to the teacher who has developed a criterion-referenced test occurs when an individual responds correctly to an item at the first administration and incorrectly to the same item at a later time. If a student can respond correctly to an item today but not tomorrow, then it is not a good item or an error in measurement has occurred. If there is an indication that individuals can respond correctly to an item at one time but not at another, then it would seem that the item is not reliable. In the criterion-referenced system it is assumed that if an individual correctly responds to the item he knows the concept that is being examined. If this consistency does not hold over repeated testing periods, then the assumption of knowledge of the concept cannot be maintained. The consistency that the teacher looks for in a criterion-referenced system is the consistency of correct response on repeated administrations of one item.

The concept of consistency does not pertain to individuals who initially respond incorrectly to an item. It may be that between administrations the individual has gained information that would help him answer the question. The consistency that is looked for in a criterion-referenced test relates only to whether an individual who has responded correctly once can do so again. Of course, one must be careful to examine the item for clues of test-wiseness that could allow an individual to respond correctly each time he sees it without possessing the skill. That is, it is possible to get highly consistent results but still have invalid results.

Usability

In the criterion-referenced system, usability and reliability are similar. The major concern in usability is to determine whether a student who responds correctly knows the material that is basic to the item responded to. If an individual responds incorrectly to an item at one time and correctly another, does this mean that the individual has learned the material that relates to the item during the interim or does it mean that the individual has learned or gained from the practice of having previously answered the item? In other words, can he respond correctly to the item without understanding the concept? The teacher can assess this possibility by requiring a student to respond to more than one item designed to assess the same information. The usability of the results depends on the assumption that when an individual responds correctly he understands the concept behind the item. If this assumption cannot be defended, then the results from the criterion-referenced test are not usable.

Item Analysis

Item-analysis procedure with a criterion-referenced test is different from that of a norm-referenced test. There is no need to determine the item-discrimination index for a criterion-referenced test, because the items are developd to discriminate only between individuals who can and cannot answer an item correctly. Therefore, the discrimination index of an item has no relevance in the criterion-referenced system. Of importance to the teacher would be how difficult a particular item is. Rather than call this the item-difficulty of the test item, we would prefer to call it the criterion-difficulty of the test item, because the item itself is the criterion. The criterion-difficulty is the number of individuals who respond incorrectly to an item divided by the total number of individuals who respond. This is the percentage of students who respond incorrectly to a test item. As the criterion-difficulty index approaches 1, the majority of the individuals are unable to answer the item and therefore do not understand the information. As this ratio approaches 0, the majority of the individuals responding to the item understand the concepts underlying the item and are responding correctly.

The teacher can interpret this criterion difficulty in a way that would determine how much more time should be spent in class on a given topic or which students require individual help on the particular content covered by the test item. Criterion-difficulty can be an extremely useful standard for the teacher when it comes to interpreting what to do with test results. An example of the criterion-difficulty index is found in Table 9.3, which gives the results of how ten individuals responded to six items. One indicates that the individual responded correctly to the item; 0 indicates that the individual did not so respond. Criterion-difficulty is determined by dividing the number of zeros for each item by the number of individuals who responded to the item, and in the example the number of individuals responding is ten.

In Table 9.3, item 6 has a criterion-difficulty index of 1. This should indicate to the teacher that an item has been included to which none of the students is able to respond correctly. Given this information, the teacher will first re-examine the item to make sure that it asks the question that was intended. Then the teacher must re-evaluate the presentation of this topic and consider alternative ways of presenting it in the future in a way such that the students can comprehend the content.

The other criterion-difficulty indices in Table 9.3 indicate that some students have attained the criterion and others have not. The teacher can use this information to advantage. For example, item 5 has a criterion-difficulty index of only .1. This means that only one student missed the item. Perhaps the teacher should work with this student individually on the content covered by item 5. On the other hand, item 3 has an index of .7. This indicates that 70 percent of the students taking the test missed it. Perhaps the teacher should plan to work with this 70 percent, providing some other task for the 30 percent who responded correctly.

Observation Data

The standards that must be used in determining whether observation data is meaningful are the same as must be used in judging internally developed tests. First, a teacher must be concerned about the content validity of the observations being made. A

Table 9.3   *Criterion-Difficulty Index*

STUDENT	ITEM RESPONSES					
	1	2	3	4	5	6
A	1	0	0	1	0	0
B	0	1	1	1	1	0
C	0	1	1	0	1	0
D	1	1	0	1	1	0
E	1	1	0	0	1	0
F	1	1	0	1	1	0
G	0	1	0	0	1	0
H	1	1	0	1	1	0
I	1	1	0	0	1	0
J	1	0	1	1	1	0
Correct Total	7	8	3	6	9	0
Criterion difficulty	.3	.2	.7	.4	.1	1

high degree of content validity can be obtained by specifically defining the behavior to be observed. Table 9.4 reports the observation of four kinds of behavior: daydreaming, active listening, passive listening, and speaking to topic. For the observation data to be meaningful, the teacher must have specifically defined these and have become convinced that they can be adequately differentiated. In addition, the teacher must define specifically the stimuli to be observed in connection with this behavior. This can be checked by employing more than one rater for an occasion. If the behavior is adequately defined, the raters should agree in their observations.

Determination of the reliability of the observation data requires at least two ratings of the same behavior. These generally result from two different observers of the same activity. It is possible for a teacher to serve as his own second rater if he has access to audio or video tape, depending on the behavior being observed. The teacher can tape the activity while observations are in progress. Later the same behavior can be observed a second time by listening to or viewing the tape. If a second rater is not available or if the activity cannot be taped, there seems to be no way to check on the reliability of observation data.

Table 9.4 presents data from two raters who have observed the same children for twelve different time periods in four specific types of behavior. The results indicate that the raters do not in all instances agree on what they were observing. One way of defining rater reliability is to divide the number of agreements of ratings by the number of potential agreements. In this example, there are sixteen possible times when the individuals could have agreed and only eight times in which they actually were in agreement. Therefore, the rater reliability for this example is .50. It is not at all uncommon for individuals to expect the rater reliability to be above .85. High rater reliability implies that the two raters saw the same things and that it is fairly certain that the observations of the one rater are consistent with the observations of the second rater.

In Table 9.4 we have gone a step further in our assessment of reliability. Because it expresses a rather poor rater reliability, we decided to determine the rater reliability with respect to each behavior. In this situation we defined the number of potential agreements as the total number of times either of the two raters indicated that a particular behavior was occurring. For instance,

one or the other of the raters indicated that daydreaming was occurring. At time segment 2, only the second rater felt this was
occurring. At time segment 7, only the first rater felt this was
occurring. These are two occasions on which they did not agree.
At time segments 5 and 8 they did agree that daydreaming was
occuring; therefore, the reliability index for daydreaming is 2
over 4 or .50. In observing the data for the different behavior in
Table 9.4, the only rating reliability that is acceptable is the rater
reliability on "speaking to topic." This would be expected because it is the most observable behavior of the four that are listed.
  Usability and observational analysis procedures are interrelated.
Suppose that a teacher would like to find out what stimuli are
creating certain behavior in the classroom. It might be that the
teacher wants to find out why an individual has begun daydreaming. This information cannot be obtained from the data
reported in Table 9.4, because the stimuli present during daydreaming are not indicated in the table. If they were, the teacher

Table 9.4 *Behavior Observation Data*

	DAYDREAMING		ACTIVE LISTENING		PASSIVE LISTENING		SPEAKING TO TOPIC	
Raters	1	2	1	2	1	2	1	2
Time segment								
1							1	1
2		1			1			
3			1	1				
4					1	1		
5	1	1						
6							1	1
7	1				1			
8	1	1						
9			1	1				
10				1	1			
11			1			1		
12					1	1		

Rater reliability $= \dfrac{\text{number of agreements}}{\text{number of potential agreements}} = \frac{8}{16} = .50$

Rater reliability per behavior
  Daydreaming $= \frac{2}{4} = .50$
  Active listening $= \frac{2}{4} = .50$
  Passive listening $= \frac{2}{6} = .33$
  Speaking to topic $= \frac{2}{2} = 1.0$

might find that the student began to daydream when students began making presentations in class. If this were observed in the data, then the teacher might be able to assist the student in overcoming his daydreaming problem.

Although it is not reported in Table 9.4, sometimes the teacher has defined specific behaviors and then does not observe them over a fairly lengthy time period. For instance, a teacher might wish to observe fighting within the classroom but over an extended time she observes none. Close observation may reveal a more subtle type of distraction however. Children may be distracted by sounds. If such behavior occurs but fighting does not, then the teacher may have selected the wrong behavior to observe. In observing results from a data summary, the teacher should always be cognizant of the fact that, if certain behavior is not being observed, then it may not be important to the particular classroom environment. The teacher may want to redefine the behavior to be observed.

The standards employed for internal measures are the same as those for external measures. The importance of standards for internal measures depends on the uses to which test results are to be put and the particular reference system to be employed in the interpretation of data. Similar standards can be employed with observation data. At all times, the teacher must remember that the attempt is to obtain data that will help children learn more effectively and efficiently.

Reflections

1. Items are selected to be included in an internally developed test primarily on the basis of content validity. In the norm-referenced testing, an item is selected according to its ability to discriminate between the high- and low-scoring students.
2. The most important type of validity for an internally developed measure is content validity. In many instances concurrent validity is beneficial if the appropriate concurrent criterion can be obtained.
3. The most common types of reliability obtained for norm-referenced internal testing are test-retest and split-halves reliability coefficients.
4. The appropriate item analysis indexes to use with norm-referenced testing are item-difficulty and item-discrimination.

5. In criterion-referenced testing, the appropriate item index is the criterion-difficulty index.
6. Consistency in observation data can be checked if more than one rater is rating the behavior or if audio or video tapes are made of the observation time period that enable the teacher to rate the same situation more than once.

Exercises

1. Determine the validity of the instrument that you developed in Chapter 8. Prepare a written defense for its validity.
2. Provide evidence that the instrument you developed is reliable.
3. Explain how the results from your instrument can be used to assess some objectives for the class.

Selected References

VALIDITY

See references in Chapter 4.

RELIABILITY

See references in Chapter 4.

ITEM ANALYSIS

Ebel, R. L. *Essentials of Educational Measurement.* Englewood Cliffs, N. J.: Prentice-Hall, 1972. Pp. 383–406. The author presents a thorough discussion of item analysis, the index of difficulty, and the index of discrimination and how they can aid in item selection and revision.

Gronlund N. E. *Measurement and Evaluation in Teaching.* New York: Macmillan, 1971. Pp. 250–56. Item-analysis procedure, interprettation and estimation of item difficulty, and item discrimination are demonstrated.

Remmers, H. H., N. L. Gage, and J. F. Rummel. *A Practical Introduction to Measurement and Evaluation.* New York: Harper & Row, 1965. Pp. 267–68. Gives a very brief discussion of item analysis, item difficulty, and item discrimination. An outline for making a simple item analysis is included.

Stodola, Q., and K. Stordahl. *Basic Educational Tests and Measurement.* Chicago: Science Research Associates, 1967. Pp. 26–30. The authors present a clear discussion of item difficulty and item discrimination.

Part Four

Application in the Schools

10

Schoolwide Testing Program

CONCERNS

1. What is a schoolwide testing program?
2. What are the purposes of a schoolwide testing program?
3. Who should be responsible for a schoolwide testing program?
4. What are the steps in organizing a schoolwide testing program?
5. How often should there be schoolwide testing?
6. When should tests be administered during the school year?
7. How should test results be reported to teachers, parents, students, and the public?
8. How does a schoolwide testing program provide for flexibility?

In each of the preceding chapters, a specific aspect of measurement has been discussed. It is necessary now to examine the development of an overall testing program for a school system. A schoolwide testing program requires that external and internal tests be administered to defined groups of students at specified times in a specified manner. The purpose of such standardized administration is to gain information about the status of the defined groups of students. In other words, a schoolwide testing program is an established procedure for assessing how the students in the school system are progressing in cognitive and noncognitive areas.

Example 10.1 presents an example of a schoolwide testing program taken from a recommendation made to a school district by a testing consultant from a publishing company. We are not necessarily suggesting that this is an appropriate testing program for a school system; that decision can be made only within the context of a particular school system.

Example 10.1   *A Hypothetical Schoolwide Testing Program*

Kindergarten   Cognitive Abilities Test for determining general educational readiness

Grade 1   Spring testing using level 7 of the Iowa Tests of Basic Skills Primary Battery (Spring 1972)

Grade 2.   Spring administration of the Iowa Tests of Basic Skills Primary Battery level 8

Grade 3   Fall administration of the Iowa Tests of Basic Skills, multilevel edition, levels format. Administration at midyear of the Cognitive Abilities Test, multi-level edition, for determining student abilities in the cognitive areas measured by verbal, nonverbal, and quantitative items.

Grade 4   Fall administration of the Iowa Tests of Basic Skills to continue the program of continuous assessment of student progress in the basic skills of vocabulary, language arts, work-study skills, and mathematics

Grade 5   Fall administration of the Iowa Tests of Basic Skills; administration at midyear of the Cognitive Abilities Test to help identify

1.   Student abilities by teachers and counselors and scheduling students for middle schools.

2.   Students with high ability in one or more of the areas measured to better educate each student

Grade 6   Fall administration of the Iowa Tests of Basic Skills, levels edition, to continue to evaluate pupil growth in the basic skills and to further individualize instruction

Grade 7 Fall administration of the Iowa Tests of Basic Skills, levels edition; administration at midyear of the Cognitive Abilities Test. At this point, the Cognitive Abilities Test can be used to help teachers identify students who may not be achieving as strongly as might be expected in relation to their cognitive ability scores.

Grade 8 Fall administration of the Iowa Tests of Basic Skills to help evaluate the effects of different curricular emphases in middle and junior high schools

Grade 9 Fall administration of the Tests of Academic Progress to measure the effect of junior high school programs to evaluate student achievement in science, social studies, mathematics, reading, literature, and composition

Grade 10 Fall administration of the Cognitive Abilities Test for use by school counselors to aid students with educational and vocational choices and other educational decision-making procedures.

Grade 11 Fall administration of the Tests of Academic Progress to:

1. Determine what progress has been made by students in the areas measured by the Tests of Academic Progress
2. Compare the students with a national population to determine how well they are performing in the areas measured in comparison with the national student population
3. Help determine what effects curricular innovations have on student achievement in the areas measured by the Tests of Academic Progress

Optional testing of all students in Grades 10 and 12 with the Tests of Academic Progress for a K–12 yearly assessment program

Why Develop a Schoolwide Testing Program?

The question that must be answered before any attempt is made to develop a schoolwide testing program is "why?" Why would a school district ever want to institute such a testing program? The purpose of any schoolwide testing program is to provide teachers with data to help them make the learning environment better for the learner. A schoolwide testing program begins with the establishment of objectives and ends not with the administration of the selected tests but with the interpretation of the results in a meaningful way. The program can be considered successful only if it results in a teaching-learning environment that better meets the needs of the students. A schoolwide testing program that does not result in improvements in the learning environment must be considered unsuccessful.

A schoolwide testing program can provide information that serves several different capacities. First, it can help the teacher assess the quality of the school's curriculum. By examining the results of a test administration to students across the district at the same time, teacher's can determine whether students at various stages in their educational program possess the skills and knowledge they should possess at that point. Teachers can then determine whether the objectives of the curriculum are being met and whether the curriculum needs to be changed in any way.

A second use for data gathered from a schoolwide testing program is to help the teacher determine student weaknesses and strengths and plan individual activities accordingly. In other words, tests can provide diagnostic information. Most testing companies recognize this function of standardized tests and are able to provide teachers with the responses of each student to each item on their standardized tests.

A third purpose for schoolwide testing data is grouping students for instruction. If the students are administered an aptitude test, for example, the scores may be used to assign students to accelerated instructional programs, to remedial programs, or to the typical instructional program. Such decisions should not be made solely on the basis of a single test score. One would more appropriately combine the results of an aptitude test, an achievement test, a grade point average, and the judgment of the teacher in deciding the instructional program to which a student should be assigned.

The schoolwide testing program can also be used to determine the satisfaction of students with the school by including some type of attitude measure. This may have to be a paper and pencil attitude measure if it is to be applied across the entire school system. Such measures have limitations, as we have discussed previously, but the results can be helpful in determining to some degree how students feel about the school in general and also about specific aspects of the school's program.

Finally, schoolwide testing data can be used to inform parents and other members of the community how well students are doing in the school program. Because the community is responsible for the school, it has the right to be informed of its success. One way of providing this information is through data gathered from a schoolwide testing program, presented in a meaningful way. The school should be certain that the members of the community will interpret the data correctly and the manner in which data is reported is critical.

The data gathered through schoolwide testing should be only one source of information for evaluation. Testing is a procedure for providing information that confirms or denies the daily observations of the classroom teacher. Schoolwide testing programs are not always viewed as providing one component of the evaluation system of a school system. Teachers often complain that administrators use the results of standardized tests to evaluate the teachers as well. That is, standardized test results are sometimes viewed as being the only information necessary for evaluating a teacher, a teaching process, or a student. Such practice is a gross misuse of standardized test results. Each test score contains an error component and many factors other than the learning that takes place in a classroom may affect scores. A student could perform poorly in a particular content area not because his present teacher is not doing a good job but because a former teacher did a poor job. Thus it is an error to judge the quality of a teacher, a teaching procedure, or a student solely on the basis of the results of a single test administration.

Responsibility for the Schoolwide Testing Program

Once a school system has decided that it needs a testing program and has established its general purposes, it is necessary to consider who is responsible for it. Since the basic purpose of a schoolwide testing program is to gather information to help in improving the educational program, the major responsibility must lie with the teachers. We would recommend that a school system interested in establishing a schoolwide testing program consider establishing a committee of teachers and administrators to define the standardized tests to be used, determine what internal measures must be developed and who should develop them, approve internally developed measures, determine when tests should be administered, establish that the staff is prepared to administer and interpret the results of the testing program correctly. Thus, such a committee should be responsible for all aspects of the testing program. Teachers and administrators have responsibilities other than testing that require most of their time and attention. If the testing program is to be successful, therefore, it is imperative that an individual be available whose major responsibility is to oversee the testing program effectively. The testing director, then, helps the testing committee reach its decisions. He should not make such major decisions as what standardized tests will be used or when the tests will be administered. He can make recommendations, but the responsibility for what tests will be used and other major decisions should lie with the teachers through the testing committee. The testing director should be responsible for carrying out the committee's mandates. Specifically, the testing director should have expertise in measurement. The testing committee should be able to turn to him for advice and assistance in making the major decisions for which they are responsible. He should also be responsible for seeing that the decisions and policies established by the testing committee are carried out.

Steps for Organizing the Schoolwide Testing Program

Establishing Objectives

After the testing committee has been established and a test director has been selected, the testing program must be organized. The first step is to establish the specific objectives of the schoolwide testing program. To do this, the testing committee must be familiar with the curriculum. Only by knowing the general emphasis or lack of emphasis of the curriculum at each instructional level can the committee determine where data gathered through a testing program could be helpful. For example, a reading readiness test may be appropriate in kindergarten if students begin to learn to read in kindergarten. It would make no sense to administer a reading readiness test to third graders in such case.

The specific objectives will help the committee establish a number of other important aspects of the testing program, including the types of test to be administered. For example, if the objective refers to what a student has already learned, an achievement test would be needed. If the objective refers to future accomplishment, an aptitude test may be appropriate. Or an attitude measure may be necessary for an objective that refers to assessment of feelings.

The testing committee decides the specific tests to be used. Here the testing director should be able to indicate which objectives can be achieved through externally and which through internally developed tests. If several external tests are available for a single objective, the testing committee will have to apply the standards for judging external tests discussed in Chapter 4. If a test must be developed internally, the testing committee must determine who should develop it. Once the test has been developed, the standards for judging an internal measure discussed in Chapter 9 will then have to be applied by the testing committee to determine the appropriateness of the test.

The specific objectives will also help the committee determine how often and at what time of the school year tests should be administered. For example, if one objective is to provide diagnostic information for the teachers to use in working with individual students, a test may have to be administered each year in order to provide current information. This objective of providing diagnostic information would probably also dictate that the appropriate test be administered in the fall of the year so that the information will be available to each student's present teacher. Another objective may be to determine the student attitudes toward school. This might require that an attitude assessment be made yearly, but, since summer vacation may affect a student's attitude toward school, it may be necessary to administer the test near the middle of the school year.

Establishing Test Administration Procedures

Once the objectives of the program have been established, the appropriate tests selected and developed, and the times of administration determined, the testing committee must establish a schoolwide testing procedure. There must be planning sessions with the teachers as to how the instruments are to be administered. The planning session should emphasize that during administration of an exam, all the teacher's attention should be directed toward the testing environment. The teacher should also become aware of the importance of the time limit that may be placed on some of the tests. The teachers should be briefed as to how they should deal with interruptions in the testing schedule. All this should be planned so that each testing session goes as smoothly as possible.

It might be appropriate for the review committee to determine whether students should experience practice test sessions in the classroom. The purpose of this would be to give students exposure to the types of items and the directions used in the test. This is not teaching toward the test; it is making students aware of testing conditions. This procedure can be incorporated into a regular school curriculum by giving students an opportunity to respond to items from an old test similar to the new ones. Preparation for taking the test can be discussed in class. Preparation procedures seem to be important, because many research studies have indicated that there may very well be a practice effect in testing situations. That is, students who have experience with a particular type of test tend to score higher than students who do not have such experience. Providing all students with practice would help to control this phenomenon.

One other very important arrangement must be made before test administration. Teachers must make the students aware of how the tests are to be used. One variable that affects the students performance is motivation to do well. Highly motivated students generally perform better than poorly motivated students. One way of promoting motivation to perform well on a test is to make sure that individual students are aware of the way in which the test results are to be used. It might be appropriate for a teacher to provide several examples of how the test results will be used to improve the teaching-learning environment for a particular student. Students who realize that the results will be used to help them tend to be more highly motivated in taking tests.

Establishing Methods for Reporting Test Results

Another step in organizing the schoolwide testing program is to determine the reporting procedures for the teacher, public, parents, and students. It is most important that the teacher receive from the testing program all results that relate to her classroom and all individuals within it. If the results of a testing program cannot be received by teachers, then the tests should not be used as an evaluation instrument. Therefore, it is imperative that the teacher be given results that relate to all the individuals in a classroom. If some of the instruments are to be used as criterion-referenced instruments, then the responses to each item must be made available to the teacher. If norm-referenced testing is part of the testing program, then the teacher must be provided with the norms. If local norms have been developed, these should be provided along with national norms.

Of major importance to the teacher is the receipt of a cumulative profile of how each student has performed on previous administrations of tests related to the content covered by the most recent test. This cumulative profile can indicate the student's progress or growth in a particular area. This is probably the most meaningful information that can be provided as long as the teacher realizes that such data is frequently unrealistic and interprets accordingly.

The testing committee should be extremely careful in reporting schoolwide testing results to the public. In general the public does not have the expertise to interpret the test results. Moreover, the mode of communication relied on by the general public is usually the newspaper, where brevity often seems as important as content but tends to produce reports that fail to indicate why tests are used. The testing committee must be careful to make sure that information given the public is thoroughly explained in language appropriate for that public. Graphic representations of data can be extremely helpful and so can reporting the percentage of students who correctly respond to each item. When norms are to be reported, it is imperative that the school testing program inform the lay reader that norms are not standards against which to make judgments but that they simply provide information that describes a particular group and that individual students may be compared against that group. It is of utmost importance that in reporting results to the public mean composite scores must be accompanied by information that describes how students distribute themselves about the score scale. The use of a single score to represent an entire class may have little meaning to the public or, even worse, the public may misinterpret the single score. Therefore, it is an important responsibility of the schoolwide testing program committee to be sure that the information that the public receives thoroughly describes the entire school program and not just score averages. It is better not to report at all than to try to avoid confusion and misunderstanding by writing reports that are too brief.

In reporting to parents, information must be comparative in nature—that is, a child's test results should be compared with his previous results so that parents can be made aware of the amount of growth that the child may have accomplished in selected areas. This type of reporting can be made with graphic representations of expected gain together with analyses of growth patterns. The child's performance is thus used as his own reference. It is important to note that not all children grow at the same rate and that it is more meaningful to parents to show precisely in what ways the child is growing.

If criterion-referenced systems are employed, then longer time periods should be used in reporting results to parents. They should be allowed to see the items their children responded to correctly and incorrectly and should be allowed to indicate whether they think the items are meaningful. In this way, the teacher can gain information about the parents' expectations for the school. But to do this the teachers must provide information either in carefully written form or as a detailed oral explanation. This usually takes more than a fifteen-minute conference allows.

It is very important that test results be reported to students as quickly as possible. In general, we believe that students should receive not numerical values as a result of a test but information similar to that given to their parents. The information should be graphic and should indicate to the student how much he has grown since the last testing period in the areas evaluated by the test. The student should realize that he is being compared against himself, and in most cases he will be able to show some growth. Test results reported in this manner can help a student evaluate himself. In discussing test items with the individual student, the teacher can decide whether he does not understand concepts or actually understands the information but simply made errors in responding. This takes a great deal of time but if tests are to be used as tools for the teacher and the student, it is important that the students be given as much opportunity as the teacher to react to the results.

Establishing Auxiliary Testing Procedures

Finally, the testing committee must determine procedures for auxiliary testing that might occur after the original testing period. The need for auxiliary testing periods occurs when observed schoolwide testing program results do not coincide with the daily observations of the teachers. This could very well indicate that the standardized test results are not appropriate and that other assessment should be made. Auxiliary tests may be parallel forms of the original test or other newly designed tests or even the same test administered again in a different setting. Such auxiliary testing should benefit the teacher in reassessment of judgments.

We are not suggesting that all students participate in all auxiliary testing programs. Such programs should be available for the purpose of gaining more information but this will not necessarily be required for all children. Some research studies have reported that only 25 percent of students need participate in auxiliary testing sessions. It is nevertheless a very important aspect of schoolwide testing.

The assumption underlying this chapter is that a schoolwide testing program must be based on the curriculum and objectives of each school system. Once objectives have been designated, it is the responsibility of the testing committee to select the instruments and prepare the teachers to administer them. Students also should be prepared to take the internally and externally developed tests. This preparation is intended to help motivate students to perform as well as they are able. The purpose of the testing program is to find out what the students know and to identify the students who are motivated; this provides realistic information about those who are not.

A testing program does not end with the administration of the test and the reporting of scores to the schools. This is really the beginning of the effective use of a schoolwide testing program. When the results have been reported to the teacher, then the process of interpretation begins. In making interpretations, the teacher can modify the students' environment to help them develop a better understanding for the objectives inherent in the testing program. If the teacher is not provided with the opportunity to critically evaluate results and report them to significant individuals in the student's learning environment, then we must question the need for a testing program in the first place. The process of discussing the results with the teachers, parents, and, in particular, students, is basic to a good schoolwide testing program. If the tests are not used for improving the learning environment for the people in the school setting, then a schoolwide testing program should not be established.

Reflections

1. A schoolwide testing program is an established procedure for assessing how the students in the school system are progressing in cognitive annd noncognitive areas.
2. Various purposes of a schoolwide testing program are to help:

a. assess the quality of the curriculum
b. assess the strengths and weaknesses of the students
c. group students
d. determine the students' attitudes toward the teaching and learning environment
e. inform the general public as to how well students are doing in the school program

3. The major responsibility for the schoolwide testing program lies with the teachers in the system.
4. The steps in developing a schoolwide testing program are:
   a. establish specific objectives
   b. select or develop the appropriate instruments
   c. establish a procedure for administering the testing program
   d. establish a planning session for all teachers in order to have a standard administration procedure
   e. establish the procedures for reporting results to all significant individuals
   f. determine procedures for an auxiliary testing program.
5. The objectives of a schoolwide testing program designate how often testing on a schoolwide basis should occur.
6. The objectives of the testing program and specifically how the results are to be used designate when testing should occur during the year.
7. Test results should be reported to individuals only when the teacher or other educators have had the opportunity to be sure that the limitations of the interpretation are explained in detail.
8. The auxiliary testing program provides flexibility to the schoolwide testing program.

Exercises

1. Review Example 10.1. Based on your experiences in this class, add or delete any standardized instruments that you believe are necessary for a schoolwide testing program.
2. Determine whether attitude measures should be used in a schoolwide program. If attitude measures are to be obtained, determine when the information should be collected.
3. Determine the most appropriate time for collecting the desired information from a schoolwide testing program.

4. How should the test results be used? Provide evidence that the amount of time spent on the testing program will be beneficial to the students and the school system as a whole.
5. For each test administered, indicate to whom and how the results will be reported.
6. Select a particular content area (for example, math) and set up a possible testing program for the school system. Be sure to describe the intent of the program and how the results from throughout the system can be used.

Selected References

SCHOOLWIDE TESTING

Ebel, R. L. *Essentials of Educational Measurement.* Englewood Cliffs, N. J.: Prentice-Hall, 1972. Pp. 531–43. Presents the problems and characteristics of testing programs designed for improvement of learning, selective admission, scholarship awards and certification of competence.

Noll, V. H., and D. P. Scannell. *Introduction to Educational Measurement.* Boston: Houghton Mifflin, 1972. Pp. 466–508. The planning of a measurement program is analyzed. Two illustrations of actual measurement programs are given.

Remmers, H. H., N. L. Gage, and J. F. Rummel. *A Practical Introduction to Measurement and Evaluation.* New York: Harper & Row, 1965. Pp. 83–115. The authors give a detailed account of the problems involved in the organization, development, and administration of a school evaluation program.

Thorndike, R. L., and E. Hagen. *Measurement and Evaluation in Psychology and Education.* New York: Wiley, 1961. Pp. 444–83. Discuss local testing programs and desirable qualities in such programs and the planning, administering, and reporting of results. It also includes tables and graphs illustrating interpretation of results.

PROFILES

Nunnally, J. C. *Educational Measurement and Evaluation.* New York: McGraw-Hill, 1972. Pp. 72–76. The characteristics and interpretation of score profiles are considered in this section.

Remmers, H. H., N. L. Gage, and J. F. Rummel. *A Practical Introduction to Measurement and Evaluation.* New York: Harper & Row, 1965. Pp. 164–76. Gives an example of how to use test results in counseling. A number of different types of score profiles and their interpretations are also presented.

Stanley, J. C., and K. D. Hopkins. *Educational and Psychological Measurement and Evaluation.* Englewood Cliffs, N. J.: Prentice-Hall, 1972. Pp. 93–97. Illustrations of profile charts are used and explained. Also ten principles concerning test score interpretation are listed.

Stodola, Q., and K. Stordahl. *Basic Educational Tests and Measurement.* Chicago: Science Research Associates, 1967. Pp. 278–80. A brief introduction to reading-test profiles is given through examples.

TEST SCORE REPORTING

Durost, W. N., and G. A. Prescott. *Essentials of Measurement for Teachers.* New York: Harcourt Brace Jovanovich, 1962. Pp. 108–17. How and how much parents should be told about test results are discussed.

Goslin, D. A. *Teachers and Testing.* New York: Russell Sage Foundation, 1967. Pp. 25–32. Some school policies and teacher practices concerning score reporting are presented.

McFarland, S. J., and C. F. Hereford, eds. *Statistics and Measurement in the Classroom.* Dubuque: Brown, 1971. Pp. 225–32. This article deals with what parents should know about test results. The idea of interpreting results in a verbal rather than numerical manner is presented.

Stodola, Q., and K. Stordahl. *Basic Educational Tests and Measurement.* Chicago: Science Research Associates, 1967. Pp. 286–93. Gives some practical methods of presenting test scores so that they can be easily understood.

11

Evaluating a School System

Why Evaluate a School System?

In the first chapter of this text, educational evaluation was defined as the process of delineating, obtaining, and providing useful information for judging decision alternatives. The purpose of evaluating a school system is to determine whether its educational programs meet the requirements set forth by the objectives established for them. If the objectives of the school system are not being met, changes must be made that will allow them to be met. Educational evaluations are necessary if a school system is to remain dynamic and adaptable to change. A major problem in conducting an overall school evaluation is to determine how the evaluation is to occur and what types of information must be collected to provide evidence that a school is or is not meeting the objectives that have been set forth for it.

When the general public asks for an evaluation of the school system, it does not necessarily expect there to be a single direct response that indicates that the system is or is not doing the job that they intend for it to do. As all teachers and administrators and most of the general public know, a school system is a conglomeration of a huge number of specialized curricula. It is possible that the science curriculum is successfully meeting its objectives but that the history curriculum is not. Students may be leaving high school with communication skills but little or no vocational skills. Such problems make it impossible for the school system to present to the public a single statement about the quality of its program based totally on objective data.

The educational community has developed procedures that will allow for gathering data about specific components of the school system. This information can then be used by the appropriate individuals in the evaluation of each specific component. It is hoped that the evaluation will allow for identification of the components that require change and those that are currently meeting their objectives successfully. The results of the evaluation of each component can be presented to the public to show how successful each component is in meeting its objectives.

Defining the Components of the School System

The procedure for defining the various components of the school system that must be evaluated begins with the statement of the general school objectives. These are usually provided by the school board as a representative of the public and provide the administration with a statement of the goals that the educational system is expected to accomplish. For example, one of the general objectives may be "to advance learning."

Once the general objectives have been defined, the professional educators assume the responsibility of defining the specific components of the general objectives. Quite obviously, a statement of specific objectives will have to be made in each content area and in each classroom. For example, "to advance learning" means two quite different things in mathematics and in English. Within mathematics, "to advance learning" means different things for a class in geometry and a class in algebra. In English, "to advance learning" means different things for a class in poetry and a class in grammar. It is the responsibility of the professional educators to determine what the general objective "to advance learning" means in each content area and within each of the specific classes in that content area. The delineation of the general objectives as specific objectives is necessary before measurement can enter into an educational evaluation.

In Figure 11.1, we have tried to show visually the process of moving from an overall school objective to the specific objectives of the individual classroom. The reader is cautioned that evaluation of specific objectives does not totally fill the requirements of an overall school evaluation. There are gaps in moving from specific objective evaluation to evaluating the overall objectives

Figure 11.1 *Hierarchy of Educational Objectives*

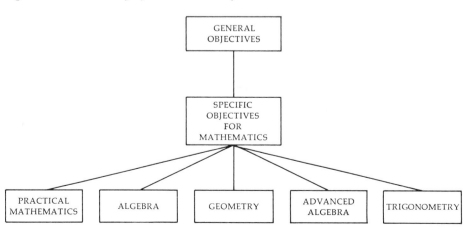

of the school system. It is the responsibility of the decision-makers to pool the information of the special components of the school system and to make subjective decisions as to whether the general school objectives are met. After a subjective decision has been made as to whether the general objectives have been met, then it is the responsibility of the decision-makers to determine whether in general the school is meeting its responsibility to the public. If it is not, they should determine which changes should be made to allow this responsibility to be fulfilled. The evaluation of a school system is a function of its components. The results of these components of evaluation are combined in a subjective manner to assess whether the system is meeting its general objectives.

Measurement in Evaluation

The role of measurement in educational evaluation can be described only after the educators within the school system have defined its specific objectives. In defining specific objectives, they also define the group of individuals and the type of behavior or knowledge to be assessed. This definition in turn determines the role of measurement in an educational evaluation. Until the specific objectives have been stated, the role of measurement in an educational evaluation is quite vague. As a result, measurement often provides information that is not useful.

Reference System

In stating specific objectives, educators must decide the type of reference system that should be employed in determining whether an objective is met. The objective must indicate whether a criterion-referenced system or a norm-referenced system is more appropriate for the concept of concern in the objective. A criterion-referenced system is designed to determine what behavior a student possesses at the particular time that a test is given or an observation is made. This type of reference system is appropriate when the particular terminal behavior that must be present at the time the test is given is specified in the objective.

In a norm-referenced system, information is obtained about how individuals who take the test compare to some norm group identified by the teacher as appropriate for the students in the particular classroom. This type of reference system is employed when the specific objectives indicate that the students are to be compared against each other or against some other known group. In the norm-referenced system, the concern of the objective must be related to how well an individual performs in comparison to others rather than with the specific traits the individual possesses.

The decision as to what types of reference systems are to be employed in the various evaluations must be made with respect to each component or specific objective. Most sound educational evaluations include objectives that call for both norm-referenced and criterion-referenced measurement. It is the responsibility of the teacher to decide which type of reference system is necessary to gain information that will assist in determining whether the school is meeting its intended goals.

External Measuring Devices

Once the behavior to be assessed has been defined in the objectives, it is necessary to determine the best way to obtain the information to be used in judging whether the objective has been met. The first source that an educator will probably look to is external measuring devices, tests developed by individuals outside the school that have been shown to be good measures of the behavior specified in the objectives. Such standardized tests usually have been developed by the major publishing houses.

To determine which external measuring devices are most appropriate for use in a particular educational evaluation, the educator must consider the validity and reliability of the instruments from which he may choose. One type of validity to consider is content validity. In assessing the content validity of a test, one must determine whether the behavior assessed by the test is one that the objectives indicate is of concern. Other types of validity are predictive validity, concurrent validity, and construct validity. Information as to the degree of each type of validity that a standardized test possesses is provided by the test publisher. A standardized test should never be selected for use without knowledge of the degree to which it possesses the type of validity of concern.

The three types of reliability of interest to an educator are test-retest reliability, equivalent-forms reliability, and internal consistency reliability. All these measures are attempts to determine whether a test consistently measures whatever it is measuring. The educator must determine from the objectives what types of reliability are of concern. The degree to which the test possesses that type of reliability must then be determined. As with validity, the test publisher provides this information in the test manual.

Another important consideration in selecting external tests relates to use of the test results. If results are not useful in relation to the objectives, then that test should not be selected. Test results must be interpretable in terms of the objectives being assessed. An external measuring device should provide scale scores that convert the raw scores on the test into meaningful indices that help the educator determine whether each of the specific objectives being assessed has been met. If the results are not useful, then the educator should not select that particular measuring device even though it is judged to be valid and reliable.

Internal Measuring Devices

If, after an extensive review of the external measuring devices available, the educator decides that no external tests assess the behavior of concern in an objective, the educator must turn to some other source for information. If external measures are not available to assist in providing information for the educational evaluation, then instruments must be developed by the individuals within the school system. This adds a new dimension to the problem of the educator, who must know how to construct internal measures that provide valid, reliable, and useful information.

To develop good tests the educator must set forth the specific objectives that the test is designed to assess. Next, the best item format for assessing each behavior included in the objectives must be determined. After the item format has been determined, the teacher develops and aggregates test items. An educator should be aware of the problems that exist in test development. The cautious educator knows that the criteria employed in judging external tests are appropriate for judging internal measures. There is little concern about the content validity of the test because the teacher who has made an assessment of external measures and found none of them to have the appropriate content validity must know what is to be assessed in the classroom. Therefore, the content validity of the internally developed test is usually not in question. Quite often the internally developed tests are criterion-referenced tests, and the content validity of the test is the most appropriate concern of the educator. If this is true, then the concept of reliability for external measures is not appropriate for the internal measure, because the internal measure assesses individuals in the class against the content of the item, whereas the external test compares individuals against other individuals and the test is intended to find out their different abilities. Another criterion to be employed with the use of internal measures is the usefulness of the data. If the individual who is going to use the data develops the test, the usability or interpretability of the test is usually not a major question.

Observational Techniques

Not all the information collected in an educational evaluation needs to be or should be collected from a test. Other procedures can be used. One is the collection of observations of what is occurring in the classroom or in the more general school environment. The teacher should be aware that most tests, whether external or internal, are developed for the purpose of assessing how the student will actually behave in a given environment. In collecting observational data, the actual environment can be observed and the effects of the environment on the individual can be isolated. By doing this the educator is collecting basic information as to how an individual will behave in a setting where the conditions of everyday life are present. Educational evaluation is not restricted to collecting test scores only. Other bits of data may be collected by observation, audio tape, video tape, general interviews, or expert opinion. This is particularly true if the evaluation includes more than just an assessment of cognitive knowledge. Since today's schools have been required to assume roles other than simply the presentation of factual information, the assessment of cognitive knowledge is not enough.

Once all the information has been collected by the measurement process, the impact of measurement on evaluation ends. As the reader will recall, educational evaluation and measurement assist the process of delineating, obtaining, and providing useful information for judging decision alternatives with respect to specific components of the entire school system. It is at this point that educational measurement ends. Educational evaluation does not end at this point. After information has been collected for the specific components of the school, it is the responsibility of the decision-makers to review the measurement data and determine whether general school objectives have been met.

In an educational evaluation, the combining of information from the special components of the school system usually provides some contradictory evidence for the decision-maker. For example, the decision-maker may find that all the objectives in reading are being met in only three of five schools in a particular school system. This type of specific component evaluation allows the decision-maker the opportunity to institute changes in the unsuccessful schools while leaving the successful schools unchanged.

If individuals view the measurement process to be the same as the educational evaluation process, then they will be evaluating only certain components of a school system. Usually this responsibility is left to the professional educators; they must determine whether the special components are being met. If they are not being met, then the professional educator can modify the system. This is not the evaluation that the general public is concerned with. The general public is concerned with the overall role of the educational institution in the community. To make the type of educational evaluation that is needed by the public, educators must use the measurement process to assess special components of the school system. The decision-makers must determine whether with this information and knowledge of the special components of the program, we can firmly state that the educational institution is meeting its responsibility to the community.

Measurement is not the same as evaluation. Measurement is the process through which useful data may be gathered for evaluation. This information is combined with information obtained in other ways to allow the decision-maker to judge the most appropriate decision alternative. Measurement involves the gathering of useful data. Evaluation requires the combination of data and judgments as to what alternative should be taken in determining future actions.

Reflections

1. The purpose of evaluation is to improve the educational environment for students.
2. Evaluation is the process of delineating, obtaining, and providing useful information for judging decision alternatives.
3. Specific objectives delineate the information to be gathered for the educational evaluation and set the criteria for judging the success of a program.
4. If the information gathered from the measurement process is valid, reliable, and interpretable with respect to the objectives, it is useful.
5. Information for educational evaluation can be collected through internally or externally developed tests or through systematic collection of observational data.
6. Measurement gathers and provides useful data. Evaluation indicates whether, and if so where, efforts need to be made to improve an educational program.

Exercises

Throughout the class you have been reviewing class objectives and developing and administering measuring devices that relate to the class objectives. Review this information and write an evaluation report of this class. Provide supporting evidence for your evaluation statements.

Selected References

MEASUREMENT AND EVALUATION

Noll, V. H., and D. P. Scannell. *Introduction to Educational Measurement.* Boston: Houghton Mifflin, 1972. Pp. 20–44. An interesting historical presentation is given of the development of measurement and evaluation from the 1900's to the present.

Remmers, H. H., N. L. Gage, and J. F. Rummel. *A Practical Introduction to Measurement and Evaluation.* New York: Harper & Row, 1965. Chapter 2. Some of the purposes of evaluation are briefly described.

Stanley, J. C. *Measurement in Today's Schools.* Englewood Cliffs, N. J.: Prentice-Hall, 1964. Chap. 2. The author reviews the development of the scientific movement in education with emphasis on measurement.

ACCOUNTABILITY

Nash, R. J. "Accountability: The Next Deadly Nostrum in Education." *School and Society,* 99 (1971), 501–04. Discusses the problems inherent in accountability and advises careful examination of the whole idea.

Greenfield, T. B. "Developing Accountability in School Systems." *Education Canada,* 12 (1972), 21–29. The reasons behind the accountability movement are related and a definition of accountability along with guidelines for achieving it are given.

"Teacher Accountability." *Nations Schools,* 89 (1972), 45–68. A compendium of articles is presented. They explore the many facets of the accountability movement.

DEFINING RESPONSIBILITIES

See references in Chapter 1.

NEEDS ASSESSMENT

Crowson, R. L., and T. P. Wilbur. "Purposes of the Michigan Assessment of Education," in F. J. Sciara and R. K. Jantz, *Accountability in American Education.* Boston: Allyn and Bacon, 1972. Pp. 387–97. The authors examine the rationale of assessment and the specific purposes of the Michigan Assessment Program.

Womer, F. B. "National Assessment of Educational Progress," in F. J. Sciara and R. K. Jantz, *Accountability in American Education.* Boston: Allyn and Bacon, 1972. Pp. 26–38. National assessment and its purposes and model are thoroughly discussed.

Appendices

Appendix A

Selected Test Publishers Directory

Other publishers not listed here are in Buros' *Seventh Mental Measurements Yearbook.*

AVA Publications, Inc., 11 Dorrance St., Providence, R.I. 02903

American Guidance Service, Inc., Publishers' Building, Circle Pines, Minn. 55014

American Language Institute, Georgetown University, 3605 O St. N.W., Washington, D.C. 20007

American Printing House for the Blind, 1139 Frankfort Ave., Louisville, Ky. 40206

Behavioral Publications, Inc., 2852 Broadway, New York, N.Y. 10025

Behavioral Sciences, Inc., 3000 Sand Hill Road, Menlo Park, Calif. 94025

Bureau of Educational Research and Service, University of Iowa, Iowa City, Iowa 52240

CTB/McGraw-Hill, Del Monte Research Park, Monterey, Calif. 93940

College Entrance Examination Board, 888 Seventh Ave., New York, N.Y. 10019

Consulting Psychologists Press, Inc., 577 College Ave., Palo Alto, Calif. 94306

Cooperative Tests and Services, Educational Testing Service, Princeton, N.J. 08540

Counselor Recordings and Tests, Box 6184 Acklen Station, Nashville, Tenn. 37212

Educational and Industrial Testing Service, P. O. Box 7234, San Diego, Calif. 92107

Educational Testing Service, Princeton, N.J. 08540

General Educational Development Testing Service, American Council on Education, 12 Dupont Circle, Washington, D.C. 20036

Guidance Testing Associates, 6516 Shirley Ave., Austin, Texas 78752

Harcourt Brace Jovanovich, Inc., 757 Third Ave., New York, N.Y. 10017

Houghton Mifflin Co., One Beacon St., Boston, Mass. 02107

Industrial Relations Center, University of Chicago, 1225 East 60th St., Chicago, Ill. 60637

Institute for Personality and Ability Testing, 1602 Coronado Drive, Champaign, Ill. 61820

McGraw-Hill Book Co., Inc., 330 West 42nd St., New York, N.Y. 10036

Prentice-Hall, Inc., Englewood Cliffs, N.J. 07632

Psychological Corporation, 304 East 45th St., New York, N.Y. 10017

Psychologists and Educators Press, 419 Pendik, Jacksonville, Ill. 62650

Psychometric Affiliates, Box 3167, Munster, Ind. 46321

Public Personnel Association, 1313 East 60th St., Chicago, Ill. 60637

Science Research Associates, Inc., 259 East Erie St., Chicago, Ill. 60611

Western Psychological Services, 12031 Wilshire Blvd., Los Angeles, Calif. 90025

William C. Brown Company, Publishers, 135 South Locust St., Dubuque, Iowa 52001.

Appendix B

Glossary of Measurement Terms

Absolute Interpretation   A method of interpreting test scores whereby a test score is considered as an indication of what skills and knowledge an individual possesses at the time the test is given. The test itself, rather than some group of students, is the reference point in absolute interpretation of test scores.

Achievement Test   An instrument designed to measure the extent to which a student has attained concepts and skills in a given content area that he could reasonably be expected to have attained at the time the test is given.

Affective   Aspects of an individual that involve emotional feelings rather than intellectual knowledge.

Age Equivalent   A score that indicates the age in years and months of the group at whose median the student in question scored on a given test. It allows for the determination of which age group a particular student performed most like on the test in question.

Age Norm   The average performance of an age group in a particular test. Average age norms can be used as the basis of comparison for the performance of a specific student.

Aptitude Test   A test designed to assess an individual's potential for performing some task or how well an individual can be expected to perform in a particular area.

Attitude Test   A test designed to assess an individual's feelings toward something.

Average   The score that is usually thought to provide the best indication of the typical performance of a group of individuals. The average may be represented by the mode, median, or mean and does not have to be a score actually obtained by someone.

Battery of Tests   Two or more tests designed to be administered together or in succession and that measure different aspects of the same attribute—verbal and nonverbal intelligence tests, for example.

Central Tendency   Another name for average or the most typical performance of a group of individuals. Central tendency may be reported as the mode, median, or mean.

Cognitive   Aspects of an individual pertaining to knowledge and understanding.

Completion Item   A test item that requires a student to supply the missing part of a statement. Completion items are often referred to as "fill-in-the-blank" items.

Composite Score   A total or overall score for an individual determined as the average or sum of the student's performance on the various subtests of a test battery.

Concurrent Validity   The degree to which the results of a test provide information consistent with an accepted contemporary criterion of performance on the variable that the test is intended to measure.

Construct Validity   The degree to which a test measures a particular, theoretically defined aspect of the variable being considered.

Content Standard Score   A test score interpreted to indicate the percentage of a set of content that a student has achieved.

Content Validity   The degree to which a test measures the content areas that the objectives for testing indicate the test should measure.

Correction for Guessing   A method for adjusting a student's score on a test by subtracting the number of items answered incorrectly from the number of items answered correctly. This is an attempt to remove the effects of guessing from a student's score and, as a result, cause the test score to provide a better indication of what the student knows.

Correlation Coefficient   A numerical index of the degree to which individuals tend to have the same relative position with respect to other scores in the group on two different variables. An index of 0 indicates that there is no relationship between the relative position of individuals on the two variables, while an index of +1 or −1 indicates that there is a perfect relationship between relative positions.

Criterion-Difficulty Index An index of how difficult the criterion in a criterion-referenced test is. It is determined as the number of individuals who respond incorrectly to a test item divided by the total number of individuals who respond to the item.

Criterion-Reference A method of measurement and interpretation that attempts to determine what skills and knowledge a student possesses at some point in time. A student's performance is interpreted relative to what he should be able to do at that stage in his development.

Culturally Biased Test A test that includes items based on experiences of a particular culture so that individuals of that culture tend to perform better than individuals with different cultural backgrounds.

Cumulative Frequency The number of individuals in a score distribution who score below a given score.

Cut-Off Score The minimum percentage of items that must be answered correctly before a student can be said to have mastered the content measured by a test.

Decile One of the nine score points in a distribution that divides the score scale into ten intervals, such that each interval includes an equal number of scores.

Diagnostic Test A test designed and administered for the purpose of discovering the strengths and weaknesses of an individual.

Difficulty Index An index of how hard it is to answer a test item correctly. It is determined as the number of individuals who respond correctly to an item divided by the total number who respond to the item.

Discrimination Index An index of the degree to which a test item differentiates between individuals who perform better on a test and individuals who perform poorly. This index is usually determined as the number of individuals in the highest 27 percent of scores who answer an item correctly minus the number in the lowest 27 percent of the scores who answer an item correctly. The difference is divided by the total number of individuals in the upper 27 percent.

Educational Objective   A statement as to the behavior a student should demonstrate at the end of a period of instruction.

Equivalent Forms   Two or more tests essentially the same in all important aspects except that different test items or a different order of the same test is used.

Equivalent-Forms Reliability   The correlation or consistency of performance of individuals in two forms of the same test.

Error of Measurement   The difference between the score a student obtains on a test and the score he actually should have received, or his true score.

Essay Item   A test item format intended to allow the student to analyze a set of information and provide a meaningful and original response.

Evaluation   As defined by the Phi Delta Kappan National Study Committee on Evaluation, it is "the process of delineating, obtaining, and providing useful information for judging decision alternatives."

External Test   A measuring device developed outside the local setting.

Foil   An incorrect alternative in a multiple-choice test item.

Frequency Distribution   A listing of the scores obtained by a group of individuals along with the number of individuals who obtained each score.

General Objective   A statement of the intent of an educational program describing the group, the changes that should occur, and the terminal behavior, in general rather than in specific terms.

Grade Equivalent   A scale score determined from a raw score obtained on a test. The grade equivalent of a particular score is the grade level of the norm group whose median (point below which 50 percent of the scores fall) is the same as the raw score.

Grade Norm   The average performance of various grade levels in a particular test. Average grade norms are typically provided for the beginning, middle, and end of each of the various grade levels and can be used as the basis of comparison for the performance of a specific student.

Group Test   A test designed for administration to several students at the same time.

Individual Test   A test designed for administration to a single student rather than to a group of students.

Intelligence Quotient (IQ)   A scaled score resulting from the administration of an intelligence test. It is generally interpreted as an indication as to how well a student can be expected to perform in school.

Intelligence Test   Aptitude tests designed to measure a student's general learning capability.

Internal Consistency   An index of test reliability based on whether an individual responds consistently throughout a test. This type of reliability is usually determined by dividing the items of a test into two groups and determining the correlation coefficient between an individual's scores on the two groups of items.

Item Analysis   Procedures used to determine whether a test item is functioning properly in a test. Item analysis commonly refers to the determination of the difficulty index and discrimination index of a test item.

Item Pool   A group of items developed to measure a particular set of content or skills. The items included on a test can then be chosen from this pool of items.

Internal Test   A test developed by individuals within the environment in which the test will be used.

Item Stem   The part of a test item that presents the situation to which a response must be given. The stem may be a question or statement to be completed or a problem to be solved.

Local Norm   The average performance of a group from the setting in which a test is given. Average local norms can be used to allow comparison against students in the same setting rather than to students outside the local setting.

Matching Items   A test item that requires an individual to match an item stem with the appropriate response.

Mastery Test   This is similar to the criterion-referenced test in that it is intended to determine the degree to which a student has attained certain concepts and skills considered essential at that point in a student's educational process.

Mean   This usually refers to the arithmetic mean when it is used in education and it is determined by summing all the scores in a group and dividing by the number of scores added. As such, it indicates the average score obtained by a group.

Median   The score point below which 50 percent of the scores in a frequency distribution fall. It is a measure of the most typical performance of a group of individuls on a test.

Mode   The score occurring most frequently in a frequency distribution.

Multiple-Choice Item   A test item that presents a student with a problem in the stem and asks him to respond by choosing the correct response from a number of possible alternatives.

Normal Distribution   A very specific bell-shaped curve. There are many normal curves, but the percentage of scores falling between various z-scores is always the same.

Norm   The average performance of a group against which the performance of a given student is compared.

Nonverbal Test   A test that does not require a student to read.

Objective Test   A test that can be scored without subjective judgments.

Percentile   One of the ninety-nine score points that divide the score scale into one hundred equal intervals so that each score interval includes the same number of scores.

Percentile Rank   The percentage of the total number of scores in a group that fall below a particular score.

Performance Test   A test that requires the individual being tested actually to perform the task in question—for example, the part of a driver's license examination that requires an individual actually to drive a car in traffic.

Practice Effect   The phenomenon that taking the test can provide an individual with knowledge about how to take that test or tests similar to it. Individuals who have experience with a particular type of test tend to score higher than do individuals who have no experience with that type of test.

Predictive Validity   The degree to which performance on a test provides information consistent with an accepted future criterion of performance on the variable that the test is intended to measure.

Psychomotor   Aspects of an individual that involve coordination of psychological and motor (muscular) skills.

Quartile   One of three score points that divide a score scale into four equal intervals, such that each interval contains the same number of scores.

Range   The number of score points between the highest score obtained in a group and the lowest score obtained by that group.

Raw Score   A score obtained on a test that has not been converted from its original state.

Reference System   A system that allows a comparison point for a given test score so that the score may be interpreted in a useful way.

Reliability   The degree to which a test measures consistently whatever it measures.

Scale   The set of values to which raw scores are converted. This scale has well-defined characteristics necessary to interpretation.

Scaled Score   Raw scores are converted to scaled scores so that the score distribution will have well-defined characteristics. These characteristics are necessary for interpretation and seldom exist in the original raw-score distribution.

Score   A numerical indication as to how well an individual has performed on a test.

Semi-Interquartile Range   A measure of variability typically reported with the median. It is one-half of the number of score points between the seventy-fifth and twenty-fifth percentiles.

Short-Answer Item   A test item that requires an individual to compose a short and precise response.

Specific Objective   A statement of the intent of an educational program. This statement describes the group, the change that should occur, and the terminal behavior in specific terms.

Split-Halves Reliability   A measure of the internal consistency of a test that provides evidence as to whether individual students maintain their same relative position when the test is divided into approximately equal parts. This reliability is usually determined by calculating the correlation of scores on the even-numbered and odd-numbered items.

Standard Deviation   A measure of variability usually reported with the mean. It is an indication of the standard or typical amount by which a score on a score distribution differs from the mean of the distribution.

Standard Error of Measurement   The standard deviation of the errors of measurement that a student would receive upon repeated testing. It is assumed that these error scores are normally distributed, and therefore the standard error of measurement is the standard deviation of a normal distribution.

Standard Score   A scaled score that relates each individual's score to the mean of the group by indicating how many standard deviations each individual is above or below the mean.

Standardized Test   A test for which the directions, time limits, test booklets, and other conditions of administration have been structured so that they are the same each time the test is administered.

Stanine Score   A scaled score in which raw scores are converted to one of nine possible scores. Each stanine represents a percentage of the total number of scores for the group in question.

Statistic   A numerical value that describes some aspect of a sample of individuals. Examples of statistics are the mean, median, mode, range, and standard deviation.

Subjective Test   A test that requires the individual who is scoring it to make judgments as to the correctness of responses.

Subtest   A specific test of a general achievement test battery designed to assess a particular set of behavior for a specific content area.

Test   A measuring device. This device may measure affective, cognitive, or psychomotor traits.

Test-Retest Reliability   The correlation or consistency of performance of individuals on the same test administered at two different times.

True-False Item   A test item that requires the respondent to indicate whether a given statement is true or false.

True Score   The score that a student would receive on a test if there were no measurement error. It provides an indication of the knowledge a student actually possesses.

Test-wiseness   A knowledge of procedures to follow in taking a test and of clues to correct answers in test items that enables the student to increase a test score.

T-Score   A system of standard scores. The mean of the T-score distribution is fifty and the standard deviation is ten.

Usability   The degree to which test results are interpretable in addition to being valid and reliable.

Validity   The degree to which a test actually measures whatever it purports to measure.

Variability   Dispersion or differences in a group of scores.

Verbal Test   A test that requires a student to be able to read in order to respond to the test items.

z-Score   A system of standard scores. The mean of the z-score distribuition is 0 and the standard deviation is 1.

Index